Human Geography in a Shrinking World

A New Collection By Duxbury Press.

The Man—Environment System in the Late Twentieth Century

General Editor
WILLIAM L. THOMAS
California State University, Hayward

HUMAN GEOGRAPHY
IN A SHRINKING WORLD

RONALD ABLER
Pennsylvania State University

DONALD JANELLE
University of Western Ontario

ALLEN PHILBRICK
University of Western Ontario

JOHN SOMMER
Dartmouth College

DUXBURY PRESS
North Scituate, Massachusetts
A Division of
Wadsworth Publishing Company, Inc.
Belmont, California

Duxbury Press
A DIVISION OF WADSWORTH PUBLISHING COMPANY, INC.

ISBN-0-87872-073-1

L.C. Cat. Card No.: 74-84839
PRINTED IN THE UNITED STATES OF AMERICA

1 2 3 4 5 6 7 8 9 10 — 79 78 77 76 75

Contents

Editor's Foreword

For almost all of us the future is more important than the past, because the future is where we expect to spend the rest of our lives. The where and when of tomorrow are thus of significance for everyone concerned with the quality of his future. Geographers have traditionally described, analyzed, and explained the past and the present. Their emphasis has been upon what mankind has done and is doing in creating human habitats, or cultural landscapes. Fortunately, there is an increasing interest in studying the future (or alternative futures) in order to improve current decisions whose results will determine mankind's future situation.

This volume is a cooperative effort by geographers in Canada and the United States. It is altogether fitting that the volume should be an international effort since a proper perspective on the results of man's actions in North America cannot be gained from one country alone. The international flavor also is represented by the volume's four organizer-editors, two of whom hold university appointments in Canada and two in the United States. Ronald F. Abler received his Ph.D. degree in 1968 from the University of Minnesota and is Associate Professor of Geography at Pennsylvania State University, specializing in intercommunications systems. Recently he has been Associate Director and Atlas Editor of the Comparative Metropolitan Analysis Project for the Association of

American Geographers. Donald G. Janelle was awarded the Ph.D. degree from Michigan State University in 1966, was for several years on the faculty of the U.S. Air Force Academy, and is now an Associate Professor of Geography at the University of Western Ontario. His interests are in spatial aspects of urban conflict, concepts of relative space, and methods of spatial forecasting. Allen K. Philbrick received the Ph.D. degree from the University of Chicago in 1949, and has been on the faculty of Syracuse University, the University of Chicago, and Michigan State University. Since 1965, he has been a Professor of Geography at the University of Western Ontario. He is best known for his volume, *This Human World* (John Wiley and Sons, 1963), and for his interest in human spatial organization. John W. Sommer received his Ph.D. degree from Boston University in 1968. For many years he made his home in Arabia and other Southwest Asian countries, but has since had a sustaining interest, and has done field research, in Africa and its cities. He is now an Assistant Professor of Geography at Dartmouth College.

I am pleased to introduce and recommend to you this volume in the series, THE MAN-ENVIRONMENT SYSTEM IN THE LATE TWENTIETH CENTURY. The ideas here expressed are representative of geography's contribution to modern thought and social action. These essays vividly demonstrate how geography has taken on a dynamic, outward-looking, cross-disciplinary, problem-solving attitude. Behavioral science methodology has become part of contemporary geography, as have more rigorous forms of analysis and a concern for proper environmental management. The purpose of the volumes in this series is to provide a forum through which the new ideas in geography may quickly reach their broadest audiences among the educated public. The series, THE MAN-ENVIRONMENT SYSTEM IN THE LATE TWENTIETH CENTURY differs from other series in several ways: it is open-ended, rather than finite, and will contain as many volumes as future developments in geography will warrant. By taking the works of geographers and bringing them to bear not only on geographic thought but also on the fruits of other appropriate disciplines, the series will be an important force for the enrichment and stimulation of human knowledge.

WILLIAM L. THOMAS

Preface

Human Geography In A Shrinking World is a collection of essays concerned with the locations of events and people during the next century. As such, it is an integral part of the exploding futuristic literature, but one that offers a viewpoint not normally developed in futuristic works. Our authors may disagree about many things, but they all agree that *where* an event will occur is just as important as *when* it will "take place." This conviction is the unique perspective that this volume offers.

Because transportation and communications are such critical determinants of the locations of social, economic, and residential activities, a concern with long-term whereness requires some discussion of these two technologies. Part I (Perspectives) consists of four chapters that analyze current and future transportation and communications technologies in relation to locational decisions. Part II (Implications) explores some consequences of the hypermobility that transportation and communications are creating. Future settlement patterns are of major importance here because of their dependence on movement technologies and because they are such fundamental patterns of life. But beyond choosing settlement patterns, we face numerous alternative ways of organizing society, government, and cultural groups. Several authors address the dilemmas of selecting among the many alternatives we have.

In Part III (Alternatives) we suggest ways of answering the

questions and dilemmas raised in Part II. Several scenarios, an urban settlement simulation, and a Delphi study are used to answer questions about future activity locations. The diverse settings and the range of geographical scales incorporated in these essays make it clear that geographical questions can be answered by futuristic methods. Yet techniques only help us answer questions; they are never answers themselves. The book's final chapters stress that point. Even if we have techniques for managing an almost paralyzing array of alternatives, it will still be impossible to make choices without becoming deeply involved in philosophical and political arguments. Futuristics may produce better decisions, but it will not make decision making any easier.

A locational decision has a long "half-life." A choice made today about the location of a park or a roadway produces opportunities or constraints for a century or more. We are making the future every day whether we do so consciously or unwittingly. Writing and organizing these essays has helped the authors and editors clarify their thinking about spatial futures and about their long-run responsibilities as citizens and geographers. If *Human Geography In A Shrinking World* helps others become more self-conscious about the long-term geographical implications of current decisions, we will be pleased and grateful.

Ronald Abler
Donald Janelle
Allen Philbrick
John Sommer

Minary Conference Center
Holderness, New Hampshire
May, 1972

Acknowledgements

Many of the essays in this volume were first presented at the Conference on the Geography of the Future held at Bayfield, Ontario, Canada, in November, 1970. The Bayfield Conference was made possible by generous support from the Canada Council and the Department of Geography at the University of Western Ontario, the host for the Conference. We deeply appreciate their help.

Numerous ideas and impressions that originated at the Bayfield Conference were refined at the Conference on Building Regions of the Future that was held at the Universite de Montreal in February, 1972. We are most grateful to Dr. Marcel Belanger and his Quebec colleagues for their efforts in organizing the second conference.

Dartmouth College made the facilities of the Minary Conference Center available to the editors for the time needed to knit the essays together, and we thank them for their contribution to the completion of the work.

Finally, several people contributed important ideas during discussions at the Bayfield Conference and on subsequent occasions. We would be remiss if we did not acknowledge the help of those who attended the Bayfield Conference but who are not represented by a paper in this volume. They are identified by an asterisk in the following list:

Participants in the Bayfield Conference, 1970.

Ronald Abler, *Pennsylvania State University.*
*Larry Bourne, *The University of Toronto.*
*Stanley Brunn, *Michigan State University.*
William Bunge, *York University.*
Hans Carol, *York University.*
*Ian Jackson, *The Department of Energy, Mines and Resources, Canada.*
Donald Janelle, *The University of Western Ontario.*
*Robert Latham, *Bell Telephone of Canada.*
Robert McDaniel, *The University of Western Ontario.*
George Macinko, *Central Washington University.*
*Ross MacKinnon, *The University of Toronto.*
Allen K. Philbrick, *The University of Western Ontario.*
*Edward G. Pleva, *The University of Western Ontario.*
*Guy Reeves, *The Canadian Council on Urban and Regional Research.*
*Lorne Russwurm, *The University of Waterloo.*
*Richard V. Smith, *Miami University, Ohio.*
John Sommer, *Dartmouth College.*
William Warntz, *Harvard University.*
Roy Wolfe, *York University.*
Wilbur Zelinsky, *Pennsylvania State University.*

Part I: Perspectives

Chapter 1

Introduction: The Study Of Spatial Futures

The Editors

The main thesis of this book is that man's technological skills are rapidly exceeding his ability to cope with the opportunities and problems they engender. Too often, opportunities offered by technology go unrealized because we cannot muster the consensus on end results prerequisite to applying technology intelligently. Equally often, when we attempt to realize goals upon which there is some agreement we are frustrated by unlooked for and unperceived side effects of our techniques.

If we hope to solve current problems and avoid future dilemmas, we must make decisions not only in the context of the present, but insofar as possible, with one eye on the effects these decisions will have on the future. As we try to guess what kinds of constraints and opportunities will exist ten, thirty, and fifty years from now, it seems clear that two current trends will persist in providing the basic frame of reference for life in the future. Individual geographical mobility will continue at unprecedented levels, and increasing numbers of people will participate in this mobility. Simultaneously, our power to communicate will increase sharply.

Human Extensibility in a Shrinking World

The last century saw revolutionary advances in mobility and communication. For instance, the meandering 1,200 mile journey down the Ohio River from Pittsburgh to St. Louis once took a full week. By 1900, railroads had shortened the trip to 600 miles or one full day; today, the 550-mile air distance is traversed in a relaxing trip of one hour. The development of information transfers at near instantaneous rates has been even more phenomenal. Peking and Washington, separated by the 45-minute path of an intercontinental missile, are only a fraction of a second apart via tele-satellite hookup. The shrinking world, or the convergence of space in time, is hereafter referred to as time-space convergence.[1] Transistor radios, telephones, and television are linking most of the world's households into a global network. The increasing abundance of mechanized vehicles has permitted much greater mobility of both people and materials. Potential interactions among households, firms, villages, and nations are increasing geometrically. In this context, time-space convergence can also be seen as human extensibility.

Instead of viewing our world as shrinking, it is perhaps more accurate to view man as expanding. Doubling the speed of travel quadruples the territory that can be reached in a given time. Since 1800 man has increased his average speed of land travel tenfold from 4 miles per hour to 40 miles per hour. This has expanded one hundredfold the area that can be traversed in a given time period. For example, compare the areas of two circles defined by 4 and 40 mile radii respectively. If one can travel directly from the centers to all points within the circles, the respective territories of access are 53 square miles and 5,300 square miles. If the number of people in this expanded system also increased at the same rate, say from 4 to 400, then the combinations of possible interacting pairs increase from 6 to 79,800. Transportation and communications improvements have provided us with global information networks, and the possible combinations for interaction among nearly 4 billion humans are staggering.

Even more staggering, however, are the perceptual lags that prevent us from adapting political, social, economic, and ecologic views to the technological realities of such interaction levels. These lags put us out of phase with our capacities for unwitting or willful mischief. Locational inflexibility, information overload, crippling bureaucracy, and short-sighted resource exhaustion are constraints that preclude imaginative solutions to problems. Too often, such constraints trap decision makers into thinking that the future must be adapted to fit the present, when a more appropriate view is that the present must accommodate many possible futures.

Futuristic Strategies

There are several strategies for revealing what lies ahead. One strategy is to convince people that mankind is in trouble; that present behavior, if continued, will lead to eradication of the species through economic depression, political revolution, war, and famine. This "scare" approach is illustrated in such recent writings as Dennis Meadows and associates' *The Limits to Growth*, Alvin Toffler's *Future Shock*, and Jay Forrester's *World Dynamics*.[2] The tactic is not new; distinguished forerunners date back to Thomas Malthus and Karl Marx.

Other approaches emphasize forecasting techniques and their applications, and do so without apocalyptic overtones. Forecasts can be normative or goal-oriented. The term normative is sometimes used to mean goal-oriented. In this volume, however, normative is used as in science to mean "according to a norm, rule, or law," as opposed to the kind of self-fulfilling prophecy of which goal orientation is a product. Thomas Malthus' prediction that mankind's geometric growth rate would outrun the arithmetic increase of his food supply, for example, was based upon a model of comparative rates of change for two interdependent variables. As such, it was a normative forecast. If the norm was wrong, the forecast was wrong. Normative forecasting, based upon extrapolating the future from past trends, is summarized by Robert Ayres in *Technological Forecasting and Long Range Planning* and by Erich Jantsch in *Technological Forecasting in Perspective*.[3]

Goal-oriented forecasting works backward from an assumed future to the present. The forecast that an American would be first to land on the moon was a product of the goal-oriented space program announced by President Kennedy on inauguration day, 1961. Commitment to a plan to place a man on the moon requires identification of strategies and allocation of present and future resources for implementing specific goals. This aspect of forecasting is reviewed by Jantsch, but Dennis Gabor covers it in greater detail in *Inventing the Future*.[4]

Nearly all normative and goal-oriented forecasting efforts have focused on the questions: What? and When? An overriding weakness in this literature is the consistent omission and neglect of an equally basic question: Where? "Where is the future?" must complement the more traditional question of "What will be when?" The conceptual separation of space (where), time (when), and events (what) has pervaded social thought for a long time. Only recently have efforts been made to integrate them conceptually in the Einsteinian paradigm of time-space.[5]

For convenience we may separate time and space from one another in measurement problems. Time is generally held constant when measuring space, and space is generally held constant when measuring time. Nevertheless, time and space are inseparable because they are different versions of the same entity. Accordingly, answers to the questions, What?, Where?, and When?, are aspects of one problem—the identification of time-space events. This time-space view of reality is implicit in this book. Although much more work is needed, descriptive and explanatory time-spatial models are emerging and they will help redress the imbalance that ignores the "where of the future."

Torsten Hägerstrand has pioneered in studies of the spread of technological and social innovations in rural areas and among nations.[6] Richard Morrill has developed predictive models that simulate the spread of blacks into white neighborhoods and residential development at the edges of cities.[7] Predictive models for a wide variety of urban changes, such as population growth, land use alterations, and transportation impacts are being refined at the University of Toronto's Centre for Urban and Community Studies.[8] *Regional Forecasting* is a landmark in both normative and goal-oriented time-spatial forecasting.[9] Soviet scholars have also shown keen interest in futurism. Rodoman, for example, forecasts that the earth's natural envelopes of air, water, and biota will one day be replaced by an "anthroposphere" of manmade structures.[10] Such examples are indicative of a widespread concern for considering space and place in forecasting efforts.

Systematic Approaches to Futures

The difference between a soothsayer and a futurist is the degree to which they base their forecasts upon an understanding of regularities in the phenomena to be forecast. Forecasting is rooted in systematic knowledge. Unfortunately there exist large gaps and inconsistencies in this systematic knowledge. The fact remains, however, that there is a parallel between the order-seeking goals of the sciences and the objectives of forecasting. Often, the forecaster is willing but the scientific underpinnings are weak, and it is worthwhile to enumerate the reasons this is so. The very reasons for our weakness in predicting the future underscore the need for a systematic base for normative and goal-oriented forecasting.

Knowledge Gaps and Conflicts

Any single forecasting objective, not to mention the holistic objective of understanding man's future, involves the comprehension of so many variables that no single viewpoint or philosophy can embrace them. The predictions required in mankind's growing hour of need concern matters of much larger scope than the domain of a single discipline or even a constellation of disciplines. The integration of science in such efforts as the unified science movememnt of the 1930s or the interdisciplinary pairs of committees of disciplines since then has proven wholly inadequate to the task. Such efforts usually have been addressed to the solution of particular research objectives and whereas they have provided important insights nothing less than a holistic intellectual effort that embraces all sciences as well as the humanities is equal to the task at hand.

It is little wonder, then, that forecasts cannot be deduced from general laws of science or from the laws of any particular science. In practice forecasts are limited specific statements concerning parts of problems, related to specific applications of scientific knowledge for particular categories of circumstance. In most cases scientific laws are insufficiently general for direct application to social policy.

This means that inductive insights yielded by specific observations appropriate to specific forecasting problems are often the only hope of success. Such limitations on the use of scientific principles in forecasting are a consequence of our ignorance rather than the inadequacy of principles or logic themselves. If we were wiser and more knowledgeable we could forecast more effectively.

We are often understandably interested in individual behavior, but forecasting success tends to be inversely proportional to the specificity of the forecast. A primary limitation of forecasting is that one may predict for the group but not for the specific individual. For example, the National Highway Safety Council can accurately predict the number of people who will die in highway accidents on a holiday weekend but are totally unable to tell which individuals will become statistics.

Many people fear science will tell them something must be a certain way even though they don't want it that way. This is the nub of the conflict between determinism and free will in the social application of scientific knowledge. Despite the desire to "will away" existing laws of nature, most people understand that the way to at least an illusion of freedom is to work with the laws of nature rather than be at odds with them.

The conflict between determinism and free will is an unsolvable one that goes far beyond the acceptance or rejection of scientific forecasting. Consider freedom and decision. Decisions cannot be avoided, but until they are made in any given situation, freedom of choice appears to exist. Actually it has been constrained by previous decisions of the decision maker and those around him. As soon as any particular decision has been made, irreversible consequences appear which give the illusion that freedom has disappeared. Actually freedom remains in the new unfolding reality and in new circumstances that emerge. Freedom and constraint are mental constructs which accompany our every conscious moment. As mental constructs, they must not be confused with reality, which is neither wholly determined in advance nor wholly subject to free will.

Predictions are partial statements about fragments of the future. Their accuracy is dependent on the occurrence of a specific event or series of events. Such occurrence, in turn, is dependent on the interaction of many independent variables. If one such variable should change, the prediction could fall flat. Predictions and forecasts are perhaps unjustly taken to task for failing to "come true."

Our knowledge of the laws of nature is so narrowly particular and so restricted along disciplinary lines that it is little wonder one doubts the ability of science to provide the necessary basis for forecasting. Our best efforts at strengthening such weaknesses lie in the development of general systems theory.[11] Systems theory correlates and integrates disparate information flows from multiple sources. In stressing interactions, flow sequences, cross references, and feedbacks, systems concepts promote understanding of complex problems.

A Philosophical Overview

Conceptual difficulties and knowledge gaps are like warning signs advising us to proceed with caution. Forecasting, for example, even when based upon the best available scientific findings, may have adverse effects on our future. We may be led to choose alternatives with undesirable consequences owing to complex interactions that are poorly understood. Forecasts, if adopted as self-fulfilling prophecies, frequently result in undreamed of consequences, a phenomenon described as the counter-intuitive tendencies of complex systems.[12] For example, the idea that the United States should have a limited access interstate highway system was originally viewed as an unmitigated blessing. Few anticipated the noise, pollution, artificial division of communities, and acceleration of urban sprawl which have been its consequences. Such potential hazards accompanied the increased accessibility originally viewed with starry-eyed euphoria. Intuitive expectations, though necessary, are not sufficient. Hard-nosed anticipations of the effects of any technological innovation on current and future lifestyles are essential steps in the search for a better future.

Convergence, Divergence, and Extensibility

Time-space convergence and human extensibility are two intuitively identified tendencies of critical importance for the decades ahead. Their consequences are so far-reaching that they merit recognition as dominant themes for study by spatial futurists.

Time-space convergence measures rates at which places are moving closer together in travel time or communication time. In a similar manner, time-space divergence measures rates at which travel or communication times between places increase. For example, travel time between airports and central cities has in some instances lengthened because of the increasing traffic congestion characteristic of many metropolitan areas. Divergence, however, is only an occasional lag in a more pervasive tendency toward convergence. Reductions in travel time between London and New York City from approximately eight days to six hours over the last fifty years illustrate dramatically the overall convergence process. This coming together by 186 hours is expressible as an average convergence of 3.5 hours per year since 1920. This figure is a gross simplification which neglects the timing irregularities of transport innovation and the asymptotic nature of the convergence process. It is nonetheless a measure of the change to which the remainder of our social, political, and economic institutions must adjust. World trade, tourism, and international conflicts are all conditioned by the new environments created by convergence, divergence, and extensibility.

To Constantinos Doxiadis, a student of human settlement forms, the ultimate in human extensibility will be for all major points on earth to be separated by only ten minutes' travel time.[13] At different scales, one might consider the convergence or divergence of jobs with homes, hospital care with households, wholesalers with retailers, and politicians with the voters who elect them. Human extensibility is an implicit consequence of changes in time-distance relationships—aside from being closer to individual voters, politicians now have access to more of them. And, as advances in communication decrease the significance of time and space, politicians may extend their images over a wider territory to more people.

Although convergence has wide impact at global as well as local scales, it has by no means released man from the shackles of space and time. The negation of distance and the effort needed to overcome it occurs at varying rates for different socioeconomic and political groupings. Extensibility expands with every advance in transportation and communications technology, but only for those who can afford such opportunities. For those possessing lesser means, time-space convergence may be negligible. In fact, there is reason to believe that convergence contributes to the polarization of the "haves" and "have nots".

In American cities advantages from transport improvements do not accrue to blacks and other minority groups as much as they do to whites. In Detroit, for example, the average distance (to say nothing of time distance) between jobs and homes has decreased for whites but has increased for blacks.[14] Does this divergence also apply to access to hospital care, educational facilities, and swimming pools? We will see somewhat later that such is the case.

Futures: By Whom and For Whom?

Aside from the problems associated with current socioeconomic and political inequities, the opportunities engendered by the convergence process pose other crucial problems. For example, which way will the scales ultimately tip? Can we ensure desirable as opposed to undesirable futures? Who is to decide what is desirable and for whom? The distinction between tolerable and intolerable futures may, in fact, be a chancy one. Utopia for one may be dystopia for another.

Rigid plans are usually the product of those in power, who generally seek to lump all of us into one future identified with their own interests. The assumption is glibly made that all share the same values. This attitude is epitomized by the expression, "What's good for General Motors is good for the country." The ubiquity of human conflict, ranging from family squabbles and sibling rivalries to world wars, exposes weaknesses in this myopic assumption. Very often, absence from the planning process of those disadvantaged by prejudice, lack of opportunity, poverty, and general powerlessness, leads to wider and deeper gaps, thus reinforcing the power and values of those in control. Plans tend to box us in, wittingly or unwittingly committing resources for a future which may be completely out of joint with what we expected.

Although plans preclude options and reduce possibilities for selecting from an infinite variety of futures, and although they entail risks, the opposite is also true. Failure to plan entails equal or greater risks. The question, therefore, is not whether we should plan, but how and for whom do we plan futures whose exact nature is yet unclear.

Assumptions for Utopia. Although future objectives should be based upon the aspirations of all men including the least powerful among us, such objectives must be weighted against and in terms of the pressing need to insure man's survival. Future human habitats must be in balance with Nature's critical constraints. With this in mind, the following humanistic goals for Utopia are suggested:

> *Preserve life and the ecosystem*
>
> *Insure the maximum freedom of choice*
>
> *Tolerate and support diversity*
>
> *Appreciate people over property*
>
> *Promote and enhance creativity*
>
> *Put things where we want them to be rather than where we think they have to be*
>
> *Develop recycling rather than linear systems for use of the earth as the home of man*

These seven suggestions will be considered in detail later, but it is apparent even at the outset that their implementation will require combining the views of humanism with those of science.

Constraints on Opportunities for Futures

Related to the key questions of What?, When?, Where?, and How?, are certain conditions which are generalized here as the constraints of location, information, stress, administration, and resources.

Location.   The location constraint is responsible for the tyranny of space.[15] Often, it seems, an invisible hand forces us to locate things where they must be. Partly in response to human values of sociability and profit motivation, the spatial patterns of human settlement are highly clustered. In subareas of many of the world's mega-cities such as in New York City's Harlem, population densities exceed one hundred thousand or more people per square mile. Others in Asia have peak densities three to four times that great. Such dense agglomerations diminish needs for transportation and insure speedy linkages among complementary technologies and human skills. Agglomeration economies accrue because of the economies of scale. Effort expended on moving materials, goods, and people over more extensive areas would decisively cut into profit margins.

Given the prevalent work ethic, the search for survival at levels of quality suitable to perceived needs prescribes where all but the most eccentric and resolute of us live. We are not free. Our locational choices are constrained by our survival instincts and by what we perceive to be the demands placed on us by society. We live where we live because we must. This is the tyranny of space; its subjects are many. The quest to maximize profit from real estate effectively allocates land uses within cities. Social prejudice and income differentials divide wealthy areas from areas of poverty.

Time-space convergence offers a potential escape from the tyranny of space. As the effort (cost) required to overcome time and distance decreases, increased locational freedom becomes possible. Within limits of land ownership patterns and institutional restrictions, it becomes much easier to live where we wish. Personality differences and human preference may become dominant locational factors. This freedom, however, is deceptive. For, by freeing ourselves from the tyranny of space we assume in its place the tyranny of communications.

Information Overload.   In order to live we must communicate. Economies based on flows of raw materials, goods, people, money, and information require highly articulated networks. The increasing complexity, specialization, and size of our institutions greatly intensify the volume of information needed to keep the system functioning. In the context of this ever increasing need to communicate, the tyranny of communications expresses itself as information overload. As we push ourselves toward and beyond the limits of effective information assimilation, we must seek new ways to identify and to ameliorate the harmful effects of information overload.

Stress.   Stress operates at individual through world scales in all human and natural systems. Psychologists have examined physical stress in the human mind and physiologists have studied stress in the human body. Similarly, sociologists, economists, political scientists, botanists, zoologists, and others have studied stress in their respective areas of competence. Without reviewing the extensive literature on this subject, the following questions concerning stress require answers if we hope to anticipate the future successfully.

> _ _ *What are the appropriate levels of stress for human and environ-*
> *mental systems?*
>
> _ _ *To what extent is creativity stress-dependent?*
>
> _ _ *Can stress be balanced by opportunities for disengagement—such as*
> *rest and leisure?*
>
> _ _ *As we increase the proportion of our time devoted to rest and leisure,*
> *will we be able to sustain higher short-term levels of stress?*
>
> _ _ *Just as the athlete trains his body and mind to absorb higher and*
> *higher levels of stress for limited durations, can we train other*
> *human and natural systems to do the same?*

Administration. Myriad flows of people, resources, goods, money, information, and power are controlled by administrative institutions known collectively as bureaucracy. There is growing concern over the responsiveness and humaneness of giant administrative systems. Bureaucracies typically consist of chain-of-command or multiple-level structures based on hierarchical flows of power and information. They resist change and demand that their functionaries be loyal to the organization—whether it be a corporation, university, or government agency. Some of the latter (for example, school districts, voting districts, counties and provinces) are products of spatial bureaucracy; they have fixed, relatively permanent boundaries and they demand loyalty to territory.

Bureaucracy is an overstressed system that is becoming swamped in its own output. More importantly, it is being challenged by some increasingly important organizational tendencies. North American economies trend toward nonhierarchical information flows and toward non-permanent groups united by opposition to problems. Although the most effective solutions to administrative constraints are likely to be political in nature, computer and communications technology could cater to growing demand for the *ad hoc* organization that is prerequisite to mass participation.

Resources. Resources constraints arise out of concern over global resource budgets and the earth's ability to sustain the demands man and the rest of the biosphere place upon it. Zimmerman defines resources in cultural terms.[16] If man neither perceives the utility of a given raw material nor has the technical competence and will to make use of it, the raw material is not a resource; thus, prior to World War II uranium had no resource value. Today, efforts are being made to convert pollutants into resources. Resources are thus ever-becoming and the limits of availability for so-called renewable (such as water) and nonrenewable resources (such as oil) are changing in response to increases in human understanding and creativity.

The limits resource constraints impose on man's future are related to the quantity of resources known to be accessible and their consumption rates in the context of cultural attitudes toward their use, reuse, and discard.

Cultural Attitudes Toward Constraints

In India very little is ever wasted—the streets and fields are picked clean of scraps of paper, wood, twigs, metal, and even dung. A use and reuse is found for nearly everything. A glance along the littered roadsides of North America clearly reveals evidence of attitudes toward material wealth and resource use distinctly different from those in India and other parts of the world. The prevailing view toward resources in postindustrial societies is linear. Resources are used, discarded, and exhausted. In contrast, cyclical use demands that resources be recycled, as in the closed system of a space vehicle. The ecology movement has made progress toward continual recycling of glass, metal, paper, wood, and water. Also recycling technology has been promoted by public outcries against institutions that encourage planned obsolescence, such as the automobile industry.

Cultural attitudes are linked with technological capabilities and they condition the significance of the aforementioned constraints. Indeed, the realization of the utopian goals listed earlier will be greatly enhanced if such attitudinal shifts as the following are achieved:

> *The tempering of profit motivations so that advances in transportation and communications will help diminish the tyranny of space.*
>
> *A change in the ethic toward work so that the tyranny of communications and resultant stress can be balanced by individually selected levels of disengagement.*
>
> *A shift toward acceptance of change rather than stability as a way of life so that the administrative constraint of bureaucracy can give way to more flexible organizational arrangements.*
>
> *An accelerated shift from linear to cyclical resource use so that the earth can accommodate its life systems at optimal levels.*

To date our locational, administrative, and resource use systems have absorbed and accommodated a considerable degree of technological and social change. This partial success is now being systematically shattered by increasing awareness of ecological and social problems, and by growing apprehension over our ability to maintain effective control of our earthly domain. Thus the attitudinal shifts suggested above must proceed in all haste.

We offer final notes of both optimism and pessimism before

launching the reader into the journey of this book. Unlimited energy resulting from nuclear fusion would greatly reduce present constraints of time, space, energy, other resource needs, and environmental pollution. If this occurs in conjunction with necessary changes in cultural attitudes, then man will have taken a giant step toward fuller realization of his personal and societal utopias. But the quantum leaps needed to compel changes in our political, economic, and social perceptions seem far off.

Putting the Contents into Context

In figure 1.1 we present a model which serves as a road guide for mapping this book's contents. The first four chapters (Part I) define and explain convergence and extensibility as the origins of stress. Because transportation and communications are such critical determinants of the

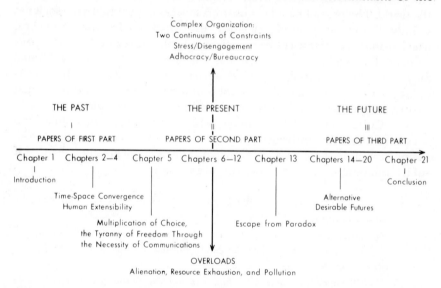

Figure 1.1   A Model of the Organization of This Volume.

As indicated by the horizontal dimension, the book focuses on the way past and ongoing processes (especially time-space convergence and human extensibility) create current opportunities and dilemmas (the vertical dimension). Our major concern is whether man can escape present paradox by fashioning appropriate means of disengagement, administration, and resource cycling, or whether the most probable alternative future is one in which convergence and extensibility generate more problems of overload than they solve.

locations of social, economic, and residential activities, it is important that we understand in detail the ways they are changing our lives and our perceptions. Part II explores direct and indirect effects of convergences and extensibility with emphasis on the stresses they can create and with attention to the explicit formal responses such stresses demand. Chapters 6 through 12 are concerned with choosing among alternative settlement patterns because of the way such patterns depend on transportation technologies and because they are such basic dimensions of human existence. Part III (chapters 13-21) describes in more detail some of the alternative futures hinted at in Parts I and II. Scenarios and simulations answer some questions about the future, but other authors raise questions concerning the ability of our resource bases to support the alternative futures envisaged in this book and elsewhere.

To some degree the path to a happy future is clear. Once we understand the basic processes that are shrinking space and creating the future, our major task lies in maintaining a positive trajectory through the present to the future. To stay above the horizontal line in figure 1.1 we must adjust our institutions and ethics in ways that will permit us to choose wisely from the array of opportunities technology will provide. We must not fall prey to rigidity and alienation in the face of multiple opportunities. Either we organize and manage our journey toward the future or we become paralyzed in which case we shall be carried helpless into the future.

Assuming we can devise strategies for avoiding alienation and exhaustion, we can talk meaningfully about alternative futures under man's control. We must look to the future not as a refuge from the past and the present, but as a desirable, anticipated destination. The difficulties of choosing among alternative futures, when any choice involves as many problems as solutions, make it clear that formulating alternative futures is more of a beginning than an end. But to make such tentative beginnings, even in full recognition of the dilemmas they in turn create, is preferable to succumbing to the dilemmas of the present.

References

1. Donald G. Janelle, "Central Place Development in a Time-Space Framework," *The Professional Geographer* 20 (1968): 5-10.

2. Dennis H. Meadows *et al.*, *The Limits to Growth* (New York: Potomac Associates—Universe books, 1972); Alvin Toffler, *Future Shock* (New York: Random House, 1970), Jay W. Forrester, *World Dynamics*. (Cambridge: Wright-Allen, 1971).

3. Robert Ayres, *Technological Forecasting and Long Range Planning* (New York: McGraw-Hill, 1969); Erich Jantsch, *Technological Forecasting in Perspective* (Paris: Organization for Economic Cooperation and Development, 1967).

4. Dennis Gabor, *Inventing the Future* (New York: Alfred A. Knopf, 1964).

5. Thomas S. Kuhn, *The Structure of Scientific Revolutions*, 2nd ed. (Chicago: The University of Chicago Press, 1970); Henry Margenau, *The Nature of Physical Reality* (New York: McGraw-Hill Book Company, 1950); James M. Blaut, "Space and Process," *The Professional Geographer* 13, (1961): 1—7.

6. Torsten Hägerstrand, *The Propagation of Innovation Waves.* Lund Studies in

Geography, Series B, Human Geography, No. 4. Lund, Sweden: Gleerup, 1952; Torsten Hägerstrand, "Aspects of the Spatial Structure of Social Communication and the Diffusion of Information," *Papers of the Regional Science Association* 16, (1966): 27—42.

7. Richard L. Morrill, "The Negro Ghetto: Problems and Alternatives," *Geographical Review* 55 (1965): 339—381; Richard L. Morrill, "Exansion of the Urban Fringe: A Simulation Experiment," *Papers of the Regional Science Association* 16 (1966): 27—42.

8. S. Golant and L. S. Bourne, *Growth Characteristics of the Ontario—Quebec Urban System*, Research Paper No. 4 (Toronto: Centre for Urban and Community Studies, 1968); G. J. A. Smith, *Transportation and Urban Design: A Systems Approach to Toronto's Future Transportation Network*, Research Paper No. 23 (Toronto: Centre for Urban and Community Studies, 1970); G. Gad, *A Review of Methodological Problems in Estimating Urban Expansion*, Research Paper No. 25 (Toronto: Centre for Urban and Community Studies, 1970); Leslie Curry, *Multivariate Spatial Forecasting*, Research Paper No. 12 (Toronto: Centre for Urban and Community Studies, 1969).

9. M. D. Chisholm, Allen E. Frey, and Peter Haggett, eds., *Regional Forecasting*, Proceedings of the Twenty-second Symposium of the Colston Research Society (London: Butterworth, 1970).

10. B. B. Rodoman, "The Organized Anthroposphere," *Soviet Geography: Review and Translation* 9 (1969): 784—796.

11. Ludwig von Bertalanffy, *General System Theory* (New York: Braziller, 1968).

12. Jay W. Forrester, *Urban Dynamics* (Cambridge: M.I.T. Press, 1969).

13. Constantinos A. Doxiadis, "Man's Movements and His City," *Science* 18 (October, 1968): 326—334.

14. Donald R. Deskins, Jr. "Residence, Workplace Interaction Vectors for the Detroit Metropolitan Area: 1953 to 1965," in *Special Publication No. 3, Interaction Patterns and the Spatial Form of the Ghetto* (Evanston, Ill.: Northwestern University Geography Department, 1970).

15. William Warntz, "Global Science and the Tyranny of Space," *Papers of the Regional Science Association* 20 (1968): 7—19.

16. Erich W. Zimmermann, *World Resources and Industries* (New York: Harper and Row, 1951).

Chapter   2

Perceptions and Technologies as Determinants of Predictions about Earth, 2050

Allen K. Philbrick
The University of Western Ontario

ABSTRACT: *Four global budgets must be balanced: energy, material resources, environmental pollution, and population. Achieving practical fusion-power reactors with a resulting reduction in energy cost would make it possible to balance the other three global budgets, but only if we also adjust our attitudes and concepts. For example, the merging of time and space (reduction in time distance) that is now possible decreases the significance of location, and we must adjust our thinking and behavior accordingly.*

The conditions prevailing on the earth in 2050 can be predicted, but such predictions must take into account changing human aspirations as well as technological innovation. To make a successful prediction, one must understand the processes on which the prediction is based. An essential process to be understood is "what does it take?" for people to match their aspirations and achievements. The human race is one huge, enlarging energy field of individual and group aspirations. The abysmal gap between the hopes of the "have nots" and those of "the haves" is the generator of the future. The locus of this change generator is in the minds of specific human individuals and groups. Maps of world industrial organization and of world hunger combined into one surface, one continuum of difference, would represent the total human perception of the differential or gap between what is (achievement), and what humanity thinks ought to be (aspiration). Such a map would be time-spatial. It would bubble with constantly changing perceptions and aspirations.

World cultures and their definable subdivisions are parts of a global mentality or "noosphere."[1] In order to predict how the gap between aspirations and achievements will be closed, the phenomena upon which this cultural change will act must be identified. Granted that the social revolution we are experiencing on a global scale represents basic dissatisfaction with things as they are, can the demands of humanity be satisfactorily met? Can the earth be so organized that there is room for fulfilling all, or almost all, of people's aspirations? There are four principal global budgets that must be balanced if the answer to this question is to be yes. These are energy, material resources, environmental pollution, and population, which represent a modern version of the four horsemen of the Apocalypse.

Gough and Eastland point out that "auxiliary energy (derived mainly from fossil fuels, water power and nuclear-fission fuels) 'opens the gate' to the efficient use of the sun's energy by helping to produce fertilizers, pesticides, improved seeds, farm machinery and so on."[2] The spiraling nature of the demands made by energy increases, food increases, and population increases on resources derived from the original use of solar energy is evident (figure 2.1). The imbalance between the standards of life in the developed countries and those of the less developed countries (to say nothing of the imbalances among groups within even the most advanced countries) is the cultural generator of social revolution.

The first answer, therefore, to the question "what does it take to match people's aspirations with achievement?" is a dramatic increase in available auxiliary energy. For purposes of predicting the condition of the earth in 2050 we must assume achievement of practical fusion-power reactors. Such an assumption is in line with the history of technological innovations over the past century. It is, of course, not certain that such power will be used wisely. Yet, fusion power must be achieved to make the first three of the four principal global budgets balanceable. Fusion power will not automatically balance a single budget, however, let alone a global one. The difficult readjustment in mental attitudes required and the spatial consequences of such readjustments are the primary concerns of this chapter.

Another process to be understood for successful predictions about 2050 is the connection between culture and human organization of terrestrial space. The present uneven distribution of human population is

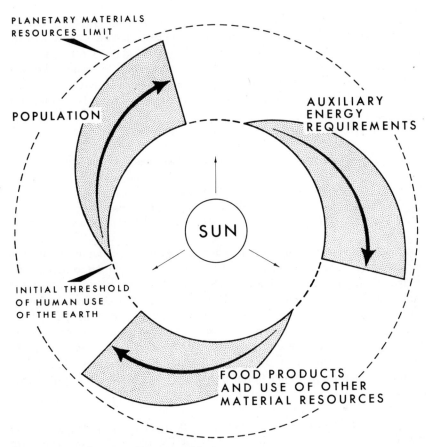

Figure 2.1 Planetary Resource Limits.
The sun is the source of all life and of most energy. The distance between the "initial threshold" and the "planetary materials resource limit" represents the terrestrial stocks of energy, food, materials, and population carrying capacity.

the result of Western economic man's cultural bias toward maximizing consumption (markets) and minimizing transport costs (distance); these values are responsible for metropolitanization and industrialization. But, following the impact of fusion power, new values will govern population distributions. These developments must follow upon the new perceptions of the future which will emerge from the current social revolution. Accordingly, the underlying question must be: What new mental attitudes will determine patterns of human organization in 2050?

Stages in Human Dimensional Perceptions

To answer this question we must know something about the context in which these future attitudes and settlement patterns will emerge.

Such a context is to be found in the changes in human perception of the spatial character of the world. In the past 500 years man's perception of the dimensions of the world have changed remarkably. Four types are discernible in a continuum of expanding dimensional perception. The last of the four perceptions is barely started, but it is the one which will be in full flower by the time an infant of today is experiencing what is predicted in this chapter.

The four types of perception referred to are:

Type Name	Primary Dimensional Perceptions
1. local	0—1 and sometimes 2
2. regional	0—1—2 and sometimes 3
3. global	0—1—2—3 and sometimes 4
4. in-and-out	0—1—2—3—4 and sometimes n

Each type's dimensional meaning is geared to a common cultural perception among a population at a given state of technological and territorial organization. Historically, such states of being represent a continuum of development. The change from one to another, however, comes as the result of complex socioeconomic mutation, a kind of cultural quantum jump. Implying a single linear continuum of development would do great violence to the ebb and flow of the history of civilizations or cultures. No intention of dismissing prehistorical or ancient historical peoples as lacking in dimensional perceptivity should be read into what follows.

Local Perception. A large proportion of the population in pre-industrial subsistence societies were primarily aware only of their own locality. This has not been the case since industrial exchange systems were developed. In a dimensional sense, one may define local perception as zero to one-dimensional. Persons with only local perceptions thought of themselves as locality bound. Movements to and from other points of focus were primarily linear in the local context.

Only a tiny minority, such as merchant adventurers, high priests, kings, emperors, "fools," poets, and wandering minstrels had vision beyond the local horizon. Yet the Roman, Chinese, Arab, Mali, and Carolingian Empires, to say nothing of others that have gone unrecorded, could not be called local. What of them? Are they exceptions? In this context, their leadership classes represent the initial organizational push toward two-dimensional regional perceptions. The very fact that they represent pulses of regional organization which subsided without achieving global proportions is noteworthy. While they existed, the overwhelming majority of their subjects remained local in their organized spatial commitments. Even today a significant proportion of the world's people possess a primarily local or point-bound frame of reference. Their numbers are declining, however, in relation to those with regional and worldwide awareness.

Regional Perception.   More than local perception emerges from local perception. The majority of the population of a region probably first experienced such perception after the English industrial revolution. Steam and the industrial revolution made production for regional distribution commonplace. Collecting resources from several places for processing and creating commodities for sale on a mass production basis made more and more people conscious of different and distant places and larger regions. Point to point movement by road, canal, rail, river, ocean, and air routes shattered the parochial viewpoint of the local village and paved the way for the two-dimensional regional viewpoint to progress to a three-dimensional global perspective.

Global Perception.   The regional view is now evident in wide-spread urban networks in all parts of the world. Gaps in its diffusion exist only here and there in developing nations. Technological developments brought about the air and the electronic ages that made the global mentality possible. Jet air transport made long-haul intercontinental travel commonplace in the post-World War II era and thereby forced people in the industrialized nations to think globally. Continuing developments such as intercontinental ballistic missiles and communication satellites have "shrunk" the globe to an instant's time-space for information and an hour's time-space for delivery of "the bomb."

> *The Russians are not "ninety miles off our shores." They are literally "up" and we from them since we occupy each other's heavens and can mutually destroy to the depth of five hundred feet anything on each other's surface.*[3]

In-and-Out Perception.   Nuclear space technology has brought human awareness to the threshold of time-space perception. Einstein's relativity theory laid the basis for objective understanding of the inseparable nature of time-space.[4] Space as the relative location of phenomena, and time as the rate of change of such relative locations in motion, are different cultural constructs of one inseparable phenonenon, time-space. Separation of spatial from temporal thinking is a cultural convention, not objective fact. Conceptually integrating time and space is as difficult for most people to become accustomed to as was the idea some centuries ago that the world was not flat but spherical.

Yet, perceptual mergings of space and time are upon us for purposes of human terrestrial organization. Electronically, we can see and hear over the entire earth almost instantaneously via satellite. It is accepted that instantaneous perception is non-simultaneous by the clock. There is nothing radically new about this. This recognition began to become commonplace with the introduction of the time-zones during the railroad era. Supersonic transports and earth satellites continue to shrink time distances in ways that are topics of conversation and head shaking wonder for older people who remember when radio was a novelty and television a dream. A perceptual state is at hand in which location at a particular point on the earth's surface is beginning to lose its meaning of fixity.

Man's experience of weightlessness in outer space due to freedom from earth's gravity and the receipt of color television pictures of the earth from the moon have profoundly affected our culture. Hundreds of millions of mankind have been introduced to the fourth-dimensional, time-space perception of looking out and looking in as a correction to the concept of up and down.

Perception Lag

One very important qualification in understanding this continuum of dimensional viewpoints is the complexity introduced by perception-lag. The four types of perception are cumulative, not mutually exclusive, since objectively each type possesses all dimensions. The phenomena under discussion are perceptions held by a very large and variable population—the whole human race.

Not surprisingly there are millions of persons for whom the dominant perception of the world is as local today as it was for their ancestors five hundred or more years ago. The difference is that such persons are probably a minority today rather than a majority. What has happened is that a majority of the population representing earlier perceptual types remained static while a growing number acquired the insights of the next perceptual type.

When the regional perception which accompanied the industrial revolution was sweeping the world with its economic and organizational consequences, a majority of the world's population still lagged behind and retained their local state of mind. Today, when we are starting what may be called the nuclear time-space perceptual state, most of humanity still perceives things in varying degrees of global, regional, and local terms.

Thus, perceptions of the world's spatial characteristics have become more complex as human population has increased in size, range of organization, technology, and affluence.

A Tri-Part Social Revolution

The social revolution we are experiencing is a three-part one. It is:
1. Sociopolitical 2. Economic-technological and 3. Conceptual-spatial.

I do not intend to predict specific sociopolitical outcomes of the current social revolution. Such outcomes are not irrelevant, but heated controversy over ideological conflict is thus avoided. I assume, therefore, successful establishment of more stable forms of popular political organization sensitive to human needs not now served by the established order, such an assumption being in line with sociopolitical innovations over the past century.

The key to balancing the global budgets of energy, material resources, and environmental pollution is the nuclear fusion option that will provide the auxiliary energy required to satisfy the aspirations of the "have nots." I also assume, therefore, successful achievement of practical fusion power reactors.

It is my purpose to deal with the conceptual and spatial facets of the social revolution, for they will determine the predictions to be made about the earth in 2050.

Growth Without Increase

It now appears that the period of rapid population and industrial growth that has prevailed during the last few centuries, instead of being the normal order of things and capable of continuance into the indefinite future, is actually one of the most abnormal phases of human history. It represents only a brief transitional episode between two very much longer periods, each characterized by rates of change so slow as to be regarded essentially as a period of non-growth. It is paradoxical that although the forthcoming period of non-growth poses no insuperable physical or biological problems, it will entail a fundamental revision of those aspects of our current economic and social thinking which stem from the assumption that the growth rates which have characterized this temporary period can be permanent.[5]

We live today in the transition period just preceding the era of growth without increase. The problem is not how to balance the global population budget, but how to bring about attitudinal changes which will make possible a stationary-state global economy capable of stabilizing "economic development, materials depletion, pollution, war, and the organization of human societies."[6] For as Hubbert has said, "the one type of behavior for this curve [the population curve] that is not possible is that of continued and unlimited growth."[7]

What does growth without increase mean? Education is the best example. Teaching represents growth on the part of both professor and student. Yet the professor has not literally transferred any reifiable substance of which he is the bearer. Nor has the student gained in the sense of weighing more or becoming two bodies instead of one.[8] Yet a process of growth has taken place. Accordingly, gross national product notwithstanding, it is conceivable that each country can continue to grow even though its population remains stable, its material resources budget does not increase, its gold reserves remain the same, and a host of other phenomena remain fixed. *Qualitative* changes might take place which would provide great satisfaction to the populations. Stabilization of birth and death rates so that the population is stationary or increases slowly is quite within the reach of any culture which collectively decides to accomplish it.

Conceptual—Spatial Predictions   Spatial perceptions have always had profound affects on the spatial organization of the earth's surface. Accordingly, we may expect continuing spatial consequences of the perceptual model described above.

My predictions are that there will be continued development of a truly global perception of the necessity to balance the four global budgets; and that there will be a further negation of time and space in terms of terrestrial organization. These spatial predictions are based on the achievement of four conditions: 1. Reduction in energy cost; 2. Reduction in time distance; 3. Growth without population increase; and 4. Appreciation of human rights above property rights.

Reduction in Energy Cost   When the nuclear fusion option is realized, energy supply will exceed the demand, and the cost of energy will drop. Such a dramatic change in the energy base of our global economy will have many long-range effects, because productivity then will be able to whittle away at the backlog of unfulfilled aspirations. Many negative pressures which now supporrt high birth rates will diminish. Long-range planning dependent upon great increases in the amount and levels of communication will be possible, because the people will no longer be bound by concerns about war, hunger, unemployment, disease, and pestilence. As a cultural drive, growth without increase might replace the present emphasis on increasing the gross national product.

In addition, fusion power can resolve both the nuclear waste disposal problem and, through the possible development of a device called the "fusion torch," might help resolve other pollution problems as well.

> *Among the inherent advantages (of the fusion system), one of the most important is the fact that the use of fusion fuel requires no burning of the world's oxygen or hydrocarbon resources and hence releases no carbon dioxide or other combustion products to the atmosphere.——Another advantage of fusion power is that no radioactive wastes are produced as the result of the fuel cycles contemplated.*[9]

It must be acknowledged that the energy assumption is basic to the other predictions here stated. If we do not succeed in the energy developments described, most of what follows will fail, for a massive increase in energy expenditures will be necessary to bring about the changes predicted in the following sections.

Reduction in Time Distance   The location of a given place is

altered every time its connectivity to other places is changed by improvements in a highway or construction of a bridge. A point's location is altered
in a more general way by the "shrinking of the earth" by technological
improvements in transport. The sailing ship transformed the seas from
barriers to connectors. The airplane made three-dimensional space a reality
above parts of the earth's surface. Moon-shot satellites capable of escaping
the earth's gravitation have made possible n-dimensional movement of life
support systems into outer space. The potential for colonizing other planets
in our galaxy has exponentially changed our perceptual horizon to in and
out instead of up and down.

Paralleling the general changes in spatial perception there has been
a steady reduction in the significance of place in industrial location. "A
central location is no longer fundamental to an economically rational
distribution of manufactured commodities to the metropolitan market."[10]

Even the city, which has always been considered the focus of
urbanized industrial culture, is changing its character. "A new kind of
large-scale urban society is emerging that is increasingly independent of
the city. . . . Paradoxically, just at the time in history when policy-makers
and the world press are discovering the city, 'the age of the city seems to be
at an end'."[11]

In North America, which is so often the harbinger of things to
come elsewhere,

> The simple answer is that our highways have become the streets of a
> dispersed city. They were designed to be bridges across the spaces between
> the cities, and as the means of connecting the city and the country. They
> have now become the alignments along which the impact of the city has
> penetrated unevenly but far outward into the more uniformly distributed
> agricultural and forested lands of the State.[12]

As energy becomes more abundant and we are able to employ greater
amounts of energy to change the form of objects, we will become freer of
the tyranny of location. We will transport fewer objects and ever more
energy. We will employ that energy to transform objects into the materials
we need at the places we wish to be. This is the spatial outcome of the
energy revolution. But this spatial outcome will occur only after our
attitudes have been altered by a full realization of the uses to which the
auxiliary energy can be put.

We are experiencing sequential waves of landscape reorganization.
The social disorganization of Europe's population rose in the sixteenth,
seventeenth, and eighteenth centuries. At the same time, the pressures at
the base of the Malthusian prediction of the early nineteenth century[13]
were being relieved by organized exploration and the exploitation of new
agricultural lands. Dispersed settlements, agricultural and pastoral,
through the world's so-called "new lands" caused the disorganization of
indigenous peoples and their biotic landscape to skyrocket with the

burning of the forests and the plowing of the grasslands. At the same time, the great prosperity of early English, European, and American capitalism was based upon the reverse spatial concentration of millions of people into industrial and mercantile cities. The earlier overseas dispersal supplied the organized resources,[14] that is, food, for Europe's industrial population concentrations.

Even as the concentrative forces of industrial capitalism were marshalling their energy in the age of steam, the stress within the system rose sharply because of the classical contradictions of capitalism.[15] Only a second and a third wave of technological innovation, vastly increasing the productivity per man in the petro-chemical and electronic phases of the industrial revolution, avoided the speedy and complete resolution of the contradictions.

Now, society's concentrated urban spatial pattern again shows every evidence of a rapid worldwide increase in disorganization. The problems of the urban ghetto, urban pollution, congestion, crime, the "drug culture", rising welfare and operational costs, as well as the sterility of suburban affluence, are in stark contrast to the aspirations of all sections of the population.

The energy revolution attendant upon successful realization of fusion energy will profoundly change our attitudes toward the necessity for concentrated spatial organization. When energy costs come down, transport costs will decline. When materials transformations become practical, the quantities of raw materials requiring transport will decrease. The economic and engineering basis for industrial dispersion will make freedom from the tyranny of location profitable rather than the luxury it is now.

The ways that technological change affects location can be demonstrated by examples in two fields: electrical power and water desalination.

A new infrastructure for electrical power transport will be built. At a recent conference on the future of atomic energy, the Chairman of the U.S. Atomic Energy Commission predicted that electrical energy networks will become global.[16] Power engineers will turn increasingly to nuclear generation of electricity. They will conserve hydrocarbons for uses other than energy production. This trend will be combined with heightened pressure to curb pollution of the environment that would result from consumption of lower and lower grades of fossil fuels. As a consequence it will become necessary to develop not only more extensive inter-regional and international power grids, but intercontinental ones as well. "Looking well into the future one can imagine worldwide power transmission networks which will take full advantage of time-zone differences and seasonal diversities to equalize the overall global daily demands for electricity."[17] Seaborg also predicts the use of laser beam technology to transmit energy via satellite.

After energy, the prime resource of all planetary life is water. If skyrocketing demands for agricultural, domestic, and industrial fresh water uses are to be met, huge quantitites of new energy will go into developing a global, manmade hydrologic cycle.[18] Desalination plants will first augment and then gradually replace the transferral of natural drainage from one river basin to another. Ultimately, if the potential for developing dry lands for settlement and support of additional billions is to be realized, we must create a manmade hydrologic cycle that will consume a huge amount of electrical energy. It will make fresh water for irrigation and all other uses ubiquitous. To be effective, such an integrated system will have to coordinate spatially the initial supplementary production sites. To distribute supplies of fresh water mined from the sea, we must select sites where land configuration and existing river channels may be combined to facilitate delivery over wide areas. There are several continental examples of potential sites where development could maximize the gains per unit of social capital invested (figure 2.2). The probable size of these required investments underscores the importance of the basic assumption of this chapter, that the fusion power option will prove practicable. Each of the four sites will be discussed briefly.

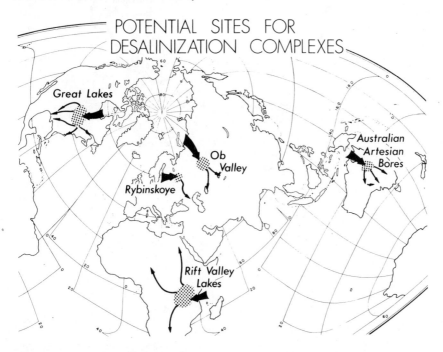

Figure 2.2 Potential Sites for Desalinization Complexes.
Ocean water desalinization plants and distribution schemes such as those mapped here would make it possible to supply large water-deficit regions with cheap water using existing river systems.

The North American Great Lakes are an ideal "nodal water region" (figure 2.3). A nodal water region is a combination of natural reservoir in relation to radial river drainage sloping *away* from the storage basin that

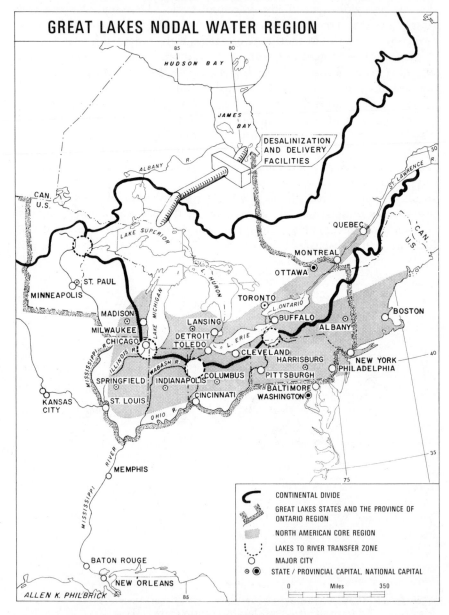

Figure 2.3   The Great Lakes Nodal Water Region.
Natural reservoirs and radial rivers that slope away from the storage basin are nodal water regions, as in the case of the Hudson Bay-Great Lakes-Ohio and Mississippi system. (From *Canadian Geographer* 8 (1964): 185.)

provides natural opportunities for delivering large amounts of fresh water to an extensive region. The distributaries afforded by the Ohio-Mississippi River system that drains the post-glacial surface of eastern North America pass through the most heavily populated, water-deficient, advanced-development region on the entire continent.

A similar low upland location exists in East Africa in the rift valley lakes region. The Nile, tributaries of the Congo, and branches of the Zambezi could distribute water widely throughout the seasonally dry savanna portions of northern and southern Africa. Seasonal drought is a serious problem in Africa (figure 2.4) and such a system would be extremely valuable in raising agricultural productivity. In Australia, the great artesian basin of southwestern Queensland could be continually charged with desalinated water from the Gulf of Carpentaria. Economic pressures will spark these developments and others like them; greater demand, more water, more production, and higher levels of economic activity will generate the affluence needed to amortize development costs.

In the Soviet Union, a modification of the Ob River proposal to create a shallow inland freshwater sea in the great trans-Ural marshes might be more sound ecologically than diverting the Ob and Yenisei from the Arctic. Even if such a scheme were combined with diversion, it could supply a great quantity of water in addition to that diverted. The difference would be in supplying the inland sea created by damming the Ob and Yenisei Rivers with desalinated water pumped over the relatively low grade from the Gulf of the Ob (figure 2.5), a distance of less than four hundred miles.[19] This distance is comparable to that from James Bay to Lake Superior in North America. The Russian plan to use diverted Ob and Yenisei water could "irrigate 50 million acres of crop lands and a somewhat larger area of pasture in arid western Siberia and Kazakhstan."

Similarly, the Rybinskoya Reservoir north of Moscow could become the valve through which desalinated water from the Gulf of Finland could be introduced into the canal system feeding the Volga. In this way, the tragic depletion of the Caspian Sea for irrigation and other purposes could be prevented without recourse to diversions from still other river basins.

A primary reason for thinking predictions of global power grids and manmade hydrologic cycles will come about is changed mental attitudes. In-and-out dimensional perception must be encouraged, utilized, and expanded. The idea that the earth is a rather tiny life-support system is increasingly persuasive. Pictures of the earth taken from the moon have convinced millions that the earth is a global ecological unit. More people were converted to resource cycling by such pictures than by all the previous exhortations and pleadings of experts put together. The famous color picture of the blue-white ball of the wet earth in a void of black is perhaps the most dramatic news picture of all time.

Since seeing this picture, many people may have become receptive to desalination of sea water in manmade hydrologic cycles as one means of

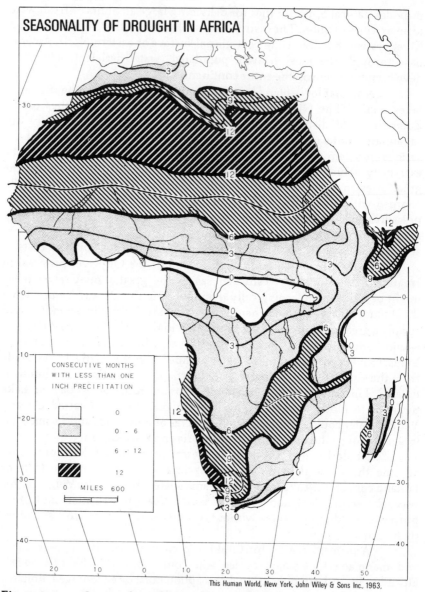

Figure 2.4   Seasonality of Drought in Africa.
The Nile, the Zambesi, and several Congo tributaries could be used to distribute
water to the savannahs of northern and southern Africa and thus alleviate seasonal
drought over extensive areas. (Reproduced, by permission of the publisher, from A.
K. Philbrick, *This Human World*, John Wiley & Sons, Inc., 1963, p. 190.)

restoring and maintaining the balance of nature. Of course, a manmade
hydrologic cycle of any magnitude will also change nature. Whenever we
do this we must study the impact carefully to anticipate the indirect as well

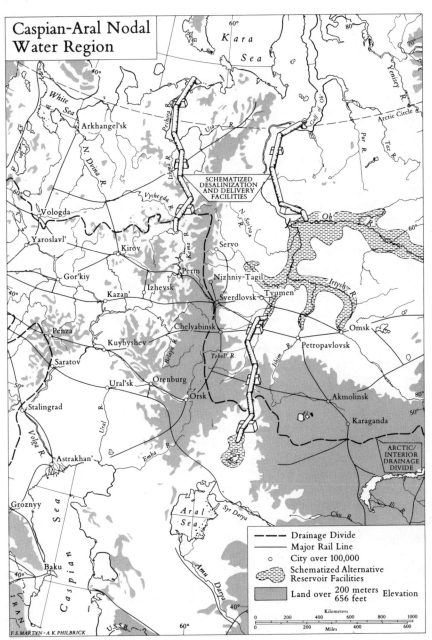

Caspian-Aral Nodal Water Region

SCHEMATIZED DESALINIZATION AND DELIVERY FACILITIES

ARCTIC/ INTERIOR DRAINAGE DIVIDE

- - - - Drainage Divide
———— Major Rail Line
○ City over 100,000
Schematized Alternative Reservoir Facilities
Land over 200 meters / 656 feet Elevation

Figure 2.5   The Ob-Yenesei Project.
Damming the Ob and the Yenesei would create an inland sea that could be used to irrigate the central Soviet steppes.

as obvious effects of our actions. This is the basic purpose of the discipline of ecology. In and out perception recognizes man's responsibility for studying the consequences of his impact upon events. This level of awareness will sharply increase mankind's rate of conversion to the necessary global perception.

Growth Without Population Increase.   Increased communication among peoples will occur at the same time that global energy transmission networks and continental fresh water distribution systems are created. This will be a likely consequence of the social cooperation necessary for such events, and a phenomenon similar to the historical development of the so-called hydraulic societies after the first agricultural revolution. Agricultural empires based upon irrigation works required hierarchical, technological, and political control. By analogy, can global systems be established without hierarchical control of a global polity? Immense increases in energy and water supply could suport a doubling population at a high enough level of living to match human aspirations with appropriate achievements. But would this help the global population budget?

Intercommunication, education, social cooperation, and the elimination of poverty and hunger can be used to promote worldwide voluntary reduction in family size and reproduction rates. That this is necessary scarcely needs saying. Failure to do so will result in a spiralling downward into chaos and bring about Malthus' prediction of war, starvation, and pestilence. Trends in human perception indicate that there is a greater probability for population stabilization than for continued rapid growth.

Appreciation of Human Rights Above Property Rights.   Human dignity requires that we appreciate human rights above property rights. This is the central issue of the social revolution in the midst of which we live. There cannot be a global polity; there cannot be the social cooperation required for successful creation and operation of global and continental systems; there cannot be a solution to the population, energy, material resources, and environmental pollution problems without an appreciation of people above property.

Such a change of attitude must occur, not so much in the spirit of ideological rule, Christian or any other, as in recognition of the soundness of all different cultural perceptions. Global intercommunication across tongues will destroy fear of difference. Successful solutions to survival problems will establish the basis for matching human aspirations with achievement. That this goal will be reached only through struggle and painful effort, if at all, there is no doubt. It is equally clear that the alternative is not simply death, which is a normal event among all living things, but extinction.

Spatial Character of Earth, 2050

What will the earth be like in 2050, a year when a child born today will be an elderly man or woman? From the foregoing description of trends in spatial perception and anticipated consequences of nuclear-industrial technology, I conclude that the basic spatial impact of the future will be a reversal in our image of where to locate.

We will continue to be focused; but we will be dispersing from earlier cultural hearths, because we will think less frequently of transporting things and more frequently of transporting energy. The phrase "the earth as the home of man" will mean more because we will be able to occupy more of its territory more effectively than at present. By using fusion power, we will water, heat, and air-condition the land to suit our requirements.

The single most important consequence, however, will be that the perception of place that has dominated us since prehistory will be lifting. We will increasingly understand that objects and established patterns of things are not just relatively located objects in a culturally defined concept of space. We will regard things and the patterns of things as events in time-space. We will witness increasing negation of the significance of place—we will overcome the tyranny of place.

References

1. Pierre Teilhard de Chardin, *The Future of Man*, trans. Norman Denny (New York and Evanston: Harper and Row, Publishers, 1964), pp. 155—184.

2. William C. Gough and Bernard J. Eastland, "The Prospects of Fusion Power," *Scientific American* 224 (February 1971).

3. William Bunge, *Theoretical Geography*, Lund Studies in Geography, Series C, General and Mathematical Geography 1, 2nd ed. (Lund, Sweden: Gleerup, 1967), p. 166.

4. Albert Einstein, *Relativity, The Special and General Theory of Relativity* (London: Methuen and Co., Ltd., 1920).

5. M. King Hubbert, "Energy Resources" in *Resources and Man*, Committee on Resources and Man, National Academy of Sciences-National Research Council, (San Francisco: W. H. Freeman & Company, 1969), Chapter 8. pp. 238—239.

6. Gough and Eastland, *loc. cit.*

7. Hubbert, *op. cit.*, pp. 238—239.

8. Kenneth Boulding, *The Image* (Ann Arbor: University of Michigan Press, 1961), p. 35.

9. Gough and Eastland, *op. cit.*, p. 61.

10. Allan Pred, "The Intrametropolitan Location of American Manufacturing," *Annals of the American Association of Geographers* 54 (June 1964): 165—174.

11. Melvin M. Webber, "The Post-City Age," *Daedalus* 97 (1968): 1093—1099.

12. Allen K. Philbrick, *Analyses on the Geographical Patterns of Gross Land Uses in the Lower Half of the Lower Peninsula of Michigan* (East Lansing: Michigan State University, 1961), p. 2.

13. Thomas Malthus, "An Essay on the Principle of Population," London, 1798,

excerpt from Sixth Edition reprinted in James R. Newman, *The World of Mathematics*, Vol. 2 (New York: Simon & Schuster, 1956), pp. 1189—1199.

14. Erwin Schrodinger, *What is Life?* Cambridge: Cambridge University Press, 1945).

15. Karl Marx and Friedrich Engels, *Communist Manifesto*, from *Marx and Engels*, ed. Lewis S. Fever (New York: Anchor Books, Doubleday & Co., Inc., 1959), pp. 6—29.

16. Glenn T. Seaborg, "An International Challenge," *Bulletin of the Atomic Scientists* (1970): 5—7.

17. *Ibid.*

18. Allen K. Philbrick, "The Nodal Water Region of North America," *Canadian Geographer* 8 (1964): 182-187.

19. Roger Revelle, "Water," in *Man and the Ecosphere*, with commentaries by Paul Ehrlich, John Holden and Richard Holm, (San Francisco: W. H. Freeman & Co., 1971), pp. 56 – 67.

Chapter   3

Effects of Space-Adjusting Technologies on The Human Geography of the Future

Ronald Abler
The Pennsylvania State University

ABSTRACT: *How will future space-adjusting technologies affect human spatial organization? Specifically, what are the geographical implications of time-space convergence and cost-space convergence in communications networks such as telephone and postal systems? One alternative future is for a continuance of local urban dispersion within larger scale metropolitinization until traditional cities disappear within a world city. But with complete time- and cost-space convergence, why even have cities? What alternative explanatory theories about space could then be developed? Perceptions about distance, space, and time become more important for spatial organization than the realities. Geographers are asked to develop sound, imaginative theories and models of spatial process and structure, apply them to what is presently known, and produce alternative spatial futures.*

Few facets of human activity remain untouched by the technologies that evoke our concern with the future, but in the spatial realm changes in transportation and communication have been more fundamental than other innovations. Our abilities to move people, goods, weapons, and information have created a world in which a robust spatial futuristics is an indispensable element of any strategy for survival. The foremost task of those interested in spatial futuristics is to forecast the effects existing and future space-adjusting technologies will have on human spatial organization, and on the way we think about our spatial futures.[1]

Relative Location and Relative Distance

Distance has always been a fundamental concern in human affairs because virtually all human and physical phenomena vary in occurrence and intensity with distance. Moreover, moving through space has always required the expenditure of time, money, and energy. The necessity to expend such resources in order to move goods, information, and people from one place to another is the single most important explanatory variable in the spatial analyst's tool kit. It is known as the friction of distance. The friction of distance is an implicit or explicit determinant of human choice and human spatial behavior in all geographical theory.

Thinkers since Strabo have been sensitive to the ability of technology to alter distance and space, but it was not until the twentieth century that relative location was identified as a spatial principle that explains the locations of phenomena and human activities. Friedrich Ratzel did more than any other individual to make relative location an element of our explanatory models.[2] The idea of relative distance is implicit in the notion of relative location, but implicit notions must be explicitly identified as general spatial principles before they can become explanatory variables. Watson argued that in the modern world distances are always relative.[3]

Modern space-adjusting systems (that is, communications and transportation) render physical maps increasingly inaccurate as representations of functional spatial relationships. Space-adjusting systems contort and convolute "real" or absolute spatial relationships in peculiar and exciting ways.

> When there are many relationships between time and space, as there are in our society, with the time required to cover the space between Washington and Chicago almost exactly equivalent to the time required to travel from Washington to one airport and from another airport to Chicago, we have what at best can be described as a confusing situation.[4]

If we wish to explain and predict spatial interaction in this situation, what is important is not absolute distances as expressed in such units as miles, but relative distances as expressed in how far apart people at different places *think* they are. The spaces in which people live are much more psychological than absolute. Time and cost are more powerful determinants of behavior than are absolute distances. Thus any attempt to forecast distributions of people and their activities over the decades ahead must be based on accurate estimates of future time and money costs of moving goods, people, and information.

Janelle's concept of time-space convergence—the rate at which places approach one another in time distance—enables us to measure changes in relative distance. Janelle calculated the rate at which London and Edinburgh converged in time-space between 1776, when the journey was made by coach, and 1966, when the trip could be made by airplane, as 29.4 minutes per year (figure 3.1).[5] Obviously, the concept of space convergence can be extended to other contexts. Cost-space convergence (or divergence), for example, can be measured by using costs of movement between the same points at two different dates. Spatial convergence can be measured for any distance-related cost or effort for which we can devise an appropriate scale. Thus, we can think of N spaces in which we might measure convergence and divergence. If we were clever enough, for example, we might be able to measure the convergence of metropolitan black and white neighborhoods in time-space and their simultaneous divergence in social-space. Time and cost by no means exhaust the dimensions along which convergence and divergence can be measured. Rather, they are two contexts for which convenient measurement scales exist.

It is well that we have such scales, for time and cost are two basic determinants of human spatial behavior. In this chapter we will explore the geographical implications of time- and cost-space convergence in communications systems. Changes in time and cost distances are more imminent than changes in other relative spaces; restricting discussion to interpersonal communications is also a matter of competence. But to anticipate a later discussion, there are good theoretical grounds for concentrating on communications. In the coming century, communications will be as powerful a determinant of human spatial organization as transportation was in the last century.

Time- and Cost-Space Convergence in Intercommunications Systems

There are a number of interpersonal media (physical channels by which two-way communication among scattered senders and receivers may be effected), but the most important are postal and telephone networks. Telegraph was once important, but is now of limited use; the number of domestic telegrams sent in the United States has declined each year since 1945.[6] Most interpersonal communications in North America now move through the postal and telephone networks, and such exchanges of written and spoken information will continue, even though facsimile, video, and computer facilities will eventually supplement postal and telephone services.

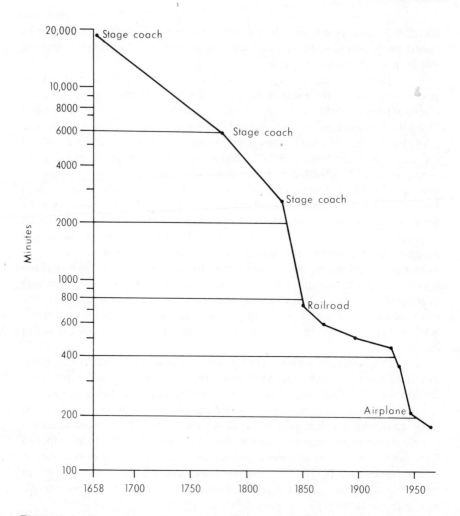

Figure 3.1   Time-Space Convergence Between London and Edinburgh.
(Adapted from Janelle, in *Professional Geographer* 20, 1968.)
Time-space convergence 1776 to 1966= 29.4 minutes per year, from the formula:

$$\frac{TT^1 - TT^2}{Y^2 - Y^1}$$

where: TT^1 and TT^2 = the travel times between the two places in year 1 and some later year 2, and
Y^1 and Y^2 = the two dates in question, thus:

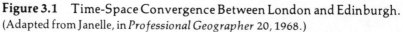

$$\frac{5{,}760\text{-}180}{1966\text{-}1776} = \frac{5{,}580}{190} = 29.4 \text{ minutes per year}$$

Time-Space Convergence   Truly national telephone service became possible in 1915 after the construction of the first transcontinental telephone trunk line.[7] Even after it became possible, placing a transcontinental call was time-consuming. It took 14 minutes to effect such a call in 1920 and required the work of as many as eight operators.[8] By 1930, improvements in network structure had cut average service speed to 2.1 minutes, and further progress brought an average service time of 1.4 minutes by 1940.[9] Automatic switching equipment reduced average service time to about 1.0 minutes in the 1950s, and customer Direct Distance Dialing has now produced a situation in which the major variable governing the time it takes to complete a call anywhere in the North American system is the time it takes the recipient to answer the phone. Dialing a long distance call and switching it through the network usually takes no more than 20 to 25 seconds. The application of electronic switching in the toll network will reduce this time even more in the future. Assuming an average service speed of 30 seconds on toll calls in 1970, time-space convergence between New York and San Francisco has been about 16 seconds per year since 1920 (figure 3.2).

Complete time-space convergence in telephonic communications

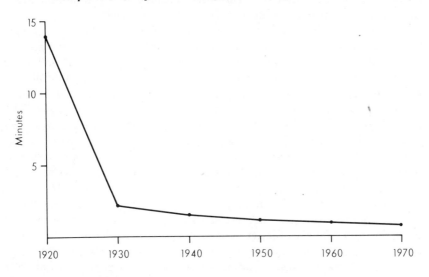

Figure 3.2 Telephone Time-Space Convergence Between New York and San Francisco, 1920–1970.

is almost an accomplished fact. There is little difference between the time required to effect a local call and the time needed to complete a long distance interconnection. Dialing and switching a local call usually takes 10 to 15 seconds. The additional 10 to 15 seconds needed to make a transcontinental call would not be considered important by most people, and even this small difference will eventually be eliminated.

In international telecommunications, the world is at a stage similar to that of the United States in 1920. Establishing a transoceanic circuit can still take a half-hour or more. International time-space convergence in telecommunications is proceeding apace, however. Direct customer dialing between New York City and Great Britain was begun on March 15, 1970, and direct dialing to the entire world will someday be possible.[10] In the same way that metropolitan telephone systems have been good models of future national systems in the United States, national telecommunications networks in advanced nations are good predicters of world telecommunications systems at some future date. Within two decades, telecommunications networks will produce complete time-space convergence on a global scale.

Complete time-space convergence—a situation in which no differences in the time required to reach near or distant points exist—shrinks areas to points. In time-space, all of North America is located at the same place. An isochrone map of telecommunications accessibility from any point in North America would have only one isochrone which would embrace the entire area tied into the continental telecommunications network. Over the last fifty years, the continent's telecommunications time-space has shrunk until every place is the same place.

Postal managers have not yet succeeded in producing complete time-space convergence. Early postal communications were very slow. Until mid-nineteenth century, mail rarely moved faster than 10 miles per hour over long distances.[11] When the Butterfield Overland Mail was established between St. Louis and San Francisco in 1858, mail could be sent between New York and San Francisco in about twenty-four days.[12] The Pony Express, established in 1860, cut the time to about twelve days.[13] By 1900, railroads reduced the time to 106 hours[14] and air mail service, inaugurated on a regular basis in 1924, cut the time to 72 hours. Today, it is theoretically possible to attain twelve-hour service between New York and San Francisco, but such speed is rarely achieved because of serious congestion in the metropolitan post offices at both ends. The Postal Service's ability to store written messages also causes complications in that collection and delivery of letter messages is periodic. A letter that misses a collection or delivery employee by one minute may wait another twenty-four hours in many cases. Assuming 48 hours to be more representative of today's average service speed, it is still true that significant time-space convergence in postal communications has been attained since 1858 (figure 3.3).

Postal engineers could produce complete time-space convergence by eliminating differentials in short-haul and long-haul movements, and the United States Postal Service seems to be moving in that direction. Since World War II postal service has deteriorated over short distances because of changes in the transportation media used by the Postal Service and because of metropolitan mail congestion. At the same time, there have been very marked improvements in long haul mail movements attributable to greater use of air transportation. The Postal Service would like to provide next day delivery for as much first class mail as possible and second day delivery for letters moving between any two points in the nation. Should local service

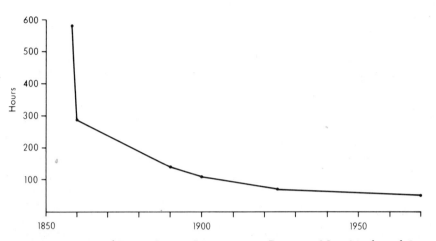

Figure 3.3 Postal Time-Space Convergence Between New York and San Francisco.

continue to deteriorate and long-haul service improve slightly, second day delivery will be ubiquitous and complete time-space convergence will have been achieved, albeit unintentionally.

The very nature of telecommunications has forced telephone engineers to design a network that creates almost complete time-space convergence. Unlike written messages, telephone conversations cannot be stored, and delaying the prompt establishment of connections in any way imposes significant costs on the network. Thus the medium itself promotes time-space convergence.

Connection time need not be eliminated before complete time-space convergence occurs. Telephone communication is not instantaneous. There still exists a threshold time which is required to establish connection with another telephone. But differences between the time needed to establish contact with a phone several thousand miles away and the time needed to make a call to the house next door have almost been eliminated. The graph of time against distance is a flat curve (figure 3.4).

Cost-Space Convergence Whereas the U. S. Postal Service has not achieved complete time-space convergence, it does offer complete cost-space convergence. A flat rate is charged for each letter regardless of the distance it is sent. This simple pricing scheme was not always in effect. In the United States, British rates that increased with distance were retained (with modifications) during the Confederation and in the early years of the Republic. In 1792, a step function of distance was legislated, which was simplified in 1799 (figure 3.5).[15] Rate reductions in 1845, 1851, and 1855 culminated in complete flat rate service at three cents per half ounce in 1863.[16] In 1883, the rate was reduced to two cents. In 1932 it was set at three cents per ounce, where it remained until 1958 when it was raised to four cents. Further increases of a penny in 1963 and 1968, and two cents in 1970

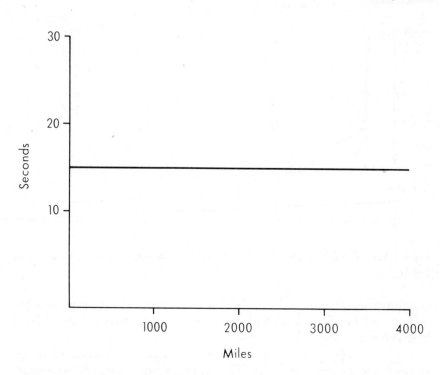

Figure 3.4   Idealized Telephonic Time-Distance Relationship.

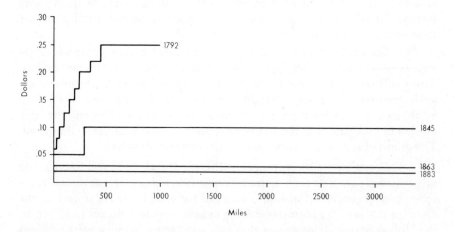

Figure 3.5   Postal Rates for Single Letters, 1792-1883.

and 1974 raised the cost to its present ten cents. Despite apparent cost-space divergence since 1932, complete convergence has existed since 1863 because distance differentials have not existed.

Telephone engineers are well on their way to producing complete cost-space convergence (figure 3.6). Between 1920 and 1970, New York and San Francisco converged at an average rate of 28.5 cents per year. While long haul rates have been dropping, short haul costs and the costs of local telephone service have been rising. Charges for calls within a 60-mile radius have risen as long distance costs were dropping (figure 3.7). As local (flat rate) calling areas continue to expand and as the basic instrument rental

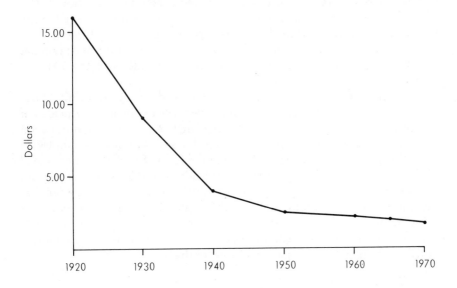

Figure 3.6   Telephone Cost-Space Convergence Between New York and San Francisco.
The curve graphed here is a linear approximation of several step-like changes between the dates plotted.

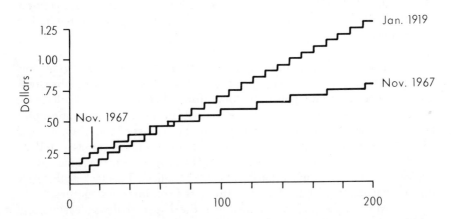

Figure 3.7   Short Haul Telephone Costs, 1919 and 1967.
Rates for calls shorter than 60 miles have risen, whereas the cost of calls over 60 miles have dropped.

for local service rises, long haul costs will continue to drop, gradually eliminating the differential between the two and producing complete cost-space convergence.

Flat rate national service already exists in the United States in the form of Wide Area Telephone Service (W.A.T.S.). For $1850 a month, business subscribers can purchase unlimited access to the national telephone network.[17] Such fees are beyond the means of the average family, but the trend toward national flat rate service is clear. Sometime three or four decades hence, a single monthly fee within the means of most families could purchase unlimited telecommunications throughout the national area.

Complete cost-space convergence is difficult to think about because it runs so contrary to spatial models. We easily accept the idea of complete time-space convergence, since instantaneous communication does not directly conflict with our world view. Although examples of complete cost-space convergence exist in the form of flat rate national mail service, local calling areas in telecommunications, and local flat rate service areas in public bus transportation, it is difficult to extend these familiar systems to national, continental, or world scales. Difficult as it may be, we must assess the effects of complete time- and cost-space convergence in intercommunications in order to make optimal use of these technologies and in order to make wise spatial choices for the future.

Two Examples of Cost-Space Convergence

The major effects of continued cost- and time-space convergence will likely be on general spatial organization and on problems of human extensibility. Before considering such impacts in detail, it is useful to review the effects of complete cost-space convergence in two instances in which it was achieved.

The Texas Common Point Territory   Because the region was served by several keenly competitive railroads, 70 percent of northeastern Texas was a "common point territory" for rail freight until April 1927. Freight rates were the same to all points within the Texas common point region from any point in the United States on or east of the Missouri and Mississippi Rivers (figure 3.8). Under these conditions, goods could be shipped from St. Louis to Corpus Christi (1,018 miles) for the same cost as shipments from St. Louis to Paris, Texas (584 miles). This lack of distance differential had important effects on the state's commercial structure.

Most important among them was the dispersal of wholesaling and jobbing centers. With respect to freight rates to the major gateways of Kansas City, St. Louis, Memphis, Vicksburg, and New Orleans, any town within the region was as well qualified to become a distribution center as any other. Small wholesaling centers arose every forty to fifty miles

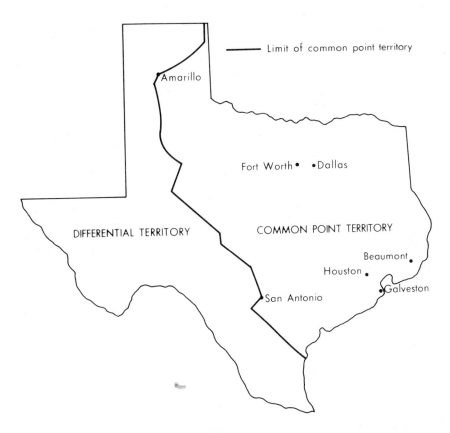

Figure 3.8   Texas Common Point Territory.

throughout the common point territory. The major variable affecting the relative sizes of such centers was the number of railroads to which shippers had access and the purchasing power of the region in which the centers were located.

The large cities of northeastern Texas objected to this rate structure, as it protected hinterlands that they might otherwise have dominated. Dallas and Fort Worth, in particular, argued that rates to them from the northern and eastern gateways should be lower to reflect their closer location to these sources of supply. Although the Texas Railroad Commission favored the common point territory in the belief that the state was better served by numerous small distribution centers, the Interstate Commerce Commission held that a more normal rate structure was in order. The common point territory was broken up into eight distance-based rate zones. The new rates reflected the situational advantage possessed by the larger north Texas cities with respect to location between the Midwest and south Texas.[18]

This unusual example of complete cost-space convergence indicates the extent to which the commercial and other functions of large cities are based on friction of distance. In the absence of frictions of cost-distance within the common point territory, Dallas and Fort Worth (as well as Galveston and Houston) could not establish the wholesaling empires to which they were "entitled." In the absence of normal distance-cost relationships, activities can agglomerate at one location or disperse equally throughout the region affected.

Alaskan Parcel Post   An unusual use of parcel post in Alaska offers similar insights. Parcel post rates in the United States increase with distance, but in a staircase fashion (figure 3.9). For computational ease, all nonlocal parcel post moving within a given Sectional Center is rated as zone 1 and pays zone 1 postage, regardless of the distance.[19] Although there is some variation in Sectional Center sizes in the conterminous states, none are large enough to cause serious rate inequities. Besides, ground transportation is available in the conterminous states, which is the normal medium by which parcel post moves.

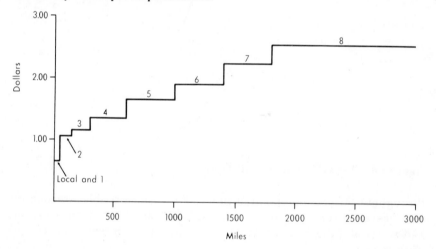

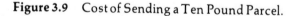

Figure 3.9   Cost of Sending a Ten Pound Parcel.

Alaska, however, has very large Sectional Centers and some very long hauls are consequently rated zone 1 flows (figure 3.10). The Anchorage Sectional Center serves post offices as distant as 1,676 miles from Anchorage, and the Fairbanks Sectional Center, which is larger than Texas, has post offices 750 miles distant from Fairbanks. The situation is complicated by the absence of any alternative to air transportation through most of Alaska. The only way the Postal Service can move mail of any class through much of Alaska is by contract air carrier. Parcel post rates for zone 1 are about half the applicable air freight rates, and consequently some rather unusual wholesaling patterns have developed in Alaska in response to what amounts to complete cost-space convergence for a parcel of a given weight.

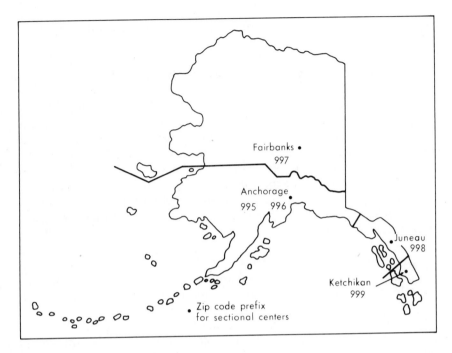

Figure 3.10 Sectional Centers in Alaska.

Commercial shippers and wholesalers now supply scattered mercantile facilities throughout sparsely settled areas of Alaska from Anchorage and Fairbanks. Of the 1,060,000 cubic feet of mail dispatched from Anchorage in 1968, 76 percent was fourth class mail (parcel post). Of the 511,000 cubic feet dispatched by air from Fairbanks, 87 percent was fourth class. Most of the parcel post consisted of stock in trade for outlying trading posts. Bread, eggs, milk, canned goods, paper products, and variety store items all moved directly from Anchorage and Fairbanks to their destinations by air at very low cost. The Alaskan air lines do not object to the diversion of what would normally be air freight to parcel post since their yield per ton-mile flown is greater for mail than for air freight.[20]

The complete cost-space convergence produced by a quirk in rate-making procedures has had effects on the location of economic activity. In the absence of any friction of distance, there is no incentive for mercantile concerns to establish a normal hierarchy of merchandising centers. With all of Fairbanks Sectional Center in the same rate zone, any point in the region can be served equally well from any other point. Fairbanks has the edge as the traditional economic capital and historic gateway to northern Alaska. But if some innovation such as submarine freighters suddenly made it less expensive for merchants to penetrate the region at Point Barrow, in the absence of changes in parcel post rates they would begin serving the entire Sectional Center from Point Barrow immediately.

To reiterate, complete cost-space convergence makes any place as economic a location to carry on commerical activities as any other place.

Mobility and Settlement in a Spaceless World

We are moving (or being pushed) into a world in which distance and relative location will be much less important than they have been in the past, a world in which their importance could conceivably become negligible. This being the case, how shall the social scientist interested in spatial behavior comport himself so as to make himself useful to his fellow human beings? The unique contribution a geographer can make is to clarify the intricate relationships between spatial structure and spatial process, with special reference to human settlement patterns, or the general spatial organization of society.

Space-Adjusting Systems and Settlement Patterns   The most important body of knowledge geographers have developed to date concerns the role of space-adjusting systems (transportation and communication) in creating patterns of human activities in space, and vice versa.

Cities arise at optimal locations for conducting the economic activities which dominate each era, within the context of the space-adjusting systems which are simultaneously dominant. In North America there have been three distinct mobility/development eras, each of which has created its own appropriate metropolitan hierarchy. Until 1850, farming (primary activity) and associated mercantile pursuits dominated the national economy, and cities located at ocean and river ports dominated the urban hierarchy, since such locations were critical nodes in the era's transportation network. Urban growth depended upon commercial expansion. As manufacturing (secondary activities) became dominant after 1850 and especially after the Civil War and as railroads supplanted water transportation, a new set of places was favored for metropolitan centers. Manufacturing cities with good rail connections grew most rapidly until about 1920. By 1920 the automobile was coming into widespread use and the national economy was shifting to a service (tertiary activity) orientation. Manufacturing employment stabilized, and the growth industries and occupations were service-oriented. Accordingly, a new set of cities rose to metropolitan status and experienced rapid growth. Manufacturing centers stagnated or experienced actual population declines.[21]

Movement systems and economic activity shifts governed the internal organization of cities as well as the entry of new locations to the metropolitan hierarchy. Prior to mechanized intraurban transportation cities were necessarily compact, densely settled, and congested because almost everyone had to walk to work. Rail technology made it possible for cities to spread out considerably after 1880. The widespread adoption of the automobile after World War II permitted metropolitan inhabitants to spread out even farther. Movement systems have been of critical importance in American setttlement history, with respect to both the external relations of large cities and their internal organization.

At the same time that mobility revolutions were changing the rules of the game for cities competing at the top of the urban hierarchy, increased personal mobility was wiping out the bottom. During the first twenty years of this century, Rural Free Delivery was sounding the death knell of thousands of crossroads settlements supported by a combined post office and general store.[22] Country hamlets and corner grocery stores in cities were next to go as better cars and roads made it possible for shoppers to reach larger centers with their greater array of goods and services and their lower prices. At all levels, the pattern of settlement has been profoundly changed by new space-adjusting systems.

We are now moving into another economic era and a new space-adjusting epoch. The occupations which Gottmann designated as the quaternary sector—jobs which revolve around the generation, transmission, processing, and utilization of information and knowledge—have since 1960 grown more rapidly than any other sector of the economy.[23] Moreover, this sector will continue to grow most rapidly in advanced economies for the rest of this century. Consider the millions of college students in the United States today. Virtually all are being trained for white-collar, information-processing occupations. Many of those who go to work without entering college choose similar occupations. The post-industrial nations of the world are fast becoming quaternary societies in which most people earn their livings by taking in each other's information.

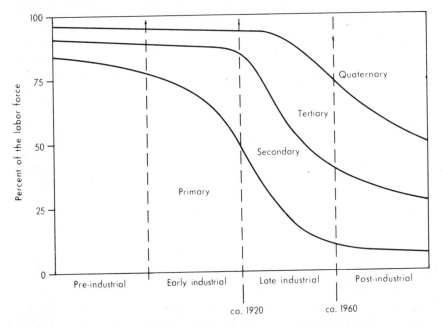

Figure 3.11 Labor Force Structure and Economic Development.

Transportation is the lifeblood of a society dominated by secondary or tertiary activities. But quaternary activities depend on flows of information and ideas. In the same way that economic health and human spatial organization in the past depended on movements of goods and people, future prosperity and future settlement patterns will depend on intercommunications systems.

The foregoing interpretation stressed the influence of transportation on settlement patterns (that is, of process on structure) for valid historical reasons. Obviously, structure also influences process. High speed, high cost routes are built between places that can afford them, which usually means large cities. Also, remember that transportation and communications systems are only conditioners, not causes, of human spatial behavior. The usual role of transportation is to make it possible or easier for people to do something they already wanted to do.

Settlement Patterns of the Future   If quaternary economic organization is supplanting tertiary organization, if communications technologies are producing complete time- and cost-space convergence, and if space-adjusting systems are necessary conditioners of human locational behavior, what future settlement pattern can we expect? The answers to this question lie in present trends and in spatial theory. Current trends will continue to operate for some time, and they can, therefore, be extrapolated into the near future. For the more distant future, however, the theories and models that spatial futurists devise become more important than extrapolations, for such models constitute the alternative futures from which society may choose.

The dominant settlement trend for 200 years has been agglomeration at lower and lower densities, and that trend will continue during the next twenty years. People will continue to migrate to cities to enjoy greater excitement and prosperity. But cities will continue to expand at lower and lower densities as versatile transportation systems make it possible for people to satisy their desires for more residential space. Contemporary additions to metropolitan areas in the United States are typically at residential densities of 9,500 people per square mile or less, whereas population densities in central cities settled in the middle of the nineteenth century ran as high as 100,000 per square mile. Residential dispersal has been a persistent trend for over a hundred years. In the United States in recent decades, cities have expanded areally at about twice the rate that they have grown in population size.

Little change in this trend will occur during the quaternary/communications era. Moreover, there is reason to believe that quaternary economic organization, more complete time- and cost-space convergence, and innovations in communications technology, will accelerate suburbanization.[24] Enough urban residents have moved to the suburbs to indicate a general preference for space amenities, even at considerable costs in time and money.

If such dispersion continues, the distinction between intraurban space and interurban space will continue to blur. If metropolitan settlement proceeds at very low densities, and if communications systems continue to provide more complete time- and cost-space convergence, or if both occur together, traditional concepts of the city will become increaingly obsolete. If society is organized around communications, and if communications are costless, every place is the same place, and it makes sense to talk about the whole world being a single city.

Such extrapolations into the near and distant future have proceeded farthest under the imaginative leadership of Constantinos Doxiadis and his associates at the Athens Center for Ekistics, who have discussed at length the coming era of Ecumenopolis, the world city.[25] If the settlement tendencies of the last century are continued along the same lines for another two centuries, something like Doxiadis' Ecumenopolis will develop. In the absence of any decision to guide events toward other outcomes, Ecumenopolis is the most probable urban future.[26]

But the point of futuristics is to determine whether or not the most probable future is the best future. Man has gotten himself into no end of trouble by following paths laid down in the past, and it is high time to question the implicit policies and choices inherent in continuation of past and existing trends. There are clear alternatives to Ecumenopolis, and it is the business of spatial futurists to identify, describe, and evaluate such alternatives.

One possibility which should be explored, for example, is whether agglomerated settlements will be necessarry at all. If truly quaternary societies evolve, and if communications systems provide complete time- and cost-space convergence, why have cities at all? If everyplace is everyplace, and if a person is as centrally located in Thief River Falls as he is in Manhattan, why have a Manhattan? Many will object that Manhattan is much more than a place to work, which is certainly true. But if the delights of Manhattan can be brought to Thief River Falls electronically via three-dimensional, life-size, holographic imagery, why make the trip? Innovations in interpersonal communications could bring us to the point of asking, as Brian Berry recently did, where reality begins and where it ends.[27]

Effects of Time- and Cost-Space Convergence on Spatial Theory

Eliminating the friction of distance removes a dimension of human geography that is so basic that it is difficult to think without it. Eliminating the friction of distance vitiates most existing spatial theory. At the same time, a frictionless world opens the door for alternative spatial theories that could prove more exciting and powerful than the largely economic theory developed to date.

Theoretical structures such as location theory, central place theory, diffusion theory, and spatial interaction theory are the foundations of our knowledge about human spatial behavior. The authors of the *Geography* volume of the Behavioral and Social Sciences Survey identified four research clusters—locational analysis, cultural geography, urban studies, and environmental and spatial behavior—as major focuses of current research.[28] Perusing the illustrations included in the B.A.S.S. volume as examples of outstanding current work verifies the absolute, rock-bottom, fundamental nature of the friction of distance as a determinant of spatial behavior. What happens to spatial theory if distance is eliminated as a meaningful variable?[29]

Location theorists would have to develop a new set of explanatory variables. All activities would become footloose, and what we think of now as minor locational factors might become dominant. Our models give primary weight to economic locational constraints, and probably for good reason. But for some time now, other factors—in many cases esthetic considerations—have become increasingly important. It is difficult, for example, to explain the migration to California in economic locational terms. Explanations that invoke environmental and social preferences are more satisfying than discussions of least cost locations, which California is not for many activities.

Similar revisions would be necessary in location theory's collective analog, central place theory. Just as cost-space convergence could make individual firms footloose, shrinking cost-space to a point would scramble the locational arrangement of commercial functions. Traditionally, increased mobility has eliminated the smallest urban places and favored higher level centers. Thus, complete cost-space convergence could produce a single service center to which consumers could resort or from which all goods and services would flow over frictionless distances to dispersed consumers. Alternatively, economic functions could be scattered indiscriminately over the earth's surface in response to noneconomic locational criteria. Whatever the compromise between these extremes, it is clear that our locational models would have to be radically modified. Even with complete cost-space convergence, there would certainly be some settlement hierarchy. But whether spatial theorists would explain that hierarchy by citing site factors, transaction flows among members of the hierarchy, or on some other basis, is unclear.

Complete time-space convergence in mass communications is already playing havoc with our models of diffusion processes. North America is now a place where some communications technologies permit almost instant diffusion, which is to say no diffusion at all. Diffusion theory is based on contact probabilities which incorporate a friction of distance. Both mass and intercommunications media are rapidly making contact probability independent of distance. Network radio and television, and declining costs of interpersonal communication have made information exchange more independent of the friction of distance than any other form of spatial interaction. Moving ideas through space no longer requires expenditure of time, a friction of distance which is the basis of diffusion theory.

While time- and cost-space convergence seemingly destroy the basis of much theory, they open alternative and exciting avenues of approach. What people *think* about distance and space is more important in the long run than the "real" nature of space and distance. Even if time-, cost-, and N-space convergence succeed in producing a functionally dimensionless world, people will continue to have strong feelings about places and what they perceive to be distance. Charting and explaining such attitudes and their effects on human spatial organization will present us with far more challenging tasks than we can now imagine.[30] A world without distance will not be an undifferentiated, isotropic sphere; because it would allow preference free reign, such a world would be immensely varied and differentiated. A day will come when we will look back with nostalgia on the simple economic spatial organization of the mid-twentieth century.

What To Do Till the Future Comes

Even if complete time- and cost-space convergence become possible, there is no guarantee that people will take advantage of the locational flexibility that technology offers. There are many undesirable aspects of metropolitan life, but cities are powerful social and cultural phenomena and human beings are herd animals. There is no guarantee that the technological possibility of complete dispersal would be followed by a massive rush to the Rockies or the Caribbean. Technological possibilities must always be assessed in the light of sociocultural probabilities.

For example, substitution of communications for travel, which is now possible, has little chance of being widely accepted. It is no longer difficult to hold business conferences via closed circuit audio-visual hookups but no businessman to whom I have suggested this alternative feels that such conferences will ever be a satisfactory substitute for personal contact. Business travel, like city life, is a way of life; people will give up both only reluctantly. Government action (perhaps a ruling by the Internal Revenue Service that business travel would no longer be considered a deductible business expense) would be required to force most business firms to curtail travel and use electronic conference capabilities. Similarly governmental incentives would no doubt be required to produce relatively complete dispersal if such a settlement pattern became feasible and desirable. And if freed from one set of constraints, people will certainly invent others; congestion and density problems could easily become as serious in Aspen or Big Sur as they are now in the cores of metropolitan areas.

Because the future is an endogenous variable in human affairs, choices must be made, policies must be adopted, and some behavioral patterns must be constrained or channeled. If we are successful in devising valid alternative spatial futures, we are still faced with the problem of what to do with them. Suppose that a future-oriented scholar has formulated five alternative settlement futures, A, B, C, D, and E, and that as far as he can tell, C is the most probable of the five. Suppose also that he perceives clear and serious dangers accompanying the development of future C, and that his considered professional opinion is that future E is more desirable. What role should he play in choosing among possible futures?

Specialists with relevant expertise must certainly inform decision makers and the public at large of the full implications of choosing each alternative. But choosing among such alternatives is impossible without recourse to morals and values. "Efficiency" is always efficiency *for* some group or *with respect to* some goals. Any assertion that some policy is "best" must inevitably be followed by the question "best for *whom?*" Decisions among alternative futures can be made only within the context of a society's values.[31] Certainly no special interest group should stipulate a society's basic assumptions. Policy choices in which equity and values are involved should be settled in the political arena, where, however imperfectly they are represented, advocates of diverse groups within a society can make their wishes known.

So what *do* we do while time-, cost-, and N-space convergence shrink space? We can make our greatest contribution by developing sound, imaginative theories of spatial process and structure, and by using them to produce alternative spatial futures for our societies. That is no mean task. This chapter takes its present form because my attempt to produce a more rigorous statement of alternative settlement futures fell flat on its assumptions. Research and theory building in social science is difficult enough; trying to build theories about something which has not yet happened raises such difficulties to the nth degree. Yet we have no choice but to do what we can. Increasingly, the alternative to a rationally and compassionately designed future that explicitly incorporates man's transportation and communications capabilities appears to be a future that is hardly worth waiting for.

References

1.   Edward A. Ackerman first characterized transportation and communication as "space-adjusting" techniques in *Geography as a Fundamental Research Discipline.* Department of Geography Research Paper No. 53 (Chicago: Department of Geography, University of Chicago, 1958), p. 26.

2.   Ratzel's comments on relative location are scattered throughout *Anthropogéographie* and *Politische Géographie.* A useful summary is G. A. Huckel, "La géographie de la circulation selon Friedrich Ratzel, "*Annales de Géographie* 15 (1906): 401—418; 16 (1907):1—14.

3. J. W. Watson, "Geography: A Discipline in Distance," *Scottish Geographical Magazine* 71 (1955): 1013.

4. Barnaby C. Keeney. "The Bridge of Values," *Science*, 3 July, 1970, p. 27.

5. Donald G. Janelle, "Central Place Development in a Time-Space Framework," *Professional Geographer* 20 (1968): 5—10. See also his "Spatial Reorganiza-tion: A Model and Concept," *Annals of the Association of American Geographers* 59 (1969): 348—364.

6. Federal Communications Commission, *Statistics of Communications Com-mon Carriers, 1970* (Washington: U. S. Government Printing Office, 1972), p. 152.

7. Horace H. Nance, "Engineering the Transcontinental Telephone Cable," *Bell Telephone Magazine* 20 (1941): 209.

8. James J. Pilliod and Harold L. Ryan, "Operator Toll Dialing—A New Long Distance Method," *Bell Telephone Magazine* 24 (1945): 102.

9. *Ibid.*, 102—103.

10. "News of the Industry," *Telephony*, Feb. 21, 1970, p. 60; J. Gordon Pearce, "Numbering Plans Get Calls Routed Next-Door and Around the World," *Telephony*, Dec. 20, 1969, pp. 24—32.

11. *Encyclopaedia of the Social Sciences*, 1934 ed., s. v. "Postal Service."

12. Alvin F. Harlow, *Old Post Bags* (New York: D. Appleton and Co., 1928), pp. 359,360.

13. *Ibid.*, p. 366.

14. *United States Official Postal Guide, 1900* (Philadelphia: Geo. Lasker, 1901), p. 845.

15. *Annals of the Congress of the United States, Fifth Congress* (Washington: Gales and Seaton, 1851), p. 3943.

16. Carl H. Scheele, *A Short History of the Mail Service* (Washington: Smithso-nian Institution Press, 1970), pp. 73, 76, 91, and 105.

17. The rate quoted applies from western Pennsylvania. Personal communication from Theodore Reigh, Bell Telephone Sales Representative.

18. These three paragraphs are a selective paraphrase from Southwestern Bell Telephone Company, *Economic Survey of Texas* (St. Louis: Southwestern Bell Telephone Company, 1928), pp. 221—224.

19. For a discussion of the organization of Sectional Centers, see Gregory L. Smith, "The Functional Basis of the ZIP Code and Sectional Center System," *Yearbook of the Association of Pacific Coast Geographers* 29 (1967): 97—109.

20. These three paragraphs abstracted from an internal Post Office Department *Memo for the Record*, dated July 18, 1969.

21. For a more detailed discussion, see John R. Borchert, "American Metropolitan Evolution," *Geographical Review* 57 (1967): 301—332.

22. Wayne E. Fuller, *RFD: The Changing Face of Rural America* (Bloomington: Indiana University Press, 1964).

23. Jean Gottmann, *Megalopolis* (Cambridge: M.I.T. Press, 1961), pp. 576 ff.

24. Jerome P. Pickard, "Is Dispersal the Answer to Urban Overgrowth?" *Urban Land* 29 (1970): 3—8.

25. John G. Papaioannou, "Future Urbanization Patterns: A Long-Range, World-Wide View," *Ekistics* 29 (1970): 368—381. This issue is devoted to the topic "The City of the Future."

26. Soviet geographers are also thinking along the lines of a world city. See B. B. Rodoman, "The Organized Anthroposphere," *Soviet Geography: Review and Translation* 9 (1969): 784—796.

27. Brian J. L. Berry, "The Geography of the United States in the Year 2000," *Ekistics* 29 (1970): 351.

28. Edward J. Taaffe, ed., *Geography* (Englewood Cliffs, N. J.: Prentice-Hall, Inc. 1970), p. 52.

29. William Warntz, "Global Science and the Tyranny of Space," *Papers of the Regional Science Association* 20 (1968): 7—19; See also Roy I. Wolfe, *Transportation and Politics* (Princeton: D. Van Nostrand, 1963), pp. 117ff.

30. For suggestions concerning some directions which might be taken, see Wilbur Zelinsky, "Beyond the Exponentials: The Role of Geography in the Great Transition," *Economic Geography* 46 (1970): 498—535.

31. Keeney, *op. cit.*, p. 27; Kurt Baier and Nicholas Rescher, ed., *Values and the Future* (New York: The Free Press, 1969).

Chapter   4

How Information Structures Influence Spatial Organization

Robert McDaniel
University of Western Ontario

ABSTRACT: *Increasing man/machine cooperation is evolving toward machine/machine information networks. There is substantial evidence of a long-term trend toward a global, cybernated space economy as the basis for a higher level of cultural sophistication for mankind. Automatic process control is the means by which man can "take charge" of his technology. The spatial implications of more complex technologies for moving goods, people, and ideas offer a fertile field for geographical inquiry.*

Human survival depends on material flows propelled by energy flows and orchestrated by information flows. Over time, these flows have become interrelated in a global network and have become continuous, though cyclical, because of frequent innovation and technological change. The dominant flows have varied over time and space as has the morphology of the system the flows serve. Until about 1750 flows of consumer goods and services were dominant and settlements crystallized around fairs, cathedrals, and seats of government. Between 1750 and 1950, flows of producer goods became dominant and new settlements arose around mines and factories. Since 1950, the dominant flow has been information, and multiversities, research and development parks, and science cities have flourished.

Related to these observations are the notions that form follows function, structure is influenced by strategy,[1] and organization is determined by tasks.[2] These concepts are also related, though somewhat more distantly, to proxemics, which is concerned with interpersonal spacing.[3] Sommer also elaborates this concept of personal space.[4] Of relevance, too, are the microspatial orderings of industrial and human engineering (ergonomics). Lorenz, Ardrey, and Morris have commented upon animal spatial behavior.[5] The production engineer is concerned with the spacing characteristics of machines as the architect is with buildings.

The common element in the preceding areas of study is a concern with information structure and spatial organization. Information structure is a system or subsystem involved in some or all aspects of sensing, collecting, processing, transmitting, analyzing, storing, retrieving, disseminating, and displaying information. Such a structure may be an animal, a machine, or a human. Spatial organization is the pattern assumed by a set of interrelated phenomena (that is a system) in four-dimensional time-space.

The main focus of this paper is upon the spatial organization engendered by the following information structures: a. man/machine (ergonomics), and b. machine/machine (automation).

This is a rather restricted set. An expanded set would include the man/man (proxemics) information structure, and the traditional man/environment interface of geography.

Change in Values

Our age is characterized by increasingly explicit man/machine cooperation. This may, however, be a passing phenomenon as we enter a period of human disengagement via automation (machine/machine interaction). Such a transition may simply be another step in the evolution of the human psyche from an internalized sense of being at the center of the universe, to a sense of encompassing the universe via electronically extended senses. Is man's mental map undergoing topological inversion or is man turning inside out?

The evolution of man's view of himself begins with his notion that the earth was the center of the universe. Copernicus demonstrated that the earth occupied a quite peripheral position, and the earth was merged with the universe; a discontinuity in man's mental map was removed. Man continued to maintain that his race was separate from animals. Darwin demonstrated man's continuous evolution from animals. But man prided himself upon his free and untrammelled will. Freud changed this by arguing that man was continuously under the influence of his subconscious mind in ways he could not fathom. Man, however, argued that ony he could think. But, as Mazlish points out, electronic computers and artificial intelligence are now beginning to erase this "fourth discontinuity" and to merge man and machines.[6]

What can man fall back on as his distinctive attribute? He may seek refuge in that unique entity, the "selfish individual."[7] But even this fifth discontinuity may be eroded as men's minds become merged through the medium of global electronic information structures.[8] A creature seems to be at its maximum effectiveness just prior to its demise, as was the dinosaur. This may be the case with the institution of privacy. Global information structures may desensitize our feeling of individuality, thus facilitating man/machine structures for global control. Whereas man/machine information structures are perceived to be a threat to privacy at present, this view may change as an image of global organic interdependence gradually dawns in man's consciousness. Westin discusses the concept of privacy at length, but it may be summarized as (a) the need for seclusion, and, (b) the need for security.[9]

Seclusion involves solitude, social distance, and intimacy, has definite spatial implications, and may be a basic physiological need. Security needs are primarily cultural, but they too have a spatial aspect. The culturally induced security needs involve such negative factors as fear of income loss or humiliation through the disclosure of deviant behavior, fear of income loss or prestige through theft of ideas, and fear of loss of face through interpersonal comparisons. The spatial aspect, especially in the past, is that man used physical distance to escape social persecution or physical assault.

As the man/machine information structure evolves toward a machine/machine information structure, however, expanded security programs and automation may greatly reduce or eliminate the security aspect of privacy. The greater flexibility simultaneously afforded spatial organization may then make seclusion, in its various dimensions, easier to attain. Indeed, our present views on privacy may come to be perceived in the future as antisocial, in that they inhibit the free information flow. Such dysfunctional concern for privacy may be reduced by the behavior control techniques advocated by Skinner.[10]

Changes in Technology

Another global trend suggests that this is the "fossil age," or at least that future historians will think so. Fossil fuels provide the energy that is propelling global society into a much higher level of cultural and technological sophistication. When this fuel is spent, spaceship earth will have experienced a shattering discontinuity.[11] This period may be analagous to a "critical mass," a "sound barrier" or a "phase shift" (figure 4.1).

Related to this explosive release of energy is the rapid development of high technology in all fields (table 4.1). Much of this technology is

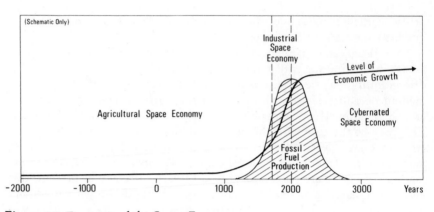

Figure 4.1 Energy and the Space Economy

Table 4.1   Summary of Some Recent Technological Trends

Information Technology:

    computers and artificial intelligence

    on-line real-time information systems

    automated process control

    communication satellites

    remote-sensing satellites

    3-D color television

    lasers

    numerically-controlled machines

    electronic terrestrial sensing devices

    electronic transmission of all five senses

Behavioral Engineering:

    with information (psychotherapy, hypnosis, conditioning, and electronic
    tools)

    with coercion (assault, drugs, and surgery)

Genetic Engineering

Biomedical Engineering

Molecular Engineering

Controlled Thermonuclear Reaction

All-Terrain Vehicles

Space Technology

Closed Cycle Systems for Food, Fuel, and Water

Weather Control[12]

converging upon 1985, in terms of economical and technical application on
a large scale.[13] It follows that the 70s is a crucial decade.

    The integration of technologies with such techniques as systems analysis leads to ever larger undertakings: space travel, jumbo jets, million-ton tankers, experimental cities, SSTs, and global remote sensing. Technology introduced on a small, limited scale often evolves into technology implemented on a global scale, as in the cases of the U. S. telephone system and the SAGE defense system.[14] Thus the numerically controlled machine tool will evolve toward the numerically controlled factory and, thence, toward the numerically controlled, or cybernated, space economy. Such an economy would be a radical departure from current conditions.

> *Mass information utilities will be only a start in the invasion and transformation of daily routines and the thought processes of individuals. The public mass displays provided by radio, T.V., and the press will evolve toward personalized information services. Purchasing and banking activities will be possible through remote input stations, and cumbersome paperwork such as checks eliminated through computerized identification and authorization procedures. Voting and opinion sampling may occur through the home console on a far more frequent basis over a greater variety of political and social issues. Individuals will have access to a growing spectrum of specialized information services and data pools, including private files.*
>
> *It may be possible to conduct most work at home through universal man-to-computer and man-to-man hookups over telephone lines whose users will be able to see one another and look at common computer-driven displays. Communication satellites will permit international tele-conferences; virtually any set of people from different parts of the world will be able to participate in the same conference and review common computer-driven information displays. As many jobs will migrate to the console-communications center at home, so will education increasingly take place at home, gradually eliminating the problems of physical distance between students, teachers, and the information they require, and progressively reducing the needs for expanding physical plants for education.[15]*

This is a conservative viewpoint. The cybernated space economy would be almost totally controlled by machines. In the light of chronic problems of poverty and starvation, running the space economy is too important to leave to man. Such a development would require revisions of our concept of work, and of our system of allocating the world's resources. Just as privacy may be an obsolete value, so employment may no longer be our economic goal. Such inversions of values have occurred previously.[16] An example of inversion of the spatial trend toward megalopolization is the growing migration out of U.S. cities into the intermetropolitan periphery.[17] Industrial locations change as the sources and modes of transporting information change. Similarly, as information sources and modes of transporting information change, new settlement patterns will emerge. Thus new information structures influence spatial organization.

In the cybernated space economy another device that may eventually merge with the numerically controlled machine tool is the on-line real-time management information system.[19] Such a system could provide automatic process control for continuous production flows.[20] Providing the links among the individual plants and institutions might be the on-line real-time computer utility[21] which would also be linked to financial, marketing, specialized commodity, and regional information systems.[22] On the consumer side of the space economy, automated marketing will become feasible.[23] Shopping via domestic remote video-consoles may require greater standardization and modularization of household goods and a consequent rise in consumer confidence. Standardization need not imply a lack of variety, but rather uniform quality. Variety will be increased with the aid of computer control. Flexible, multipurpose machines may return some food and clothing manufacturing to the home.

Complementing such production and marketing developments would be automatic electronic highways, solids pipelines, centralized railway traffic movement and locating systems, remote controlled, automatically guided aircraft and ships, and the global resource-sensing satellites. Some of these elements of the cybernated space economy are currently operational.

It is interesting to speculate upon the spatial implications of these developments. This is not easy because the effects of chemical, social, biological, psychological, mechanical, and electronic developments, with their mutual interactions, will almost certainly be counterintuitive. What may be required is a global simulation model such as that developed by Forrester.[24]

However, such spatial changes as the evisceration of the urban centers with a decline in retailing, office work, and centralized entertainment, and an increase in open space are possible. Manufacturing centers may disperse as markets migrate out of the cities and raw materials become more available through the practice of molecular engineering. Dispersal may be facilitated by efficient, small scale nuclear power plants, and fuel cells and global broadband communication nets. Scale, localization, and urbanization economies may be nullified by decreased emphasis on production, cheaper transportation and communication, individualized waste disposal and recycling, and electronic protective surveillance. Information services such as schools, counselling activities, libraries, and non-surgical medical practice may be incorporated into electronic data banks. For security and more effective environmental control, many of these activities may disappear underground.[25]

Change in Methodology

The historical trend in the physical and biological sciences seems to have been as follows:

Description$\longrightarrow$Theory$\longrightarrow$Analysis$\longrightarrow$Engineering$\longrightarrow$
Design$\longrightarrow$Molecular Manipulation or Artificial Substitutes

In the social sciences we have reached the threshold of the "design" stage, as we begin to experiment with various social forms (such as communes and T-groups) and with simulated experiences (through hallucinogenic drugs, reconstructions of the past, and public pornographic films). But if we take research in genetic, biomedical [26] and behavioral engineering,[27] then we must be willing to evaluate the impact of the "programmed" information structure of "engineered" or "designed" man upon spatial organization.

In geography and regional science, however, we are still in the "Description—Theory—Analysis"stages, busying ourselves with central place theory, regionalization, movement, computer mapping, network analysis, growth poles, and so on. But to what end? Perhaps academic freedom has become academic license in that scientific research, without regard for social implications, may destroy mankind.

The traditional scientific method is no longer appropriate in the age of electronic information and organic interdependence. Current research follows the classical paradigm and studies the past for insights into the present. We must forge a new methodology that anticipates social and technological innovations and their implications.[28] We may then present society with alternative futures to insure that present decisions are compatible with the chosen future. Our theories will "explain" the future, not the past, and as the future unfolds we shall test their validity.

Control of Change

A key question is whether society should launch a grand project to build a cybernated space economy, or simply let it grow. Conversely, ought we to forbid its development on the grounds of some higher values?

Businessmen considering automation often seek only to automate their present manual procedures instead of redesigning their total system. Similarly, the geographical profession may be taking too limited a view of its responsibilities and capabilities. We are prone to rear-view vision in that we study past trends. This may be connected with the current emphasis on quantitative and behavioral research. It is difficult to get hard data on the future.

Assuming that it is a realistic goal, the question of whether to build a cybernated space economy must be answered in light of human aspirations. A major human concern is the resolution of conflicts, whether they be intrapersonal, interpersonal, persons vs. organizations, supply vs. demand, man vs. environment, or man vs. machine. Many existing conflicts arise from the pressures of a constraining industrial, scarcity-based economy which has forged a strong value link between work (or, at least, a job) and income. There is a growing movement to weaken this link, led by futurists such as Theobald and Fuller.[29] Theobald advocates the guaranteed income. A cybernated space economy, incorporating automation and guaranteed income, would increase human flexibility in making desirable spatial adjustments that minimize conflict. Bunge suggests that society and its environment should be designed to protect children.[30] Since there is substantial evidence that values are formed during the first six years of life, this may well be the critical factor to control.

Forbidding the development of a cybernated space economy is unrealistic in light of current trends, and technology may be beyond control.[31] The best course might be to attempt to consciously control the natural evolution of a cybernated space economy with the aid of mathematical models, and with extended popular participation in decision making through the medium of interactive home consoles.[32]

Change in Social Space

The dehumanizing aspects of the man/machine information structures that prevail in the modern industrial economy may stem from the economy's spatial organization. Alexander suggests that lack of intimate contact leads to mental disorder and the autonomy-withdrawal syndrome. His solution, as befits an architect, is the appropriate spatial design of housing.[33] However, the possibility of communicating to work and school instead of commuting offers an alternative way of keeping families and friends together if it is desirable to do so.

Chimpanzees subsisted primarily on large fruits and were forced to scatter over large areas to secure them; hence they failed to organize into families or other stable social structures.[34] On the contrary, gorillas fed upon abundant and accessible stems, leaves, roots, and bark and could live in small, permanent groups. The search for jobs (or commuting to work) is analogous to searching for food. The need, in a modern economy, to move far and frequently contributes to a decline in the rate of meaningful human contact. In a cybernated space economy that one might "plug into" from any point on earth, people could live wherever and with whomever they wished.[35]

The decreasing time-lag between invention and manufacture, and the apparently increasing rate of technological advance suggest that we are still below the inflection point of an S-shaped growth curve. Because of their global, all-encompassing nature, development of the models, techniques, and technologies pertinent to a cybernated space economy would probably bring us to the inflection point. From then on, "automation will not spend itself until society is nicely organized into one well-meshed, producing-consuming unit."[36] As we move into the postindustrial millennia, perhaps a cybernated space economy will become the placenta that nurtures a rebirth of man. Evidence indicating a long-term trend toward a global, cybernated space economy is substantial. In view of the many spatial discontinuities such a trend will engender, the cybernated space economy and its sociospatial implications offer a fertile field for speculation and research within geography and regional science.

References

1. A. D. Chandler, Jr. *Strategy and Structure* (Cambridge, Mass.: M.I.T. Press, 1962).

2. D. Klahr and H. J. Leavitt, "Tasks, Organization Structures, and Computer Programs" in *The Impact of Computers on Management*, ed. C. A. Myers (Cambridge, Mass.: M.I.T. Press).

3. E. T. Hall, *The Hidden Dimension* (New York: Doubleday, 1966).

4. R. Sommer, *Personal Space* (Englewood Cliffs, N.J.: Prentice-Hall, 1969).

5. K. Lorenz, *On Aggression* (New York: Harcourt, Brace and World, 1966); R. Ardrey, *The Territorial Imperative* (Boston: Atheneum Books, 1966); and D. Morris, *The Human Zoo* (New York: McGraw-Hill, 1969).

6. B. Mazlish, "The Fourth Discontinuity," *Technology and Culture* 8 (1967):1—15.

7. A. Rand, *For the New Intellectual* (New York: Random House, 1961).

8. P. Teilhard de Chardin, *The Phenomenon of Man* (New York: Harper and Brothers, 1959).

9. A. F. Westin, *Privacy and Freedom* (Boston: Atheneum Books, 1967).

10. B. F. Skinner, *Beyond Freedom and Dignity* (New York: Alfred A. Knopf, 1971).

11. P. F. Drucker, *The Age of Discontinuity: Guidelines to Our Changing Society*, (New York: Harper and Row, 1968).

12. P. London, *Behavior Control*, (New York: Harper and Row, 1969).

13. H. Kahn and A. J. Wiener, *The Year 2000* (New York: Macmillan, 1967).

14. R. F. Abler, *The Geography of Intercommunication Systems: The Post Office and Telephone System in the United States*, (Ph.D. diss., University of Minnesota, 1968); and H. Sackman, *Computers, System Science and Evolving Society* (New York: John A. Wiley, 1967).

15. Sackman, *Ibid.*, p. 36.

16. Kahn and Wiener, *op. cit.*

17. B. J. L. Berry, "The Geography of the United States in the Year 2000," *Ekistics* 29 (1970): 339—351.

18. R. C. Estall and R. O. Buchanan, *Industrial Activity and Economic Geography* (London: Hutchinson, 1961).

19. D. C. Carroll, "Implications of On-Line, Real-Time Systems for Managerial Decision-Making," *The Impact of Computers on Management*, ed. C. A. Myers (Cambridge, Mass.: M.I.T. Press, 1967).

20. J. C. Emery, *Organizational Planning and Control Systems* (Toronto: Macmillan, 1969).

21. D. F. Parkhill, *The Challenge of the Computer Utility*, (Reading, Mass.:

Addison-Wesley, 1966); and S. D. Popell, *Computer Time-Sharing* (Engle-wood Cliffs, N.J.: Prentice-Hall, 1966).

22. R. McDaniel *et al.*, *The Erie Research Project: Construction of a Multi-Purpose Data Bank*, A Report to the Regional Development Branch, Ontario Department of the Treasury and Economics (London, Ontario: Department of Geography, University of Western Ontario, 1970).

23. A. F. Doody and W. R. Davidson, "The Next Revolution in Retailing," *Harvard Business Review* 45 (May—June, 1967): 4 ff.

24. J. W. Forrester, *World Dynamics* (Cambridge: Wright-Allen Press, 1971; M. S. Moyer, "Shifting Marketing Power in Packaged Goods Industry," *The Business Quarterly* 37 (Autumn 1969): 38—46.

25. N. Calder, *The Environment Game* (London: Martin Secker and Warburg Ltd., 1967).

26. A. Rosenfeld, *The Second Genesis: The Coming Control of Life* (Englewood Cliffs, N.J.: Prentice-Hall, 1969).

27. London, *op. cit.*; and Skinner, *op. cit.*

28. E. Jantsch, *Technological Forecasting in Perspective* (Paris: Organization for Economic Cooperation and Development 1967); D. Gabor, *Innovations: Scientific, Technological and Social* (Oxford: Oxford University Press, 1970).

29. R. Theobald, *The Economics of Abundance* (Pitman, 1970); R. B. Fuller, *Ideas and Integrities* (Englewood Cliffs, N.J.: Prentice-Hall, 1963).

30. W. Bunge, (lectures series while Visiting Professor of Geography, University of Western Ontario, 1970).

31. J. Ellul, *The Technological Society* (New York: Vintage Books, 1967).

32. S. Umpleby, "Citizen Sampling Simulations: A Method for Involving the Public in Social Planning," *Policy Sciences* 1 (1970): 361—375.

33. C. Alexander, "The City as a Mechanism for Sustaining Human Contact" in *Environment for Man: The Next 50 Years*, ed. W. R. Ewald, Jr. (Bloomington: Indiana University Press, 1967); R. L. Meier, *A Communication Theory of Urban Growth* (Cambridge, Mass.: M.I.T. Press, 1962).

34. R. DuBos, *Man, Medicine and Environment* (New York: Mentor, 1968).

35. R. F. Abler, "What Makes Cities Important," *Bell Telephone Magazine*, (March/April, 1970),

36. D. T. Bazelon, *The Paper Economy* (New York Random House: 1963), p. 357.

Part II: Implications

Chapter   5

Choosing Alternatives in Confronting the Tyranny of Technological Freedom

The Editors

ABSTRACT: *Time-space convergence provides us with enough increased choices to overload decisionmaking capacities. When the decisionmaking process breaks down, people seek to escape decisions completely. Organizational ability and flexibility prevent overchoice and its resulting stress from developing. Chapters 6 through 12 explore the variety of choices confronting society and cosider explicit formal responses to stress. If man hopes to maximize his freedom of choice, four spatial conditions are required: (1) maximum diversity in living environments; (2) maximum ability to participate in diversity and minimal coercion to participate; (3) harmonizing information and energy flows with institutional forms; and, (4) human control of the mechanisms of change.*

New technologies always cause unforeseen problems and new freedoms are always accompanied by duties and responsibilities. As options multiply and old restraints are resolved, we become subject to the dilemma that proved fatal to Buridan's ass, who starved in indecision between two equally delectable haystacks.

Technological innovation is gobbling up and compacting previously expansive space so that the places where people wish to go are being brought closer together: Abler's isolines move inexorably toward each other, Philbrick's power sources promote locational independence, and McDaniel's cybernated space economy coordinates a symphony of change. Such processes increase spatial choice dramatically and simultaneously impose a responsibility to choose well. Yet, in order to choose well, one must choose more quickly. In a field of ephemeral wild flowers that blossom one morning and disappear the next, one must pluck quickly if a few are to grace one's table. So too the investor, buyer, industrialist, or person seeking recreation under conditions of time-space convergence must take advantage of choices as they occur. The opportunity cost of hesitant decision making increases exponentially as space is shrunk. Therefore, the responsible optimizer must shoot from the hip—faster and faster, and this induces stress.

Creative Stress and Overstress

The act of creation is most often stimulated by intermittent or persistent stress. Stress plays a central role in innovation by individuals and societies, but, as Philbrick argued, innovation is dependent on human perceptual abilities. When the interaction of stress and ingenuity is balanced there is an upward spiral of creative activity which enlarges man's range of choices. Warntz addresses this point in the next chapter, "The Pattern of Patterns," but he goes on to note the adverse consequences of what he calls "high sociological intensity."

Rampantly increasing choices, so beneficial in many ways, can also bewilder the mind, push man to the point of overstress, and create a tyranny of freedom in which creativity is stifled by confusion. A reduction of options would relieve overstress but fewer choices would also diminish combinatorial potential as Philbrick notes in "Cumulative Versus Mutually Exclusive Regions in the Future" (chapter 7). Clearly, it is necessary to straddle the fulcrum of stress while contemplating the chaos and the inertia which rest on either side. Man's ability to balance is enhanced by his ability to organize and reorganize effectively and efficiently.

A Process Model of Human Response to Choice

Inspiration for our simple model comes from Karl Deutsch.[1] The model (table 5.1) is a simplified version of the more elaborate scheme (figure 1.3) that serves as a kind of roadmap for this book. It summarizes the basic processes now at work and man's response to time-space convergence: time-space convergence leads to increased choice, which generates innovation up to a point. But increased choice eventually overloads decision making capacity, and results, if decision making organization breaks down, in an attempt to escape from and reject the decision making process.

Table 5.1   Stress and Opportunity

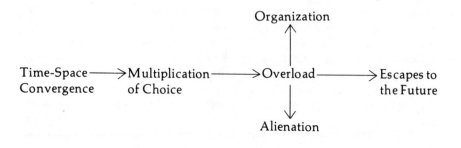

Organizaion and Alienation

Persistent stress induces organizational complexity; persistent overstress induces organizational rupture and dispersion. Under the jackhammer impact of overstress, the earth becomes tattooed with new bureaucracies, most of which emphasize sterile stability. Bureaucracy proliferates because phasing out vestigial human organizations is a difficult task, as Janelle points out in chapter 8.

Bureaucracies are organizations for decision making characterized by hierarchy, relatively stabilized division of labor, loyalty to whatever is being organized, and relatively permanent boundaries. They emphasize stability and seek to perpetuate their own existence. Their emphasis on stability dooms them either to ineffectiveness because they rapidly become anachronistic, or to coercive enforcement of stability because someone in authority does not believe or want them to be anachronistic. When traditional organizations respond ineffectively to overstress, then ad hoc organizations must take over. Once an organization has lost utility, it must wither away.

We will depend on organizational ability and reorganizational flexibility to prevent persistent overstress. If bureaucracies fail in their task individuals and societies will flee from overstress and refuse altogether to take part in the decision making. Total rejection of decision making would be tantamount to rejection of the future. Although this is an alternative, it is not viable. While there are many escapes *to* the future, there is no escape from the future, save death.

Maximizing Human Choice: Four Form Principles

The chapters of Part II concern man's freedom of choice, or lack thereof. We assume that man prefers a maximum range of choices because this creates opportunities. But what does maximum freedom of choice imply? Some guideposts are needed, and Dr. Larry Bourne has provided them by reducing specific goals to four "form principles."[2] A form principle describes the shape, structure, or spatial arrangement of things. Form principles are subgoals subordinate to the more general goal of maximum freedom of choice. The four form principles are: maintaining diversity of living environments, promoting participation, matching expectations with reality, and keeping control over the mechanisms of change.

Diversity of Living Environments   Creating diverse living environments that are easily adaptable and flexible is an important way of providing freedom of choice. Diversity increases as accessibility increases, but some people are afraid that human extensibility promotes "sameness" everywhere. Some fear a future of robot-like human beings differentiated only by identification numbers, who live in Levittowns where homes are differentiated only by their street numbers. They foresee indistinguishable cities, nations without regions, and homogenized culture realms. A world in which surprise is minimized appears to be repugnant to man as we understand him, yet he is creating a world in which shopping centers, airport complexes, groupings of stores, gas stations, motels, and other shops are identical from city to city. This production-line similarity extends to the food in chain restaurants, the goods in shops, and the trained behavior of employees. It seems that modern man has sought to minimize uncertainty through comfortable sameness. Our aspirations and our actions are perhaps contradictory. The apparently contradictory desire for surprise and similarity is in part a matter of scale. Similarity is created at one scale so that costs may be reduced. Those participating at this scale use the fruits of these cost reductions to participate on a wider scale, over greater ranges. For example, one might purchase gasoline at the same cut-rate establishment time after time in order to fly to the Bahamas on the savings, or on the accumulated green stamps. Such scale tradeoffs partially resolve the paradox, but they do not close the issue for those concerned with the principle of environmental diversity. The shrinking planet continues to yield to human mobility, and a concerted effort will soon have to be made to preserve the individuality of people, places, things, and ideas. Zelinsky and Abler explore some of the tensions between diversity and homogeneity in chapters 9 and 10.

Maximum Ability to Participate   While we are developing maximum ability to participate in and partake of diversity, we must simultaneously minimize the necessity for participation. Production of new items does not insure diversity if an individual cannot choose freely to use or to reject them. If choices are doubled but individuals are forced to participate in them, that is only half as satisfactory as a situation in which an individual can participate or not at will. In a monopolistic situation such as one can find in a state-run industry in a centrally planned economy, individuals or organizational units *must* purchase an industry's products to make that industry viable. Under these conditions choice is not increased even if the products are absolutely new. Goods should be allocated for people, not the reverse. Or, in Philbrick's terms, people should be appreciated over property.

Managing Institutions and Information   The third form principle states that institutional and information channels should be managed so that they converge and become one. Decision making structures should conform to the activity patterns of the people who use them so that energy loss is minimized. Increasingly flexible organizational structures must be devised to accommodate the rapid preference shifts that will accompany increasing freedom of choice. The goal, then, is to fit the spatial needs of humanity with society's managerial capacities.

That man has heretofore had difficulty achieving this goal is news to no one—expectations regularly exceed capabilities because aspirations exceed capabilities. Unreasonable expectations may be attributable to political or managerial leaders who have raised mass expectations by overestimating current resource capabilities or the capabilities of institutions they would organize if elected or appointed. Sometimes this is done in ignorance; in other cases it springs from a desire to control people at any cost. In either case, assymmetry between expectations and reality causes stress and diminished faith in existing organization. If overstress is persistent, reorganization occurs, hopefully in the direction of symmetry.

Some warning flags concerning inflated expectations are implicitly raised in Bunge's essay on Detroit. Sommer's apocalyptic visions of Fat Cities must be judged in the light of the urban raw material now available out of which we are to fashion hedonopolis. Bunge forcefully reminds us that a present—often a sordid one—is always with us and that our futures depend as much on solving current sociocultural problems as they do on overcoming technological and perceptual lags. World cities, Fat Cities, or no cities are edifying visions, but unless we can reconcile the present with such futures by specifying the details of the transition from here to there, we are likely to be frustrated. We will not reach our goals if we pay too much attention to expectations for the future and not enough to present problems or to the interim between now and the future.

Although we are familiar with inflated expectations, we know less about shortfall, which occurs when capabilities exceed expectations, and innovations are foregone because they are not tried. Shortfall is common in centrally planned economies where production thresholds are set, sometimes satisfied, but rarely surpassed. This appears to be in concert with the third form principle of matching institutions with human activity, but it violates the first principle concerning maximization of diversity. Open systems of competition seek to optimize choices while closed systems of regulation seek to satisfy an a priori level of choice.

Control of the Change-Makers Man must maintain control over change so that human efforts are not wasted. Man may become so overridden by unguided change that he will relinquish control to a cybernated faceless master. He would thereby sacrifice responsibility and choice. And an uncontrolled system can easily become as coercive as one in which coercion is the avowed intent of its managers.

Human extensibility has increased with developments in communications technology, but the wisdom of the messages sent has not necessarily increased. There is no automatic net gain even though society is released from location constraints and is thereby provided opportunities for greater reflection. One reason wisdom has not increased is the misuse of communications systems by cynical leaders to produce inflated expectations. Another reason is the alienation resulting from overload. Lightning-like change overwhelms our ethics and cosmologies, our images of our place in the world. To prevent the alienation that results from losing such images, we must retain the ethics and symbol systems that provide context for our actions, relevance for our religious aspirations, and feelings of belonging in the land upon which we walk.

With the fourth form principle we place qualifications on the more general goal of maximizing freedom of choice. Place, belonging, history, context, relevance, and symbols are always changing. Yet perhaps they should change at a slightly slower rate than strict adherence to the third form principle would require. Slightly offsetting the confrontation of information and institutions would provide man with a cushion of more slowly changing symbols about him.

Conclusion

The four form principles are united under the goal of maximum freedom of choice, which is in turn related to the four main themes in this book—the constraints of *location, information, administration,* and *resources.* The interfaces between these four constraints and the four form principles are the focus of chapters 6 through 12.

References

1. Karl W. Deutsch, "On Social Communication in the Metropolis," *Daedalus* 90 (1961): 99—100.
2. Larry S. Bourne, (1970). Professor Bourne suggested the four form principles during discussions at the Bayfield Conference.

Chapter   6

The Pattern of Patterns: Current Problems as Sources of Future Solutions [1]

William Warntz
University of Western Ontario

ABSTRACT: *The gaps between what is now and what might be in the future are the sources of the energy needed to transform the past and the present into the future. Maps of spatial potential of population summarize the locations of existing gaps and are useful guides to the elimination of the inequities they portray. Considering gaps and potential solutions in the context of general systems theory makes it possible to build powerful models of the processes that create what will be out of what is.*

Some speak of geography as an academic discipline and dedicate themselves to improving and refining its intellectual concepts. Others take geography to mean the spatial aspects of terrestrial reality; they note the existence of grave social injustices and seek to redress them. Whichever our view, we must be mindful that "the only real source of power in the world is

---

[1]Portions of this address were presented as the Keynote Address for the Bayfield Conference on the Geography of the Future. At that time, Professor Warntz was Director of the Laboratory for Computer Graphics and Spatial Analysis of Harvard University.

the gap between what is and what might be."[1] I can think of no other nineteen word statement that more accurately assesses the nature of the world and our attempts to organize knowledge about it. The statement contains five major terms to be emphasized: source, power, gap, what is, and what might be.

In the physical and biological sciences these elements are known in rigorous detail and are successfully applied. The key that integrates these ideas and that unifies science is the concept of energy, with its appropriate space-time considerations and its intension-extension equations. In that part of science of concern to "social scientists," the ideas are pertinent if the energy patterns of intension and extension are expressed as aspiration and perception. Overarching all these patterns stands the promise of the pattern of patterns—a general systems theory. Given the state of the world, systems theory can no longer be regarded as a diversion for dilettantes; it is now a requirement for human survival.

What Is

For any geography of the future we must discuss what might be if we allow current trends to continue and what might be if we try to shape the future into something better than it now promises to be. In both cases knowledge concerning *what is* has high priority. It may seem that the present world is not worth knowing—only worth changing. But to change it one must know it.

Welfare Gaps   For the most of the 3.6 billion men, women and children inhabiting the planet, life means suffering and deprivation on the fringes of technologically advanced nations. Malnutrition is common. In affluent areas the average person consumes four pounds of food a day. In much of the world, however, a pound and a quarter is the average daily consumption. In the so-called developing countries, the infant mortality rate is 110 deaths per thousand live births compared to a rate of 27 deaths in the so-called developed world. In the developed world man can expect to live to be more than 70, while the average man in many developing countries is allotted only 42 years and in Africa, about 35 years. Illiteracy is widespread; an estimated 800 million people can neither read nor write. And one might add that 70 percent of the illiterates in the world are women. There are now 100 million more illiterates than there were twenty years ago, although the illiterate population is declining as a percentage of total world population. Unemployment is chronic and is increasingly a lifelong condition. Over 20 percent of the world's male labor force is permanently unemployed. Inestimable millions are underemployed. The distribution of income and wealth is lopsided and in some countries it is becoming more so. In India 12 percent of the rural families control more than half the cultivated land. In Brazil, 10 percent of the families control 75 percent of the land.

Two-thirds of the world's preschool children suffer from malnutrition that is physically disabling. It affects them permanently, both physically and mentally. A very long list of similarly depressing deficits could be compiled. Explanations for this state of affairs usually relate levels of technology and resource availability to number of people, so that overpopulation, underpopulation and optimum population are discussed in these terms.

The gaps listed above can be closed. The technology exists, but the determination to do so may not exist. The affluent will not close the gaps unless they are pressured to do so. But the aspirations of certain deprived groups are being increased by their own perceptions of the gaps. Once these gaps are perceived then a new source of power comes into existence; the gaps will be closed.

Ecological Gaps   In the affluent nations we are witnessing the development of a gap between the present environment and an optimum environment. We must be concerned with the degradation of the social and economic environments as well as degradation of the physical environment. We all know of air and water pollution. We all know about the pyramiding of poisons in food chains. If food chains at their lowest level ceased being poisoned as of this instant, the maximum effects would not be observable for many decades to come. So also with degradation of the social environment. We do not yet have precise knowledge concerning the long-term effects of such pathologies as noise pollution, alcoholism, drug abuse, coronary thrombosis, mental disturbances, and suicides.

The United States and the adjacent populated fringe of Canada are perhaps the most overpopulated parts of the world in terms of per capita abuse to the ecosystems. Sociological intensity or "pace of life" in a given region may be measured by determining the rates at which socially and economically significant decisions are made. These include the rate at which commercial transactions occur, the rate at which information is processed, the rate at which people commit suicide, the rate at which businesses fail, and the rate at which we abuse the physical environment. In fairness it must be added that sociological intensity includes the rate at which the creative arts produce. We are learning much about sociological intensity. The interaction of people with people has both positive and negative aspects. Unless there be high levels of sociological intensity the creative and performing arts do not prosper. On the other hand, the rate of alcoholism shows high spatial correlation with sociological intensity. Populations that operate at high levels of sociological intensity are more apt to generate alcoholics than are those operating at lower levels. This suggests that the amount of information a population must process, the number of decisions they must make, how often they write checks, how many automobiles they contend with in driving to and from work, and so on, constitute varying degrees of stress.

Potential Surfaces: The Pattern of Patterns

The spatial potential of population is an index of sociological intensity.

A population potential surface reveals socioeconomic terrain. As a spatially continuous surface it shows the structures of exchanges relating to social and economic phenomena. Potential itself is a measure of influence at a distance or of macroscopic aggregate accessibility to a population. When we consider the entire population distribution of a country not as groups about points but rather as a density distribution in the plane, then the total potential of population at any given point c is

$$V_c = \int \frac{1}{r} G dA.$$

GdA signifies the density of population, G, over any infinitesimal element of area, dA, and r the distance of each said element to the given point c. The integration is extended to all areas of the plane where G is not zero.

It may be useful to think of total population influence in yet another way. Each person's influence may be represented by a pile of sand, with the height of the pile highest at the place the person occupies and decreasing away from him. Suppose there is a similar sandpile around the place of residence of every individual. Now let all this sand be superposed. At any point the total height of the sand will be the sum of the heights of all the individual sandpiles. The total height is a measure of total population influence at that point, and a contour map or a physical model may be made of the entire surface.

Rural population density, for example, varies empirically as the square of the potential; rural non-farm population density as the cube; rural non-farm rent varies as the first power; farmland values vary as the square; railroad track density varies as the first power; rural free delivery route density varies as the three-halves power; density of wage earners in manufacturing varies as the fifty power; and death rates vary as the square root of the potential.

Similar relationships have been established with respect to telephone network density, rail-line density, road density, market areas, administrative areas, farm sizes, alcoholism, mental disorders, the "velocity" of money, bank check clearances, first class mail, patents, telephone calls, and so on. Potential of population is a measure of sociological intensity—the rate at which decisions are made and information is processed.

The concept of potential of population integrates individual "microscopic" behaviors to yield a "macroscopic" behavior type simple enough to fit a numerical index. Because it substitutes behavior type for behavior, potential is both a highly simplifying and a strongly unifying concept. The idea of potential carries with it a field theory—a system of related factors (gradient, "energy," population density, and so on), each of which projects two basic "dimensions," population and distance, in its special way.

Income Potential   Since the idea of potential of population was first developed[2] it has been clear that not all people could be assigned equal "weights" in the formula for influence. Many people are not "standard Americans" in terms of ability to attract, interact, and influence at a distance. "Social mass per capita" in an area represents an appropriate "weight," or corrective factor. The mass of goods required to support and sustain modern civilization is great indeed; these goods are known as social mass. In the United States the per capita mass of such goods amounts to two or three thousand tons, including such things as houses, railway and highway roadbeds, public buildings, automobiles, bridges, dams, water pumped into aqueducts, and locomotives. Amounts vary throughout the world.

Statistics measuring per capita mass of artificial goods in different places are not readily available, but an acceptable substitute is obtained by weighting people by income. The pattern in figure 6.1 is such a mapping for the United States.

Potential and Power for Change   Potential of population brings about change. Change must be directed toward closing certain gaps. The gap between the "haves" and the "have-nots" is being perceived. The aspirations are there, and the means exist to reduce the gap. Another gap, which afflicts the so-called affluent nations, is that between the actual environment which exists as a consequence of wealth and the ideal environment that is more suited to perpetuating the human species.

Global Welfare Gaps

To close global welfare gaps in constructive rather than destructive ways represents a great challenge. Consider two global mappings, one of population potential (figure 6.2) and one of income potential (figure 6.3). Imagine a global field that is a continuum of ratios of the Income Potential field (in equivalent U.S. dollars per mile) to the Population Potential field (in persons per mile). The units of the resulting ratio would be dollars per person and would therefore be dimensionally consistent with per capita income. In its way, such a mapping would be yet another index of income inequalities at the global scale.

Figure 6.4 is such a mapping and figure 6.5 is a generalization of it. The sphere of the human condition has two poles, New York and Peking.

On this sphere of influence, the lines of force, that is, the gradient paths of steepest slope, converge on both poles. Figure 6.5 shows only the broad general features of the configuration; other details exist in virtually infinite regress. A suggestion of the detail that might be shown if sufficient data were available for the whole world is the pattern produced by Geoffrey Dutton (figure 6.6) who is now engaged in a long-term study of spatial and temporal patterns of population and income change in the United States.

To return to the global scene, figure 6.7 is another mapping of figure 6.4, this time with a broader contour interval plotted on a mercator projection. Not only are the isolines of per capita accessibility to social mass shown, but also the orthogonal lines of force. A halving circle for global income, population and land area is also plotted. Both poles of the world are identified in terms of the intensity of collective material well-being, taken macroscopically.

A Path Toward What Might Be

If one goal of a United Nations is to achieve economic equity for the world's citizens then a map such as figure 6.7 is a useful chart for determining general directions to that goal. Geoffrey Dutton (in converstion) has discussed the utility of such a map for the United States. One can imagine a much more ambitious application of similar concepts and data. If social potential surfaces maintain steady state configurations like fluvial and other open systems and if equivalent distributions of income and population are reasonable goals for international social policy, then, through the use of concepts outlined in this chapter as well as through data on population growth, migration, and economic growth, a programming model could be set up that would derive hypothetical future income and population distributions probable under given sets of policies and constraints. The results would take the form of potential surfaces that could specify the relations of masses of population more or less accurately depending on their order. Naturally, the more control points used the more differential equations would be needed to trace interactions through the system. If the programming challenge could be overcome, however, such a model would be a unique application of systems theory in the social sphere. Optimality principles could then be extended from organismic biology to human ecology, for if open systems are convergent and equifinal, many aspects of the future are implicit in the parameters of the present.

References

1. John Platt, "What We Must Do," *Science*, November 28, 1969, pp. 1105–1121.

2. John Q. Stewart. "The Development of Social Physics," *American Journal of Physics* 18 (1950): 239–253.

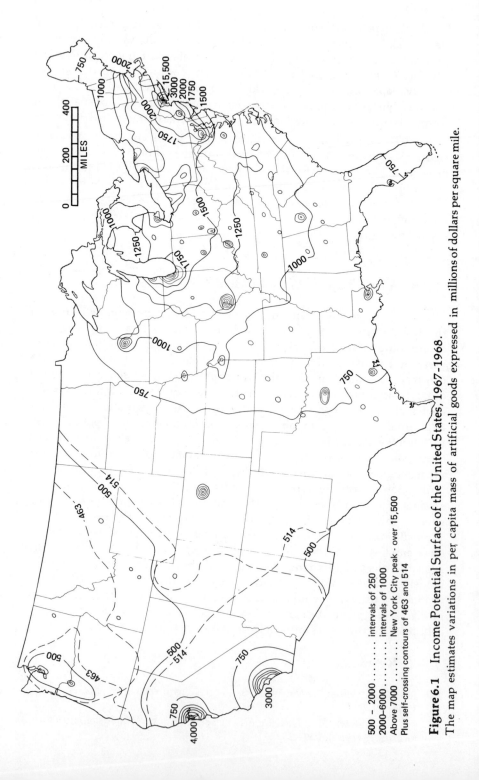

500 – 2000 .... intervals of 250
2000-6000 .... intervals of 1000
Above 7000 .... New York City peak - over 15,500
Plus self-crossing contours of 463 and 514

Figure 6.1 Income Potential Surface of the United States, 1967-1968.
The map estimates variations in per capita mass of artificial goods expressed in millions of dollars per square mile.

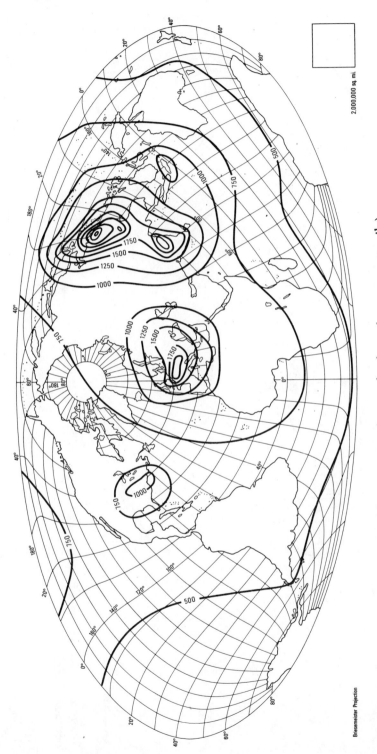

Figure 6.2   World Population Potential circa 1960 (in thousands of people per square mile).

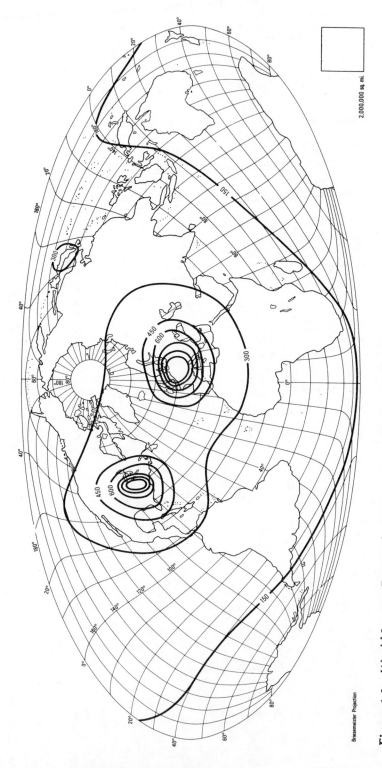

2,000,000 sq. mi.

Briesemeister Projection

Figure 6.3 World Income Potential circa 1960 (in millions of U.S. dollars per square mile).

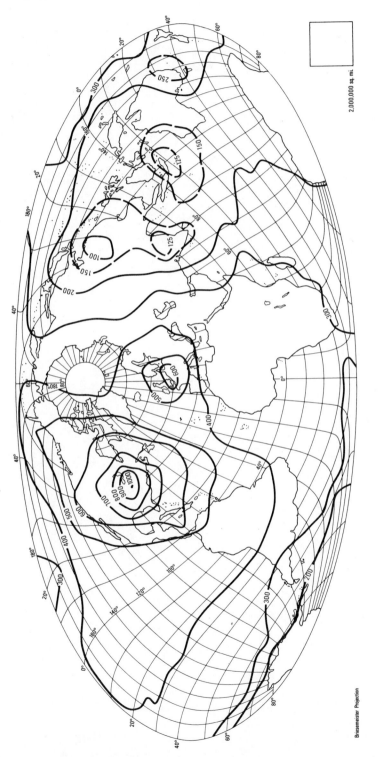

Two Poles of the Human Condition

per capita accessibility to social mass

2,000,000 sq. mi.

Briesemeister Projection

Figure 6.4 Ratio of Income Potentials to Population Potentials circa 1960 (in dollars per person).

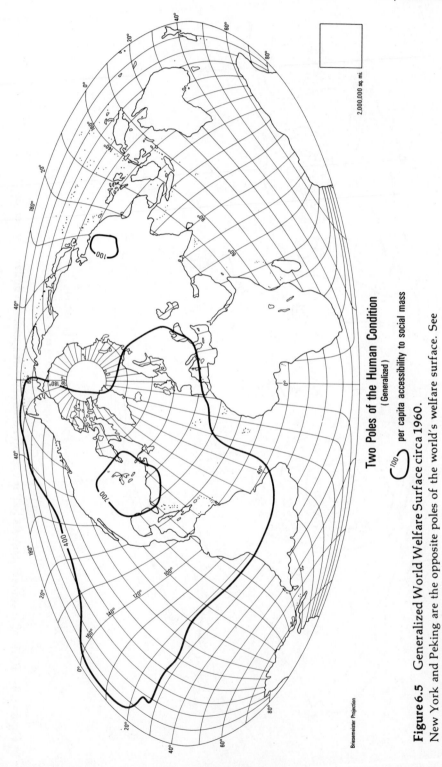

Figure 6.5 Generalized World Welfare Surface circa 1960.
New York and Peking are the opposite poles of the world's welfare surface. See
figure 6.4 for the detailed surface.

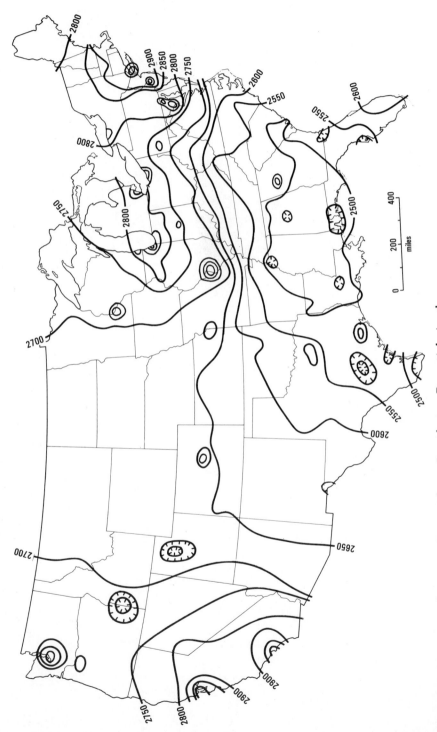

Figure 6.6 Ratio of Income Potentials to Population Potentials in the United States, 1967 (in dollars per person).

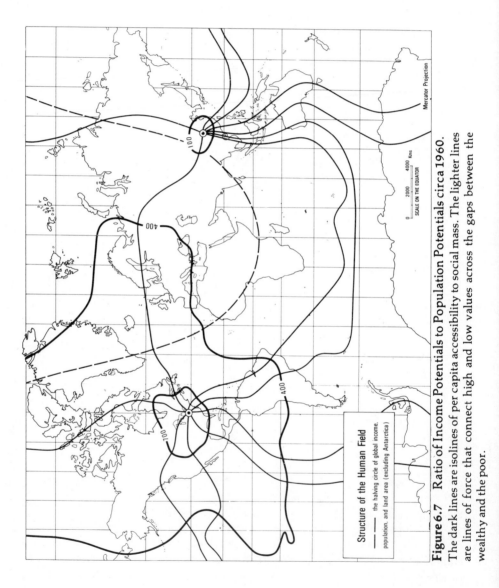

Figure 6.7 Ratio of Income Potentials to Population Potentials circa 1960.
The dark lines are isolines of per capita accessibility to social mass. The lighter lines
are lines of force that connect high and low values across the gaps between the
wealthy and the poor.

Within the figure:

Structure of the Human Field
— the halving circle of global income.
— population, and land area (excluding Antarctica).

Mercator Projection

SCALE ON THE EQUATOR
0   2000   4000 Kms

Chapter   7

Cumulative Versus Mutually Exclusive Regions in the Future

Allen K. Philbrick
The University of Western Ontario

ABSTRACT: *Nearness, separateness, and connectedness are related yet distinct concepts. Their possible combinations are demonstrated with the Venn diagram, and their usefulness for describing territories occupied by multiple human cultures is discussed. We can construct models of spatial contacts among cultures in regions of the future by permuting two cultural attitudes (active-passive and negative-positive) for each of three intercultural contact situations: attachment, containment, and displacement.*

To anyone who wishes to include rather than exclude, cumulative rather than mutually exclusive regionalization is more useful, whether one is trying to make the most efficient use of space or to treat people equitably and with the greatest possible respect.

From a theoretical standpoint, regionalization is a kind of classification. Diagrammatic spatial figures may be used to describe either classification problems or the partitioning of space. Such partitioning of space allows us to deal with the complex interrelationships among things in their relative locations. Such matters are fundamental in creating regions.

Two closed figures not touching are mutually exclusive and completely accounted for by their names (A and B in figure 7.1, part a). This is obviously not the case with overlapping circles (figure 7.1, part b).

In the latter case only cumulative notation of regionality identifies all combinations. The use of geometric spaces demonstrates the interchangability of space partitioning and classification.

In figure 7.1, part c, the names A and B refer to the circles in their mutual exclusion (see items 1 and 2), but they fail to account for the part of

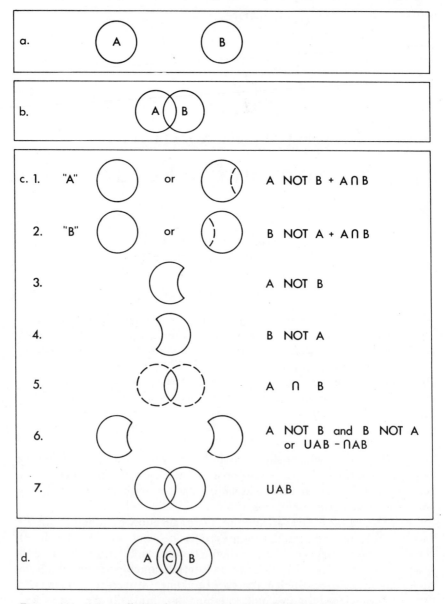

Figure 7.1 Mutually Exclusive Versus Cumulative Regions.

A which is not B (item 3), the part of B which is not A (item 4), the intersection of A and B (item 5) and the unions of A and B, including and not including the intersection of A and B (items 6 and 7).

The diagram can be redrawn (figure 7.1, part d,) so that the two facing lunes and the lens representing the intersection of the two circles appear in all possible combinations regionally, and may be regarded in a mutually exclusive listing as A, B, and C. The Boolean algebraic combinations which cumulatively account for all possible identities are the seven combinations of any three variables in any classification.

a

b

c

ab

bc

ac

abc

These are the same accumulations described previously in words with respect to the two overlapping circles, A and B, (figure 7.1, part c).

What does such an elementary review of set theory have to do with creating regions? especially with human regions? Territorial relationships among people are not simple. The successful creation of regions representing cumulative relationships among people requires accommodating all the various identities of which mankind is composed. When there is considerable cultural diversity among peoples, the number of combinations required for such accommodation increases rapidly.

Accommodation of cultural identity in spatial partitioning requires that we consider nearness, separateness, and connectedness. These concepts are implied in the mutual exclusion of circles A and B but are more explicit in the overlapping Venn diagram circles (figure 7.1, part b).

Nearness, Separateness and Connectedness

Nearness, separateness, and connectedness are closely related but distinct concepts. Nearness is a function of proximity. Subjectively or objectively considered, nearness involves a measure of closeness in a continuum from near to far. Nearness may be measured in terms of number of linkages or in terms of the total lack of connection. Separateness is not a function of nearness or proximity. Separateness means to be divided from, disjoined rather than joined. Connectedness is more than the opposite of being separate; separate entities can be connected and either near or far from one another.

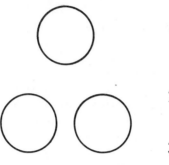

1. <u>SEPARATE</u>

2. <u>NEAR</u>
    SEPARATE

3. <u>NEAR</u> AND <u>SEPARATE</u>

4. <u>CONNECTED</u>
    NEAR
    SEPARATE
    NEAR AND SEPARATE

5. <u>NEAR</u> AND <u>CONNECTED</u>

6. <u>SEPARATE</u> AND <u>CONNECTED</u>

7. <u>NEAR</u>, <u>SEPARATE</u> AND
    <u>CONNECTED</u>

Figure 7.2   Nearness, Separateness, and Connectedness.

Again the rigor of cumulative logic can handle all the distinctive combinations of the three concepts. Just as with A, B, and C, things may be:

> *near,*
> *separate,*
> *connected, or*
> *near* and *separate,*
> *separate* and *connected,*
> *near,* and *connected, and finally*
> *near, separate, and connected, as well (figure. 7.2).*

The Dynamism of Nearness as Measured by Separateness-Connectedness

But this analysis does not end the matter. The use of the cumulative possibilities of such territorial concepts colors the creation of regions. If one

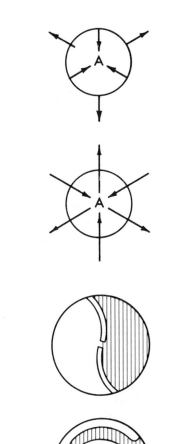

a.   INCLUSION
EXCLUSION

b.   PERCEPTUAL
PERMEABILITY

c.   SEPARATE (NEAR)
WITH MINIMUM CONTACT

d.   SEPARATE (NEAR)
WITH >
MINIMUM CONTACT

Figure 7.3   Inclusion, Exclusion, and Contact.

defines a circular territory as bounded, it may be regarded as separating a near place from a more distant one, an internal from an external territory. The definition then becomes an included portion as distinct from an excluded one. (figure 7.3, part a). The arrows facing inward express nearness, cohesion, unity, convergence, and inclusion; the arrows facing outward express separateness, disparateness, disunity, divergence, and exclusion.

Figure 7.3, part a represents more than a possible geographical surface; it may also represent the subjective personal space of the psyche. In terms of intuitive subjective self, internal and near lie within. They are the conscious and subconscious identity of each person as separate from, though connected with, the external and separate objective world. Each of us occupies a perceptual space behind a set of sensory and corporeal/territorial boundaries. Individually, each of us is geographically separate, near, and connected. The individual is the fundamental starting point in creating regions.

Our personal ability to function in society is dependent upon the permeability of our sensory boundaries. The arrows crossing the circle in both directions in figure 7.3, part b express our personal participation in the world around us. Our individual ability to be near others is a function of our skill at maintaining separateness and connectedness in a flexibly balanced state. Our success is also measurable by our ability to allow others to maintain a similar balance and by their capacity to allow us the same.

Separateness/connectedness as a cumulative measure of nearness may be diagrammed as a continuum illustrated by the shapes in figure 7.3, part c and d. Separation may exist with a minimum of contact between equals, or with greater than minimum contact. Still another way of expressing nearness through separateness/connectedness is through linkages. In the hierarchical pattern shown in figure 7.4, the number of links separating the focus, A, from successive tiers of B's and C's, shows the C's

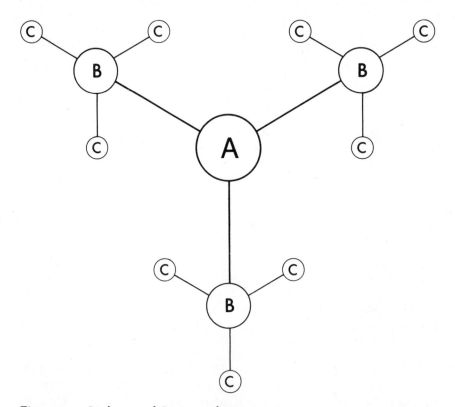

Figure 7.4   Linkage and Connectedness.

to be connected by two linkages with A whereas the B's are connected to A with only one link.

Maximizing Information

Creating regions involves more than a matter of territory. Rather, it is primarily a matter of information and communication, on the basis of which persons representing diverse backgrounds operate within varying territorialities. Mutually exclusive classes derived from heterogeneous and diverse phenomena are often mistakenly utilized as a generalization technique. Often this is done to reduce complex distributions to simple terms. Mutually exclusive categories usually result in loss of important parts of the total data sets (table 7.1). By contrast cumulative classification, making use of an identical number of categories, accommodates 100 percent of the information (table 7.1).

Table 7.1 Relative Loss And Preservation of Data by Use of Mutually Exclusive Categories and Cumulative Categories

Objective Diversity	Dominant Item classes	Data Items Lost	Cumulative classes
A B B	B	A	A + 2B
B A A	A	B	B + 2A
C C B	C	B	2C + B
A B C	None	A B C	A+B+C

Cumulative Hypothesis for Creating Effective Multicultural Regions

Designing regions that maximize the inclusion of persons within the society for which a territory is provided will most likely succeed by using cumulative classification and cumulative regionalization. Only in this manner can the paradox of nearness-separateness-connectedness, which implies a very large number of possible combinations, be resolved. Such designing must recognize the limitations of form in the search for specific accommodations for each multicultural requirement. Designers must also recognize the need for multicultural solutions in the relationships between private and public spaces.

The individual person has the greatest capacity to adapt and utilize finite sets of spatial arrangements in ways that will enable him to retain his identity in a cumulative hierarchy of parts. The least among us must be accommodated. Every individual, regardless of age, tongue, physical differentiation, past experience, beliefs, degree of education, status, or station must have maximum freedom of choice.

Only in cumulative territories can men be free to be exclusive while adhering to the principle of inclusion. Toward this end we must build cumulative and not mutually exclusive information and communication systems as the basis for a cumulative territoriality among mankind.

A World More Complex Than Ideal

One obstacle to the application of these ideas is that human relationships are more complex than ideal. Analysis of actual contacts between cultural groups with different sets of experience reveals great extremes and differences. These extremes and differences have been the bases of great evils perpetrated by the strong upon the weak. Current regional patterns present a wide range of negative and positive contacts as well as aggressive and non-aggressive behavior. If we are to talk of creating regions for the future, we must recognize and resolve the great issues of exploitation and denial of identity which make a mockery of idealized solutions.

Spatial Interfacing of Cultures

As human cultures proliferate in number, in individual size, and in territory, the world is host to countless cross-cultural contacts. Not all are confrontations; but in the absence of understanding of the nature of cultural spatial interfacing, those contacts which are hostile are dramatic and dangerous.

To further such understandings a method of modelling inter-cultural spatial contacts is needed. Two separate aspects must be combined in such a model: the variation in attitudes of individuals and groups on the one hand, and the varieties of spatial contacts accompanying the exchange of ideas.

Active/Passive, Postive/Negative Attitudes   A four cell matrix (figure 7.5, part a) provides places for two variations for each of two poles of attitude. On any given issue, one's attitude may be active or passive and negative or positive. In a cumulative sense, therefore, there exist four necessary combinations:

Active-Postive
Aggressively promoting a position in favor of something.

Active-Negative
Aggressively opposing something.

Passive-Positive
  Passively agreeing with but simply accepting something.

Passive-Negative
  Resignedly accepting something one disagrees with.

The arrows across the boundaries indicate that attitudes can change.

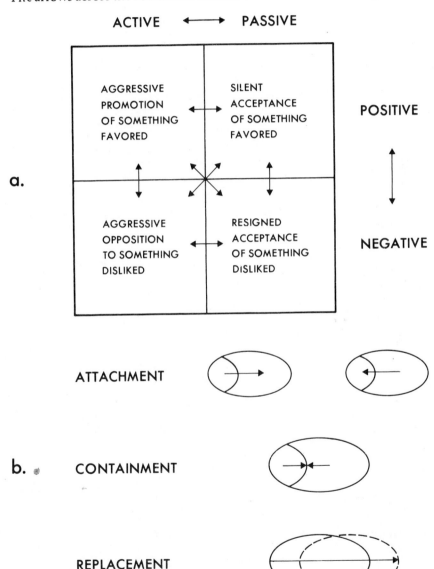

Figure 7.5 Attitudes and Connectivity.

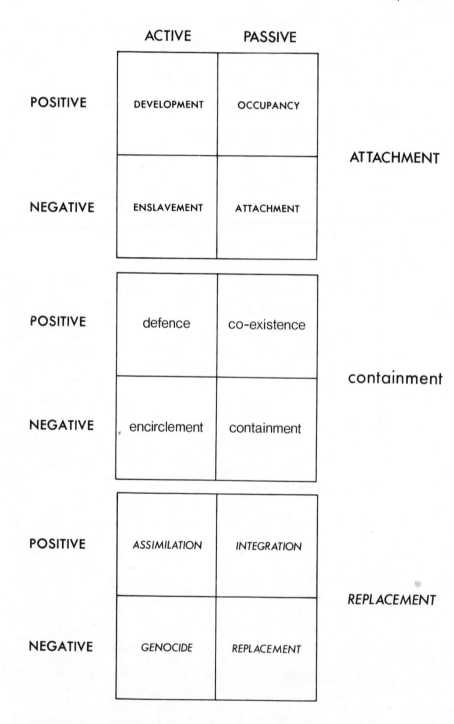

Figure 7.6 Attitudes and Regions

Attachment, Containment, and Replacement Insofar as the above attitudes apply to spatial contacts, there are three kinds of spatial interfaces that describe existing situations. These are labelled attachment, containment, and replacement (figure 7.5, part b). In cases of attachment, the arrow indicates which of two groups is attached to the other. Containment means stalemate or stand-off. Replacement is a resolution of pressure in favor of one group by intrusion upon the space of another; one group replaces the other in the latter's territory.

Spatial Interface Model When one combines attitude with attachment, containment, and replacement, each attitude creates four different expressions of each of the three types of spatial events (figure 7.6).

Under *attachment* which is defined as passive/negative, active positive is *development*, passive positive is simply *occupancy*, while active negative is the much stronger word, *enslavement*.

Under *containment* which is deemed passive negative, active positive is named *defense*, while the passive form of positive stand-off is *co-existence*. The active negative is the stronger concept of *encirclement*.

When it comes to *replacement*, which is deemed passively negative, the active positive form is *assimilation*, passive positive *integration*, while the active negative is the most extreme position of *genocide*.

One may, of course, quarrel with the choice of words in figure 7.6; but these words do illustrate the variabilities of attitude with respect to different spatial consequences of cultural contact.

Application in the Objective World In figure 7.7 the double matrix summary of the ideas presented in this chapter suggests two potential uses of the model in creating regions for the future. The first is

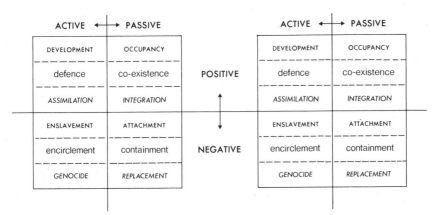

Figure 7.7 Attitudes and Regions for the Future.

analytical, the second is predictive.

The matrices identify each of the attitudes theoretically possible with respect to any given issue involved in the spatial interaction of cultures A and B. They simultaneously make it possible to assess the frequency of each and to analyze the cumulative position of the cultures with respect to one another. The arrows in the margins of the model demonstrate the way in which attachment may become containment which may give way, in turn, to replacement.

On the basis of existing trends and pressures within each culture, the model may be used to assess the potential for stable or unstable contact situation, between any two. Obviously, aggressive cultures attempt to keep others they deal with in a state of passive acceptance, with all the loss of identity and self-respect such a state implies. Equally obviously, when people react and become actively negative toward their oppressors, they develop attitudes and aspirations of a postive nature with respect to their own territoriality.

Such varying attitudes can be described; their relative strengths and directions of change can be assessed. Only if we face the reality of distress existing among the disadvantaged and oppressed of the world can we lay the foundation for building better regions for the future.

Chapter   8

Spatial Aspects of
Alienation and the
Phasing Out of
Bureaucracy

Donald G. Janelle
University of Western Ontario

ABSTRACT: *The industrial revolution stimulated a gradual but per-sistent consolidation of social, political, and economic control into fewer units of larger size. There are, however, parallel tendencies toward individual differentiation via specialization of role or division of labor. More fluid spatial behavior in the form of increasing residential mobility, decline in commitment to local communities, and growing interaction with regional, national, or international interest groups creates new lifestyles that conflict with current bureaucratic systems. Responding to ad hoc voluntary citizen action groups oriented to solving problems requires an increased flexibility and expansion by bureaucracy to embrace them. Adhocratic administrative regions must replace bureaucracy if we hope to integrate current lifestyles and ephemeral special interest groups with efficient and responsive government.*

Units of human organization vary in size from the family at one level to the United Nations at the world scale. These organizations are defined by the shared needs of their members and are designed to meet various physical, social, and spiritual needs. The household is the most fundamental of these units; it is thus a part of all higher level human organizations. Although an individual family has some direct control over the extended family, the local church, and similar institutions, control decreases and becomes more indirect at successively higher levels. In the extended family, each component household ideally has $1/n$ of the power, where n equals the number of households. At higher organizational levels the average fractional control exercised by each household diminishes as it becomes further and further removed from the places in which control is vested.

Separation of the Parts From the Whole

In competitive societies, moreover, control is seldom equally allocated among all families. Forces within man's interrelated social, political, and economic systems allocate status, power, money, and goods differentially. Thus, although households represent undifferentiated wholeness at one level, some households assume greater dominance over the system than others and thereby gain access to higher levels of control. This centralizing tendency results in leading parts that dominate the system's behaviors. Thus, a question warranting careful consideration in any attempts to design viable human habitats is: To what extent can a household be removed from a position of control over the whole (whether the whole be a block, a city, a state, or the world) and still consider itself a part of the whole? Or, to what extent is the whole becoming more and more separated from its parts? To answer this question I refer to existing trends toward organizational agglomeration and individual differentiation. In the context of prevailing economic motivations, these trends are complementary. At the same time, however, they run counter to the ideals of participatory democracy. In an era of emergent bigness some will argue that participatory democracy is outmoded and that some omnipotent, unitary power should control the globe for the betterment of the whole. Others will suggest that technology makes it possible to restore pure democracy in the form of on-line, real-time control by individuals and households.

Toward Closed Systems and Global Control   The industrial revolution stimulated an organizational trend that is still accelerating. Each successively higher unit of organization is gradually increasing its power over greater numbers of subunits. The shadow of unitary control gradually but persistently falls over national, continental, and world units. Earlier units of control are either discarded or absorbed in pursuit of perceived economic gains and holistic planning. In North America rural and neighborhood schools have been consolidated into fewer units of larger size, family farms have been aggregated into superfarms, independent stores have given way to chain organizations, and small workshops have been progressively amalgamated into factories, industrial conglomerates, and multinational corporations. Metropolitan governments gradually extinguish the control formerly vested in component municipalities, and regional government may eventually supplant metropolitan government. As Scott Greer has noted, groups which order work, education, recreation, and other activities are becoming ". . . increasingly dominated by bureaucracies that fuse through organizational absorptions and expansions into cartels of one sort or another;" control over individual behavior is shifting from the primary group structures of society to secondary groups that organize such activities as work, religion, and politics.[1]

The primary economic advantages that accrue from increased consolidation of control are economies of scale, which in turn greatly facilitate holistic planning. This is particularly true when problems transcend individuals and localities. Problems such as pollution control and providing water and transportation are dealt with more efficiently at municipal, metropolitan and regional levels than on a household-by-household basis. But holistic planning can be used to cover up or to ignore problems at more local levels. Jane Jacobs has suggested that "a region is an area safely larger than the last one to whose problems we found no solution." This is ". . . much like saying that a large insurance company is better equipped to average out risks than a small insurance company."[2] The objective of holistic planning by industry, government, and other large bodies is to convert seemingly open systems into apparently closed systems. In the face of increasing mobility and human interaction, this obsession for control leads inevitably to global units of human organization similar to the global cybernated space economy suggested by McDaniel in chapter 4.

Toward Differentiation of the Parts   Such global control units have many advantages and they may even be necessary for the long-term survival of man. But trends toward larger control units must be evaluated in the context of parallel tendencies toward individual differentiation. John Kenneth Galbraith observes that one of the noteworthy accomplishments of modern economic society is the taking of ". . . ordinary men, informing them narrowly but deeply and then devising an organization which combines their knowledge with that of other similarly specialized but equally ordinary men for a highly predictable performance."[3] In many respects man has proceeded from a state of relative homogeneity to a state of increasing differentiation, articulation, and hierarchic order. The same specialization of labor that gives identity to the individual sets him apart from others; it allows extension of self and makes aggregation of individuals into larger units of human organization necessary. Increasingly, man is faced with mutually dependent forces of division within unity. Separated functions require cooperative, unifying organizational structures; pervasive agglomeration of such support structures, whether they be corporations, labor unions, or governments, have effectively stripped the individual of control over the system.

Such loss of control propagates alienation (figure 8.1). Increasing individual specialization and larger control organizations result in greater differentiation of the parts from the whole. This in turn increases individual alienation and produces higher stress levels in affected societies. The remainder of this chapter considers spatial implications of these combined trends in light of other social trends and suggests counterforces for restoring workable relationships.

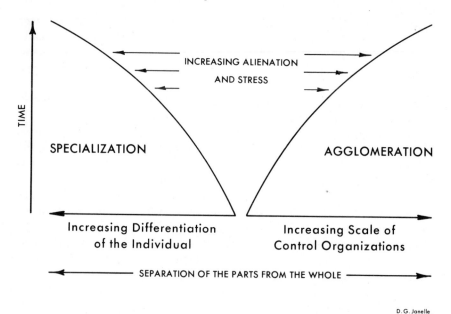

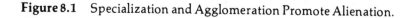

D. G. Janelle

Figure 8.1   Specialization and Agglomeration Promote Alienation.

Organizational Implications of Changing Patterns in Spatial Behavior

Competitive and cooperative agents which divide space and allocate it for various uses are the geographical manifestations of agglomerative and fragmentive forces. In general, geographical areas change as a consequence of two processes. First, the things which make up areas can change in place. For example, people rooted in an area for a lifetime will continually alter their lifestyles to match their stage in the life cycle; they may adopt new values and ways of doing things. Second, people may filter in and out of an area and alter the area's composition either in kind or in degree. The second process has been dominant in producing revolutionary regional changes in North American societies. Such changes include:

1)   Widespread mobility. Fixed human occupance is a thing of the past. Household mobility is producing increasingly open spatial systems. Associated with greater residential mobility are higher turnover rates in community ties, friendships, goods, and jobs.[4] Also evident are preferences for rental rather than ownership, and portable as opposed to fixed life needs.

2.)   Noncommitment. Given current mobility levels a decline in commitment to residential community or locality of residence is not surprising. Many people no longer identify with a residential community, and local decisions are increasingly made by a few rather than the majority. "Allegiance to a city or state is now weaker for many than the allegiance to a corporation, a profession, or a voluntary association."[5]

3.)   Noncontiguity. Finally, there is a growing noncontiguity in household communities of interest reflected in decreasing communication among neighbors and abandonment of what Greer refers to as "inclusive spatial groups."[6] Interest groups are increasingly made up of individuals scattered over regions and continents.[7]

These changes are divisive forces which increase the isolation of the individual from immediate neighbors as well as from higher levels of social and political organization. Such changes permit individuals greater selectivity in defining interest groups and they engender differentiation among groups. Such changes have additional implications that run counter to prevailing systems of societal organization—both spatially and nonspatially. New lifestyles and changing activity patterns suggest that unitary, hierarchic control systems are less useful than they once were. New organizational structures that will accommodate mobility and its consequences must be devised.

Emerging Patterns of Spatial Adhocracy   In spite of fluidity, people who live close to each other share some interests by reason of location regardless of their sense of community or neighborliness. Interests and needs may be fleeting or of longer duration. A latent community of interest may be aroused for group protection in the face of crises, for example. Spatially defined groups may form in response to floods, water shortages, slum landlords, threats of urban renewal, proposals for sewerage treatment plants, or residential invasions by unwanted groups. Individuals who disagree on other issues suddenly become one. Since household locations differ, it is not unusual for colleagues on one issue to be bitter opponents on another. Ephemeral and multiple coalitions of power develop in which any single individual may play different roles at different times

The regions which result from these alliances are temporary also. They are voluntary groupings of people loyal to problems rather than to fixed territorial units. Over the last several decades, singleminded citizens' groups have disrupted ordered grievance- and conflict-resolution systems by ignoring boundaries set by bureaucrats. The failure of present systems to cope with spontaneous, ad hoc expressions of vested interest is evident in the long and expensive attempts to adjudicate the location of freeways in North America over the last two decades.[8] It is unlikely that human activity patterns will revert to their sedate and more easily predicted past. It is increasingly apparent that bureaucracy must change. Public offices, business, industry, and other societal superstructures continue to ignore citizen interests in their annoyance over the disruptive nature of public action groups. Yet, maintaining status quo organizational principles must result in continued failure to solve problems caused by rapid environmental changes. A hypothetical example illustrates the disparity between present organizational structures and community-of-interest-regions (figure 8.2).

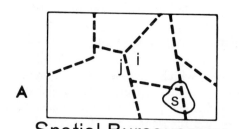

i and j are individual households.
S is an area defined by a strong community of interest (e.g., an ethnic ghetto). It presents a united stand on most problems.

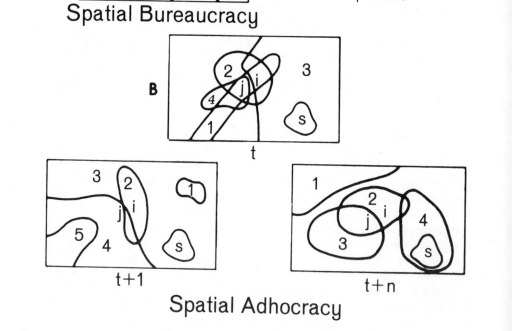

Figure 8.2   Spatial Bureaucracy Versus Spatial Adhocracy.

Many territories are divided by political or administrative fiat (figure 8.2, A). Boundaries are relatively permanent, and hierarchic power flows exist, as in political wards in a city or in counties of a state or province. Through time, agglomerative forces may lead to aggregation of these units under unitary control, such as the replacement of municipalities with metropolitan government. Extending fixed boundaries has been the usual strategy for dealing with problems associated with increased mobility. An alternative is to devise government and administrative regions that respond to ever changing needs (figure 8.2, B). Voluntary and temporary structures should be based dominantly on lateral rather than hierarchic communications. What is needed is adhocracy, not bureaucracy. We can easily imagine a structure in which at time t, individual household i may be united in activist agreement with household j on issues 1 and 2, but in opposition on issues 3 and 4 (figure 8.2, B). Their respective positions at time t + 1, however, may be completely different. Under current organizational structures, individuals in agreement on an issue may be denied full expression of their combined power by an arbitrary political line. A divide-and-conquer mechanism works to the advantage of higher level organizational structures. Spatial bureaucracy fosters feelings of powerlessness and alienation at household levels; efforts toward individual and community control are frustrated.

For reasons of income, societal pressure, or choice, not all households have shared equally in trends toward greater mobility. The area labelled S in figure 8.2 represents a spatially defined community consisting of households sharing similar lifestyles and goals and dedicated to long-term community survival. Ethnicity has traditionally defined segregated populations, such as blacks and Chicanos in American cities and many minority nationalities in Canadian cities. To combat pervasive assimilation forces many of these people have mounted determined campaigns to secure effective community control. Community control is an anti-bureaucracy movement intent on returning goal formulation to more basic levels of human organization. Many individuals buck prevailing trends by seeking out residential areas expressive of their own values and interests. Artist colonies and minicults define distinct spatial units possessing social and political cohesiveness. Community control is an effective means for challenging forces of alienation; it warrants official sanction rather than censure.

Conclusion

Increasing differentiation of individuals and the increasing scale of society's control organizations have combined with greater mobility to alienate individuals and produce stress. Ad hoc citizen action groups and long-term efforts to secure community control are forces for combating alienation. Enlightened administrators must seek to recognize, formalize, and condone adhocracies as valid expressions of vested interest.

Rapid advances in communication and transport technology have promoted bigness and agglomeration of power and control. The same technologies could be used to restore a large share of control to smaller units of human organization. A perfect adhocracy would require instantaneous, free, and total information flow, and it would require of all persons equal ability to use information to his or her best advantage. A guaranteed "living level" income for every household would also be necessary to remove economic and political obstacles to effective participation. But, just as bureaucracy, participatory democracy, and free market mechanism have failed to realize their highest ideals, it is also unlikely that adhocracy will yield perfect self-organizing systems.

Although Bennis has suggested that bureaucracy is waning, it will not wither away completely.[9] Thus we must expand organizational structures to embrace their fields of interaction. At the same time, however, we must recognize that rapid environmental changes warrant more kinetic organizational structures than we now have. Such structures are particularly important at local and regional levels, where coalitions are often fleeting and complex. Ad hoc mechanisms offer more possibilities for resolving individual and group conflicts than do bureaucracies. Unimpeded by arbitrary boundaries and jurisdictional divisions, adhocracy draws upon multiple individual and group interests to keep conflict manageable, to take advantage of bargaining opportunities, and to improve chances for mutually advantageous compromise. Phasing out cumbersome bureaucratic structures and providing adhocracies based on convergence of information structures and institutional forms will augment individual participation in control of man's destinies.

References

1. Scott Greer, *The Emerging City: Myth and Reality* (New York: The Free Press, 1962), p. 55.

2. Jane Jacobs, *Death and Life of Great American Cities* (New York: Random House, 1963), p. 432.

3. John Kenneth Galbraith, "Technology, Planning, and Organization," in *Values and the Future,* ed. Kurt Baier and Nicholas Rescher (New York: The Free Press, 1969), p. 361.

4. Alvin Toffler, *Future Shock,* (New York: Random House, 1970).

5. John Dyckman, "The Changing Uses of the City," in *The Future Metropolis,* ed. Lloyd Rodwin (New York: George Braziller, 1961), p. 154.

6. Scott Greer, *op. cit.,* pp. 37—38.

7. Melvin Webber, *et al., Explorations into Urban Structure* (Philadelphia: University of Pennsylvania Press, 1964).

8. See the many discussion papers by Julian Wolpert and his associates at the University of Pennsylvania on conflict in locational decisions. Several papers have been issued since September, 1970.

9. Warren Bennis, "Beyond Bureaucracy," *Transaction* 2 (1965): 31—35. See also
    Warren Bennis, *Changing Organizations* (New York: McGraw-Hill, 1966).

Chapter 9

Personality and Self-Discovery: The Future Social Geography of the United States

Wilbur Zelinsky
The Pennsylvania State University

ABSTRACT: *Important changes will occur in the American landscape as highly mobile individuals seek personal fulfillment and self-realization by selecting what they perceive to be optimal physical and social environments. For the affluent, economic constraints are becoming subsidiary to personal preferences, and traditional cultural regions are being replaced by voluntary regions composed of self-selected residents. Examples on a large scale are Southern California, Texas, and Peninsular Florida. On a smaller scale, there are military subregions, educational centers, pleasuring places, New Bohemias, and communal colonies.*

There are problems in identifying and studying emergent social groups of geographical interest. A possible solution is to analyze through time and space the memberships of the numerous truly voluntary associations devoted to "causes" and to amenities. Another research direction is to map the consumption of selected personality-sensitive goods and services, for example, special interest magazines and pet ownership.

The emergence of the atomistic, mobile individual in quest of personal fulfillment is a great structural change that promises to make the human geography of the near future wrenchingly different from the familiar patterns of the past. In speculating about the nature and meaning of this change I propose: (1) to simplify and isolate the phenomenon in question by ignoring as far as possible other major changes going on around us and (2) to invert a standard ploy of the historical geographer, who recreates the past by observing sequestered, fossilized landscapes, and to scout out the landscape of the future by identifying avante-garde regions and trends.

My working hypothesis is that the exercise of individual preferences as to values, pleasures, self-improvement, social environment, physical habitat, and general lifestyle has begun to alter the spatial attributes of the population of the United States to a significant extent. To avoid misunderstanding, it should be stated that the spatial structure of advanced societies has been and is largely shaped by historical inertia, livelihood pattern, age and gender, kinship considerations, ethnic, racial, and religious loyalties, and the sociocultural effects of the immediate neighborhood and the larger culture area. No one can fully liberate himself from such entanglements. But there is another factor that may be supplementing these traditional forces: the self-realization of the highly mobile, atomistic individual searching out what he or she perceives to be an optimal location in physical and social space.

There is a growing feeling, shared by many sensitive observers of current events, that the 1950's and 1960's witnessed the beginning of far-reaching changes in the relations between man and place and in the ways people view themselves and their larger environment. The invention and adoption of novel technologies, especially in communication, coupled with new modes of economic and social activity have progressed so rapidly that quantitative change may have produced qualitative change. If we accept as axiomatic the notion that the spatial structure of society is both cause and effect of spatial and nonspatial processes, and that a different constellation of spatial patterns is specific to each major social system, then there is considerable theoretical and practical value in plotting the geographical outlines of the incipient future. This essay is a reconnaissance of things to come, an attempt to chart the social contours of that outpost of the future known as the United States.

The dominant motif in mid-twentieth century human geography has been emphatically economic. We have assumed that the ruling consideration in people's spatial behavior is the maximization of economic utility, subject to some traditional value systems and to the constraints imposed by the man-environment system. We now need a new set of assumptions based upon the existence of a style-setting population numbering many millions for whom economic criteria are secondary to other considerations. Given the existence of a sizeable group whose ordinary material needs have been met and who also have access to advanced technologies of production, consumption, transport, and communication, what are the new rules for spatial behavior? Perhaps exploring the locational attributes of the "personality factor" will offer some clues. And perhaps these clues will contribute not only to a future-oriented human geography, but also to a more realistic general theory of post-industrial society.

If the "personality factor" must indeed be reckoned with in understanding the future social geography of affluent communities, then intriguing questions arise. What generates the personality gradients that might be plotted in physical and social space? Is it the normal sorting out of genes and chromosomes through the processes observed in population genetics? Or are subtler new forms of conditioning occurring during childhood and adolescence, beyond the traditional processes of close replication of personalities of parents, siblings, and neighbors? The geographer can approach such questions via the following route: Is significant migration, either transient[1] or permanent, being generated by those locational advantages believed by persons of similar bent to inhere in particular places? Perhaps certain kinds of people have affinities for certain kinds of locales. Conversely, there may be something in the ambiance of specific places that engenders specific personality traits. To what degree does the inner man select the place, and to what degree does the place select the inner man? Is a new set of social regions gestating through migratory and other processes?

The basic assumption of a recently begun study is that individuals are sorting themselves out regionally with increasing independence from social ancestry and early upbringing, and in accordance with temperament, taste, psychological style, or some other such entity which I call the "personality factor." The most accurate label for the psychological attribute that will be analyzed geographicaly is Cattell's "sentiment structure," which he defines as:

> "... major acquired dynamic trait structures which cause their possessors to pay attention to certain objects or classes of objects, and to feel and react in a certain way with regard to them."[2]

There are extraordinary difficulties inherent in defining, measuring, and interpreting human personality; and a huge literature on such problems has accumulated during the past few decades.[3] Close attention will be paid to the various personality classification systems and, in particular, to the "source traits" identified by Cattell and Eysenck through factor analysis.[4] It will be interesting to see whether the personality traits that seem to be related to the spatial configuration of the emergent postindustrial society are the same as those identified in standard testing procedures, or whether injecting a geographical dimension will reveal psychological elements or "sentiment structures" that were previously undescribed.

It is necessary to gather longitudinal as well as contemporary data to discover how the personality factor operates through time as well as across space. Thus, special efforts are being made to collect and analyze diachronic material to see whether the personality factor has been increasing in strength in recent years, and, if so, how and where. Even a tentative answer may throw some light on one of the deepest issues in American social and cultural geography—the deceptively simple question of the extent to which regional cultures are converging or diverging.

There are severe, time consuming problems in data procurement and analysis that hamper attempts to identify the spatial causes and consequences of the putatively free expression of personal preferences. Neither the problems nor the possible solutions can be set forth with much confidence for the simple reason that this research lacks direct antecedents. But a few preliminary ideas can be put forward.

Two strategies are used. One is to delimit emergent *voluntary regions* in the United States. The other is to locate, analyze, and interpret less visible communities of likeminded individuals who somehow cohere in physical or social space. Such communities are of quite recent origin, but they may well add a distinctly new character to the nation's social structure.

The Voluntary Regions of the United States

The culture areas of the world, past, present, and future, can be usefully divided into two classes on the basis of their origins.

The first and more numerous class is the *traditional region;* virtually all culture areas that existed prior to the Modern Period were traditional regions. Traditional regions are relatively self-contained, endogamous, stable, and long-lived. Individuals are born into traditional regions and remain there physically and mentally; there is little in- or out-migration. Accidents of birth automatically assign each individual to a specific caste, class, occupation, and social role. Intimate, symbiotic relationships among people and between human beings and habitat develop over many centuries, creating modes of thought, behavior, a visible landscape, and a human ecology highly specific to each locality. The usual processes of random cultural mutation, accidents of history, slight intermixture of peoples, and diffusion of innovations prevent total stasis or equilibrium and complete internal uniformity. But it would be fair to say such regions are based upon blood and soil. In extreme cases, traditional regions are synonymous with particular tribes or ethnic groups.

The second class of culture areas, *voluntary regions*, is still emergent, hence not yet clearly recognized. It is coeval with modernization in Northwest Europe and with the emergence of the individual as an essentially free agent. The earliest, largest, and, to date, most advanced experiment in constructing voluntary regions has gone on in North America. There the traditional spatial and social allocation of individuals through the lottery of birth is being gradually replaced by relatively free choice and self-selection in terms of lifestyle, goals, social niche, and place(s) of residence. This new freedom has been evident from the earliest days of serious North American settlement onward. The colonists were motivated by religious, social, political, and idiosyncratic considerations. But, with minor exceptions, they migrated as individuals or single families and gravitated toward those places perceived as best fulfilling their aspirations; there they mingled with strangers from many widely scattered places, who had similar tastes and proclivities. The process is beautifully exemplified in the establishment of the Great Basin Kingdom by the Mormons. A tightly structured, homogeneous society was created by self-consciously selecting and routing likeminded people with highly diverse backgrounds from the Eastern United States and Western Europe to a remote, empty region; it was a self-sorting of people and the fabrication of a synthetic, monotonic culture area with a vengeance. Similar processes were at work during the initial colonization along the Atlantic seaboard and later during the advance of the frontier, but less visibly and distinctly because of considerable random migrational jostling.

Once an American area was effectively settled and had achieved economic and social stability, there commenced a series of processes analogous to, but less pervasive than those typical in traditional regions. Emotional and social roots were put down; man and habitat influenced each other; diverse peoples met, merged, and hybridized their ways of life; influences were exchanged with the outside, and eventually a new culture area crystallized. The older American case simulates but cannot match premodern culture areas in intensity and longevity. With sufficient isolation American regional cultures might have developed persistent lives of their own. But frequently the same forces of individualistic choice that lead to a culture area's birth also promote its erosion and obliteration. The more enterprising elements in the population drift away to greener pastures and relict culture areas become the stages upon which new forces operate and newer voluntary regions take shape.

It is possible today to be a solid citizen of metropolitan New England, San Diego, or Philadelphia and yet be utterly oblivious to the historical cultural identity of those places. The currents of voluntary migration are many and varied and they remain preeminently economic in character, but increasingly the quest for pleasure and the amenities influences migrational decisions.[5] One might argue forcefully that the spatial sum of millions of such decisions in a "mass-cult" society is toward sameness from coast to coast and the progressive blotting out of local deviation. But increasing evidence points in the opposite direction—to new voluntary regions quite distinct in shape and structure from the older traditional regions. Some are ephemeral in the extreme, others promise durability. In aggregate, they present a new geometry of culture, a shifting, kaleidoscopic choreography of mobile individuals seeking ideal havens in their journeys of self-discovery.

There are two subsystems of culture areas in contemporary America. There is the older set of places, originated during and just after the period of first effective settlement, now largely relict. Some still prosper, but all are hybrid creatures that combine elements of the traditional areas with those of the voluntary regions. Partially superimposed over the older traditional regions are the many new voluntary regions. Some are still quite indistinct, with scarcely any functional connection with their predecessors.

A new geometry of cultural space has begun to materialize in the United States. Traditional spatial parcels of relative homogeneity are being replaced by a multilayered sandwich in which numerous strata of variable thickness span the entire country. Formerly a person seeking cultural variety would move horizontally along the earth's surface from one place-bound group to another. Now, a person can find variety with very little physical motion by shifting vertically in cultural space from one layer of the sandwich to another, or by hobnobbing with selected communities by means of telecommunications. Truly revolutionary changes in physical, social, and mental mobility have fractured and reordered the dimensional packages in which cultures operate. In some places a particular stratum, or subculture may thicken so markedly that that group dominates the locality. When this occurs, a voluntary region has come into existence.

Because economic, social, and demographic data-gathering systems are not yet attuned to the existence of voluntary regions, much discussion concerning them remains speculative, based on scattered observations, hints, and hunches. This lag in awareness is illustrated by the dearth of hard data on tourism, recreation, and leisure-time activities. Such activities are very important to students of voluntary regions and also to businessmen. But we are not yet reconciled to the pagan notion of regarding them as serious concerns. There is also the matter of spatial and temporal scale. Most emergent regions are as yet tiny or fragmented; many are also ephemeral. These are inadequate reasons for ignoring the emerging voluntary regions. Smallness or spatial irregularity may simply reflect a new spatial geometry of postindustrial communities about which very little is known. Furthermore, there is no natural cutoff on the temporal scale. All spatial structures are dynamic and evanescent. The cultural group that coheres spatially for five days or five hours is just as real, and perhaps as interesting, as one that persists for five hundred or five thousand years.

There are, however, at least three extensive tracts within the United States that appear to be voluntary regions and show signs of relative stability: Southern California, Texas, and Peninsular Florida. (Weaker cases can be made for the Upper Rio Grande and one or two other Western subregions.) Southern California and Texas began as agricultural and ranching frontiers, with later accretions of higher economic functions. More recently, it has become evident that the large volume of in-migration has been controlled by factors other than efforts to optimize economic welfare. The latter remain important, but more and more of those bound for Southern California and Texas seem to be seeking congenial surroundings and likeminded individuals. The popular impression that the Southern Californian is self-selected for certain personality traits and the similar conviction among Southerners about Texas-bound migrants merit careful investigation.

The basic conditions for the voluntary region appear to be met. Social regions determined by the traditional factors of circumstance of birth and social heredity are being replaced by aggregations of likeminded, mobile, atomistic individuals acting upon personal predilections. The cultural personalities of Southern California and Texas are decreasingly defined by their nineteenth century infancies; instead, they are constantly being redefined with the arrival of more strangers and the formulation of new attitudes and cultures. In Peninsular Florida there is virtually no nineteenth century cultural residue to be expunged. The influx of settlers, many from the South, but a large portion from the non-South, has been continuously improvising a fresh cultural milieu. We still have no clear picture of the emergent regional culture and subcultures of an area with no *raison d'être* other than the presence of people. But there is little doubt that the people pursuing Florida's varied amenities and their own self-discovery are building something far different from the culture areas of Colonial America or pre-modern Europe.

At the micro level, there exists a diversified array of voluntary regions. Here we will briefly discuss only a few categories that are conspicuous and also adhere to conventional notions about spatial contiguity and concentration. Several possibilities are omitted because their existence is still too speculative and their unusual spatial attributes too difficult to specify with the limited data and techniques at our command. Let us proceed from the traditional to the relatively avant-garde.

Military Subregions There is nothing newsworthy about the existence of a professional military population with its own way of life and its spatial enclaves. There are analogous groups in other countries, some much less advanced than the United States. We can also assume a universal tendency for the military subpopulation to be self-selected for certain attitudes and personality traits. What is special in the United States is the size, solidity, territorial extent, population, and local impact of the larger military establishments. The military subculture suffuses and dominates sizeable metropolitan areas such as San Diego, Colorado Springs, Columbus, (Georgia), Norfolk, Annapolis, and Pensacola. Paramilitary research and development centers such as Los Alamos, Oak Ridge, Huntsville, and Cape Canaveral are variants of the general class. These places along with many others constitute one large, discontinuous region or network of places whose interchangeable components are in constant, intimate connection with each other.

Education Subregions Close connectivity among numerous widely scattered points is even more obvious in hundreds of colleges and universities with their faculties, students, and hangers-on. Economic factors are present, but are largely subsidiary to taste or personality. Again, there are analogies abroad and local examples in our own earlier history. But again also, the millions of students and faculty, their rapid growth since 1945, and the intense social and cultural development of college towns and college ghettos within larger cities is unprecedented. Not every college generates its own microregion: many are too small, too overpowered by the larger society, or are meeting places for commuting students and faculties. But many burgeoning institutions of higher learning have acquired and cling staunchly to their own idiosyncratic personalities. The similarities among these places and their inhabitants are far closer than their relations with local traditional regions or with other spatially discontinuous, national subcultures.

The Pleasuring Places   This luxuriant category includes all places occupied by people in quest of pleasure, surcease, or self-improvement. Assuredly, no other nation or epoch has spawned so great a variety of ephemeral and permanent amenity-oriented communities. The following subcategories do not begin to exhaust the possibilities, nor are they mutually exclusive; many localities fall into two or more classes.

In a few years, every physically attractive amphibious region will be thoroughly exploited. Even now there are few suitable, undeveloped, privately owned tracts remaining along the Atlantic, Pacific, or Great Lakes coasts, and the Gulf Coast is also rapidly filling up. The same is true of the glaciated lake country of the Northeast and of lakes and artificial reservoirs in other parts of the country. During a warm season that varies from two months in the far north to the entire year in the far south, millions of Americans gravitate to the waterside for swimming, fishing, boating, surfing, beach combing, sunbathing, cavorting in the sand, or just to stare at seascape and shore. Each community is generally elongate and only a few hundred yards in depth, and each tends to have its own social characteristics and peculiar subculture. The amphibious communities as a group have a personality all their own; and many, although only seasonally active, are so vigorous that they dominate their localities.

Many heliotropic (sun-seeking) regions are amphibious regions, but others, especially in the warm, cloudless Southwest, are high and dry. A large fraction of the retirement subregions, notably those in Florida, Arizona, and California, are either heliotropic or amphibious. But a considerable number of retirement regions are being developed, mainly for commercial gain, in other parts of the country as well. This spatial segregation of the aged (on a scale beyond the conventional old people's home) is a new phenomenon still neglected by geographer and sociologist.

Montane regions with adequate slopes and snow and within range of large metropolitan populations eager for skiing and other snow sports have undergone rapid development in recent years, especially in New England, New York, the Rocky Mountains, and the Sierras of California. Indeed, the elaboration of the ski subculture has been so intense in much of Vermont and nearby states that a genuine transformation of the region's culture seems to be in progress. The social and economic impact of the pleasure seekers here, as in other pleasuring places, has been quite profound.

One kind of amenity-oriented subregion that seems well rooted in European antecedents is the equine region. These are, or at least have been, markedly British in character. There are now numerous areas where breeding and rearing horses, riding, and hunting are a way of life. The most intensive regions are in southern megalopolis, especially in the Piedmont adjacent to Washington and Baltimore, the Kentucky Bluegrass, and in northern Florida. These areas appear on J. Fraser Hart's unpublished map of horse-breeding farms, one of the few cartographic clues to the location of special interest voluntary regions currently available.

The subcategory labeled Forbidden Fruitlands is not peculiar to North America. These are the areas where activities normally classed as illegal—gambling, prostitution, nudism, unrestricted liquor consumption, open homosexual behavior, and certain sports are local attractions. Without question, Reno, Las Vegas, the Lake Tahoe resorts, and other urban centers of Nevada are examples, as are the international twin cities along the United States-Mexican border, and the towns along several of our interstate lines. Again, disreputable activities may be combined with more legitimate ones in hunting, fishing, or seaside areas. The transient populations that frequent such areas and the service groups who cater to them create a unique cultural ambiance.

There are many temporary aggregations of persons of common taste or purpose that impose more than fleeting impacts upon places; the rallies of cyclists or hot-rodders, "wilderness" camping, rock festivals, summer music camps, revival meetings, and the like.

Two categories of voluntary regions are unquestionably North American in character and in current expression, if not in ultimate origin. "New Bohemias" are distinctive neighborhoods near the centers of larger cities that have attracted urban folk who relish diversity, unconventional behavior, and exotic stimuli. They are complex in ethnic, racial, class, and age structure, and it is easy to oversimplify this complexity by tarring them all with the "hippie" brush. With the possible exceptions of the prototypical Greenwich Village and North Beach neighborhoods, New Bohemias are products of the 1950s and 1960s, and are still emerging, sometimes spontaneously and sometimes by design. Examples are Chicago's Old Town, the Beacon Hill-Back Bay section of Boston, Atlanta's Peachtree Street, N.E., the Vieux Carré of New Orleans, Vancouver's Gastown, Rittenhouse Square in Philadelphia, Georgetown and Dupont Circle in Washington, and Cincinnati's Mount Adams. In places such as Berkeley, Seattle, Minneapolis, or Toronto, the university neighborhood coincides with the New Bohemia; in other cities the two sections lead separate existences.

During the past decade, many communal colonies have sprung up in all parts of the country. Examples abound in urban as well as rural settings and there is considerable range in their size, organization, purpose, and type of membership. Many take pains to avoid detection and they are not readily susceptible to synoptic analysis. Perhaps the only attributes they have in common are communality of property, some rejection of the values and rules of the larger society, and an adherence to the principles of simple living and decent poverty. Whether these communes are a continuation of the numerous short-lived utopian experiments that flourished during the past century or whether they have sprouted independently out of the inner core of American culture is not clear. It remains to be seen what, if anything, they herald of the future cultural landscape.

Emergent Clusters in Social, Psychological, and Other Spaces

Voluntary regions, however novel their content, are more or less traditional, that is, territorial, in structure. A more radically novel phenomenon is the emergence of other social groups whose existence is predicated on specific common interests or "sentiment structures." Cohesion is less a territorial clustering than agglomeration in other dimensions of experience—less a matter of elbow-rubbing than a meeting of minds. Observing such groups offers difficult problems, the first of which is amassing data that identify them.

With rare exceptions, the standard data sources used by geographers are of negligible utility in an enterprise of this sort. Vital statistics, occupational, educational, religious, ethnic, linguistic, class, political, and economic attributes are largely products of traditional causative factors. For the individual, they reflect the accidents of time and place of birth, social inheritance, and the operation of economic and political forces beyond his control. Some standard phenomena, such as religious affiliation, choice of college, and residential architecture are assortative of individual personality. But such choices are constrained by strong nonpersonal factors. One strategy would be intensive interviewing of a large, carefully selected sample of the population in question. Unfortunately, the technical expertise for such work is rare or nonexistent among geographers. Moreover, highly artificial testing situations might generate dubious results. Unobtrusive measures of personality traits or tendencies are much to be preferred. The productive uses of this approach to graphing psychological and cultural change through time (for example, Richardson and Kroeber's analysis of the physical dimensions of women's gowns over a two-century period, or McClelland's study of the fluctuations in the achievement factor as revealed by the contents of elementary school readers, literary texts, and ceramic ornamentation)[6] suggest the possibility of equally rich discoveries in the spatial realm.

The following data sources may meet the standard criteria.

Voluntary Associations   Many adult Americans belong to voluntary associations. In many instances, however, membership is obligatory in varying degree because of conditions of employment, profession, or parenthood. To narrow the field down to the *purely voluntary* associations, those to which loyalty and interest are spontaneously extended, without social or economic coercion or hope of material advantage, one must exclude trade unions, professional societies, commercial associations, criminal organizations, ethnic clubs, church-related societies, *local* athletic boosters, adolescent gangs, neighborhood organizations of all sorts, and probably fraternal lodges. I would also ignore associations with severe membership qualifications such as veterans clubs, alumni groups, Alcoholics Anonymous, country clubs, those including only descendants of specific groups (for example, the D.A.R.), those of specific national or regional provenance (for example, the Iowa clubs of California or the *vereins* of Central and Eastern European immigrants), and those which are all-inclusive or fuzzy in structure, such as the major political parties, the P.T.A., Red Cross, or automobile clubs.

Two major categories of truly voluntary associations that draw their clientele from a broad spectrum of society remain: those which are ideological in the widest sense of the term; and those devoted to pleasures and leisure-time interests unconnected with ancestry, nativity, occupation, family, or local obligations. In brief, the two categories are those devoted to "causes" and to amenities. The first set promotes all manner of specific issues—political, social, charitable, intellectual, and esthetic. The second group may overlap the first in specific instances. Its clientele are "amateurs" (in the strictest sense of the term) banded together to reinforce their enjoyment of such activities as sports, crafts, hobbies, non-professional science, the popular and fine arts, and the adulation of celebrities. Elements of self-improvement are present in most groups in either category. In any event, consider the rewards of analyzing through time and space the membership of the National Rifle Association, various temperance groups, cycle clubs, leading conservation and preservation societies, the James Dean cultists, the S.P.C.A., or genealogical enthusiasts, to take a few examples.

It can be assumed that the decision to join (or not to join) such organizations says something revealing about basic personality structure. This assumption should be tested, but two immediate reservations must be made. Potential members do not have complete and perfect knowledge of all organizations in which they might be interested, nor is access open to anyone upon application. No organization is totally free of racial, ethnic, class, economic, religious, or sexual bias. In working with such material, methods will have to be devised to control for such biases. A major directory of associations exists for the United States.[7] Many organizations selected for my ongoing study are willing to provide detailed information on the location and certain other characteristics of their members.

Patterns of Consumption for Selected Goods and Services   The analysis of consumption patterns is one of the most severely neglected phases of economic geography. But analyzing such patterns would offer important insights for social, cultural, and economic geography.[8] It is hypothesized that over and above the staple items or those for which demand is determined by income, class status, education, size-of-place, and other familiar variables, there are commodities and services for which appetites are generated to a significant degree by *qualitative* differences in personalities. Again, care must be taken to correct for economic, social, and cultural factors that structure market areas for such items. It may prove difficult to control the warping of demand induced by advertising or the spatial frictions intrinsic to distributional systems. Furthermore, some innovations may be caught mid-flight, in the process of diffusing from points of origin outward to their ultimate limits.

What are some possible items? Special interest magazines; specialized book clubs; fan mail; the wide variety of greeting cards (and perhaps buttons, posters, and bumper stickers, all of which serve as informal Rorschach Tests); specific types of phonograph records and tapes; jukebox plays; the various categories of antiques; wallpaper; certain elements of clothing, ornament, diet, drink, and stimulants (unrelated to ethnic or religious considerations); color preferences for various items (such as autos, household appliances, men's shirts, lipstick, hair dye); certain craft and hobby goods; athletic games; card, board, and other indoor games; and a wide variety of pets.

Taking just these last two categories, I am reasonably certain that meaningful differentiations among people in social and physical space are evident through their expressed preferences for pets, and that these preferences stem from basic elements of personality as well as social considerations. In a real sense, pets select people. Some of the foregoing notions are implicit in an unpublished pair of maps prepared by Professor J. Fraser Hart of the University of Minnesota. They depict the "horsey set" in the United States using the surrogate measure of number of breeding farms. Anyone who has done field work in two of the more highly elaborated equine tracts of the country—the northern counties of Virginia and the Bluegrass of Kentucky—realizes that the pace-setting elites of these areas are self-selected for something beyond wealth or high social standing. If data could be compiled concerning different types of horses—and thus different horse-people—some interesting patterns and associations in social space might emerge.

Similarly, tropical fish fanciers, various types of bird-lovers, and the immense universe of dog-owners can be disaggregated to our profit. Not only do dog-people differ as a group from horse-people, cat-people, and from non-dog-people in general, but there are decided distinctions among devotees of the various breeds. The overlap among Afghan, dachshund, and beagle people is quite limited. Fortunately, usable records on various breeds of canines and other pets may reach back over several decades. As with pet-owners, so too with practitioners of bowling, sailing, model trains, bingo, scrabble, hot-rodding, or bird-watching. There may be interesting, distinct clusters of devotees in physical and social space that reveal personality factors.

I am reasonably confident that large quantities of personality-sensitive consumption data can be collected. The more obvious sources are mailing list companies, radio and television networks, advertising and marketing research firms, opinion polling organizations, academic data banks (concerned primarily with political and social phenomena), grocery and department store chains, mail-order firms, magazine publishers, manufacturers, wholesalers, and trade associations. Most such data will be packaged in terms of areas of business establishments, with rather little directly related to the individual. Thus the familiar dilemma of "ecological inference"—of guessing individual behavior from the average attributes of a larger population—arises. Recently there has been a large volume of published and private research directed to individual consumer psychology and behavior, but none of it appears to have utilized a spatial perspective. Conversely, the numerous analyses of marketing areas have duly noted demographic and economic characteristics, but have not been attentive to personality traits.

This essay is a specimen of that most maddening literary genre, the piece that cannot be ended except with the words: "To be continued." Research has been initiated along the lines suggested above and the preliminary results are exciting. The strategy has been to exploit the most readily accessible data within the two major categories: membership in truly voluntary associations; and readership of special-interest magazines (drawn largely from Audit Bureau of Circulations, 1971 and Standard Rate and Data Service). Statistics have been collected at the state level for a total of some 163 groups and periodicals for the period 1970-71, and are being subjected to a variety of mathematical and cartographic manipulations. Despite the coarseness of the areal units employed, the first stages of this analysis support the suppositions ventured here regarding the emergent social geography of the United States. They have also produced some interesting surprises. Further comment must await the detailed report I hope to complete in the near future.

References

1. Conventions of members of (truly) voluntary associations, summer chamber music camps, outdoor sports rallies with national drawing power, rock festivals, and the like may all provide temporary spatial clusters of soulmates

of more than fugitive interest. Similarly, touristic attractions may segregate like-minded people spatially, if only fleetingly: the clienteles for Disneyland, Harpers Ferry, and Mount Rainier seem quite distinct.

2. Raymond B. Cattell, *The Scientific Analysis of Personality* (Baltimore: Penguin, 1965), p. 161.

3. Although there has been a good deal of work on cross-cultural differences in personality, there seems to have been almost none on the spatial distribution of personality traits within the territorial range of a single cultural group.

4. Cattell, *op. cit.*; and H. J. Eysenck, *Structure of Human Personality* (London: Methuen, 1960).

5. Wilbur R. Thompson, *A Preface to Urban Economics* (Baltimore: Johns Hopkins Press, 1965), pp. 198—199.

6. J. Richardson and A. L. Kroeber, "Three Centuries of Women's Dress Fashions: A Quantitative Analysis," *Anthropological Records* 5 (1947): 111—153; David C. McClelland, *The Achieving Society* (Princeton: Van Nostrand, 1961).

7. Frederick G. Raffner, Jr. *et al.*, eds, *Directory of Associations*, 3 vol. (Detroit: Gale, 1968).

8. The two best statistical sources (published by the U.S. Bureau of Labor Statistics in 1963-66 and the National Industrial Conference Board in 1967) are derived from the same 1960-61 sample survey. They offer areal coverage that is far from ideal, but still suggestive of interesting possibilities in the geographic analysis of the consumption of selected commodities. Thus the figures on per capita expenditures for such things as dungarees, motorcycles, pet food, comic books, and craft and hobby goods, as given for four Census Regions, display an areal pattern that cannot be accounted for in terms of income, ethnic factors, physical habitat, or any of the usual explanations. In a similar vein, Mr. Albert Bellini, a student of mine, has been analyzing the areal pattern of various types of liquor, wine, and beer consumption over the past three decades, for the nation as a whole, by states, and for the state of Pennsylvania by individual State Liquor Store area. Although ethnicity, purchasing power, and other familiar factors, along with the diffusion process, explain much of the variation, there is still an interesting unexplained set of residuals that may somehow be related to the "personality factor."

Chapter 10

Monoculture or Miniculture? The Impact of Communications Media on Culture in Space

Ronald Abler
The Pennsylvania State University

ABSTRACT: *We return to an earlier theme, the effects of different communications media. Whereas chapter 3 attempted to forecast the consequences of communications innovations in the realms of economic geography and its theory, this chapter is concerned with effects of traditional and new media on culture and culture regions. Mass media promote homogenization because messages flow from the few to the many, whereas interpersonal media promote differentiation. Mini-communications (low-cost media directed to small, specialized groups) will probably promote more and more subcultural diversity, but increased cultural diversity does not necessarily imply increased spatial diversity.*

Communications media are the most potent space-adjusting techniques that man commands, and their increasingly intensive use will

Reprinted with slight changes from *An Invitation to Geography*, ed. D. Lanegran-R. Palm (New York: McGraw-Hill, Inc., 1973), pp. 186-195, by permission of the publisher. Copyright © 1973 by McGraw-Hill Book Company.

inevitably affect human spatial behavior and the behavioral regions (culture and subculture realms) with which cultural geographers concern themselves. We normally assume that communications promote cultural and spatial homogenization. But careful examination of ongoing and probable future developments in communications suggests that media innovations may promote cultural diversity and spatial differentiation.

Spatial Interaction and Culture

The cultural character of any locality may be regarded as the constantly changing product of the interaction of two sets of forces: those tending to promote uniformity or homogeneity with respect to the larger region or the entire world, and those promoting diversity and heterogeneity, thus making the locality less like any other.[1]

Isolation from other groups in geographical space is the strongest force promoting cultural diversity. The absence of interaction with different peoples reinforces and preserves culture traits. The isolation of the Georgia and South Carolina Sea Islands, for example, has preserved the continuity of the Senegambian and Congo-Angolan culture of the blacks who were brought there as slaves almost three hundred years ago.[2] If a cultural or subcultural group can avoid contact with dissimilar peoples, it can remain distinct or become even more unique. Closed information pools produce cultural differences.

We would expect that a process of spatial interaction like communication would reduce differences among groups because it can destroy the isolation upon which cultural diversities depend. Indeed, the global communication patterns which developed with European expansion have reduced the amount of cultural diversity in the world. Languages, religions, and even peoples have disappeared with the direct and indirect effects of Western global control and the elimination of isolation by Western communication and transportation technology. A prominent political strategist speaks of the "global city."[3] A popular social commentator describes "The Demise of Geography," assuming that "place . . . is no longer a primary source of diversity."[4]

Yet despite tremendous increases in information flows, cultural differences among peoples and places are not dissolving as fast as we might expect. There are even indications that groups are becoming more unlike. We encounter new self-consciousness and militance among formerly docile groups, while new groups form along regional, ethnic, age, and other lines. Brzezinski writes of the global city, but is worried about global ghettos.[5] Toffler thinks we are experiencing nothing less than an explosion in the number of "subcults."[6]

Such contradictory evidence and continued evidence of differ-

entiation amid homogenization make it clear that the effects of communications technology on cultures and their spatial arrangements are more
complicated than we thought. To get some idea of what the spatial pattern
of cultures will be like in the future we must examine the effects of different
communications media more carefully than we have in the past.

Communications Media and Culture

Communications media can be cross-classified into mass and
interpersonal media, and into formal and informal categories of each (figure
10.1). Formal mass media usually require prepared channels and are
essentially one-way information delivery systems. Few people act as
senders in the mass media; most people can only receive what the few
transmit.

	MEDIA	
STRUCTURE	Mass	Interpersonal
Formal (Interposed channel)	Publishing, Press, Radio, Television, Stage, Cinema; University?	Postal, Telegraph, Telephone, Amateur Radio?
Informal (No formal or institutionalized channel)	Didn't exist until recently. Now mimeo, Xerox, "Underground," film, etc.	Conversation, Non-verbal communication.

Figure 10.1   Cross-classification of Communications Media.
Means of communication can be classified by two criteria: *media*, either mass or
interpersonal, and *structure*, either formal or informal. Therefore, telephones are
interpersonal and formal, while photocopy publication is mass and informal.

Until recently, there were no informal mass media. Now facsimile
technology permits everyone to be his own publisher, and the success of
the underground press, theater, and cinema in the last decade indicates that
democratization of those media is underway.

Interpersonal media allow two-way communications. The average
person can be a sender as well as a receiver of information. The informal
interpersonal media are the most ubiquitous of the lot, whereas the formal

interpersonal media are for the most part used only in economically advanced nations.

Mass media, especially formal mass media, promote homogenization. Messages flow from the few to the many, making receivers more like the senders. Interpersonal media promote differentiation. Messages can flow from many to many, and because people tend to address interpersonal messages to other people like themselves, interpersonal channels reinforce differences.

Contemporary mass media seem to make homogenization inevitable. Regional dialects disappear as "correct" speech patterns are learned from the mass media.[7] Exposure on national network programs makes slang phrases instantly ubiquitous, and national advertising promotes uniform tastes and patterns of consumption. Media coverage of events such as the Apollo moon landings can knit much of the world into a single audience:

> *Global circulation of cultural styles and artifacts, through new forms of communication and distribution, has engendered shared attitudes and experiences in their use. Interpenetrating and diffusing through locally diverse cultures, these common elements form part of a transnational (that is planetary) culture.*[8]

National and planetary cultures, however, may be transitory. It is becoming apparent that the mass media have peaked in importance. Innovations in communications technology indicate the development of sophisticated interpersonal media that Gumpert calls "mini-comm."[9] The costs of acquiring or using mass media channels are dropping rapidly at the same time that capacity is expanding and costs are dropping in the formal interpersonal media. As a result, smaller and smaller audiences with increasingly more specialized tastes can be reached with mini-media.

The evolution of mini-comm is most easily seen in printing, where individualization has been evident for decades. There now exist tens of thousands of specialized periodicals devoted to almost every conceivable interest and topic. In addition to local newspapers and regional editions of magazines, the "underground" press now includes some two hundred papers with an estimated six million readers and its own wire service. Even books are now custom-made. Publishers will produce a book if as few as one hundred sales are guaranteed, and the day of the complete do-it-yourself book in which each individual book's contents can be prescribed or chosen is not far distant.[10]

The broadcast media are also becoming more flexible. Whereas there were 32 black-oriented radio stations in the United States in 1956, there were 130 in 1970.[11] The American Broadcasting Company now offers advertisers four demographically distinct networks, claiming that "any resemblance to traditional radio networks is purely coincidental."[12] The capacity of such media to reach small groups has been constrained by technical limitations in broadcasting and by high equipment costs. Existing

and future innovations will greatly lower costs, bypass technical limitations, and thereby make *narrowcasting* possible.

Foremost among the innovations that will make small-group
narrowcasting viable is Community Antenna Television (CATV). CATV
originally served isolated places where television reception was impossible
without centralized antenna facilities. Soon, however, CATV began to
penetrate markets already served by one or more television stations, and the
innovation has been diffusing up the nation's urban hierarchy since 1949.
By the early seventies, CATV was entering the largest metropolitan areas.[13]

CATV provides between twenty and sixty (depending on the kind
of equipment used) television channels, as contrasted with the twelve
available on the UHF broadcast band. With CATV, the cost of providing
each channel drops enormously. Once the cable network is installed, the
cost of each additional channel is simply the cost of another television
camera. CATV thus permits programming flexibility which is impossible
in broadcast television.

> *Whereas a local broadcaster may not be able to justify programming aimed
> just at ballet enthusiasts, or the local Negro community, or aficionados of
> sports cars, a regional or even a national cable network might be developed
> which could enhance its appeal significantly through such specialized
> programming.*[14]

CATV systems are starting to narrowcast high school football and
basketball games, city council meetings, and numerous other events which
cannot be broadcast because they appeal only to small, often highly
localized groups.[15] Soon we can expect two-way transmission capability
and switching capacity to be available in local, regional, and even national
CATV networks, making it possible for anyone to be his own television
producer for an audience of any size, just as facsimile technology makes it
possible for anyone to be his own publisher.

The evolution of such specialized media is not wholly unprecedented. Foreign-language newspapers and ethnic radio programming were
once common-place elements of American mass communications. But the
ability to reach *very small* groups at low cost and, even more importantly,
the ability of *anyone* to act as a sender of information will be unprecedented. Such capabilities are eliminating meaningful distinctions between
mass and interpersonal media, and formal and informal channels.

People normally prefer to communicate with people like themselves. Interpersonal and informal mass media have helped differentiate
people into distinct groups by reinforcing their respective attitudes and
information sets. Because media innovations make the traditional mass
media more like interpersonal media, we can expect them to promote
cultural differentiation. Besides facilitating the intensification of age, lifestyle, income, ethnic, and other groupings, communications media also
make it increasingly difficult to achieve national political consensus by

promoting a politics of confrontation among such groups.[16]

The new media themselves, then, contain an important bias of communication which will probably promote greater cultural and subcultural diversity in the future. The democratization of communications is the revolutionary change which may make communications a differentiating rather than a homogenizing force. The effect of minicommunication and improved interpersonal communication will be to make society more individualized in its interests and tastes.[17]

Spatial Possibilities and Probabilities

How this increasing cultural diversity will be organized in space remains unclear. The same advances in communications that enhance diversity also eliminate the necessity for groups to agglomerate in space to maintain cohesion and distinct identity. Whether increased cultural diversity necessarily implies increased spatial diversity remains to be seen.

Without distinct territories cultures usually perish quickly. Even homeless groups like the Jews survived only in the pseudohomelands provided by the urban and rural ghettos they occupied between the Diaspora and 1949. The inability of cultural or subcultural groups to survive without a distinct territory leads us to equate the two. We think cultures have to have territories and that regions must have distinct cultures. Traditionally, spatial proximity has been the only settlement pattern that permitted the intense contact needed to preserve cultural distinctness.

McLuhan feels that the media have created a tribal world and that the United States will "break up into a series of regional and racial ministates."[18] Tribal existence is predicated on a land base.[19] Geographers and interpreters of current events have recently noted strident demands for "government by turf" in urban areas. Many North American cities are divided into distinct tribal turfs, more or less immune from control by central government.[20] Ethnic, racial, and other groups are now moving to provide social and educational services for themselves. At the same time, they demand greater control over those services provided by governments in their turfs. There is evidence, then, that increased cultural diversity implies greater spatial diversity.

Alternatively, many small groups now forming and reinforcing their respective differences are nonplace communities. "Swinging Singles" can plug into likeminded groups equally well in Miami, San Francisco, St. Paul, or Chicago. Similarly, the interests of a Harlem black militant and a Watts black militant in advancing the cause of black people everywhere may be more important than their residence in two different ghettos. Melvin Webber noted the possibility of community without propinquity by way of communications, and the resulting existence of two kinds of communities: one kind is firmly rooted in place and neighborhood, while nonplace communities are independent of location, neighborhood, region, or even nation.[21] Mobility and electronic communications create nonplace communities composed of affluent, well-educated, specialized people who can afford high costs of mobility and communications. Place-based communities are organized around informal interpersonal communications and are composed of less affluent, less educated residents of inner-city neighborhoods (figure 10.2).

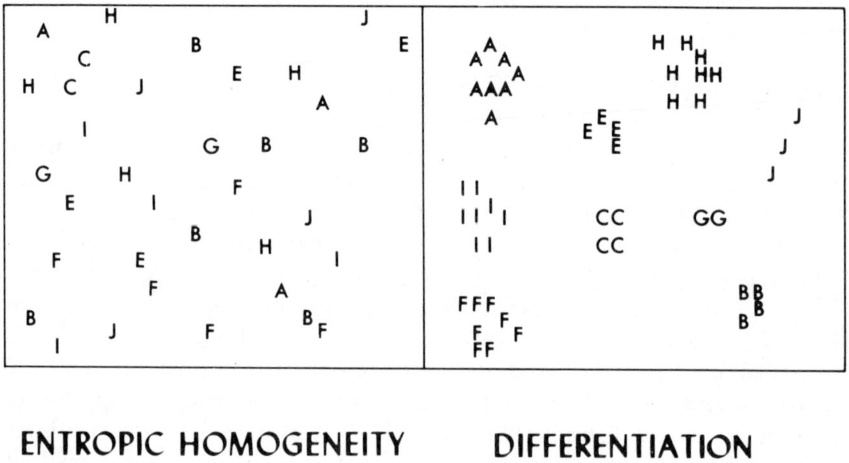

ENTROPIC HOMOGENEITY   DIFFERENTIATION

Figure 10.2   Future Spatio-cultural Alternatives.
Communications media can promote an entropic spatial homogeneity as easily as they can promote spatial differentiation. A, B, C, etc., represent members of different cultural or subcultural groups. Minicommunications media enable them to live in nonplace communities as easily as they could live in place-based communities.

The scrambling of traditional media categories and the development of nonplace communities combine to make the spatio-cultural future cloudy. We observe increased local and regional sensitivity at the same time that we note the development of supraterritorial groups whose shared interests and values override the locations of individual members.[22] Advanced communications technology can keep members of nonplace communities in close touch with each other regardless of location.

The "wired city" model of the future illustrates the spatial ambiguity inherent in advanced minicommunications. It will soon be possible for residents of a metropolis to receive and transmit all communications through a coaxial cable network. The increased ability to form nonplace communities of narrow interest will be counterbalanced by increased local and neighborhood programming. Reston, Virginia, for example, has already begun local programming over its CATV system.[23] Proposals have arisen to provide neighborhood and special-interest pro-

gramming by way of CATV in metropolitan areas.[24] Truly flexible media
can promote regional diversity just as easily as they can promote mixed
homogeneity.

Moreover, the two are not mutually exclusive. Minicommunications can simultaneously promote nonplace interest communities and place-based residential communities composed of people with
diverse interests. Individual geographers often develop both regional and
systematic specialities and seem to derive no schizophrenia therefrom;
there is no reason not to expect others to divide their attention between
narrrow topical specialities and local affairs. Indeed, a combination of
global, nonplace interests and local, place-based concerns would be the best
of all possible worlds.

Whether the spatio-cultural future is an entropic homogeneity, a
bewildering diversity of place-based groups, or a pleasing and judicious
combination of the two, minicommunications will be necessary conditions
of each alternative. But minicommunications are not in themselves sufficient conditions for any of the alternatives. The bias of minicommunications seems to make the non-place-based model more probable, but the ultimate effects of such media depend on the uses to which
societies *choose* to put them. If we choose to promote spatial diversity, we
can do so, and conversely, if we choose to promote non-place-based
interest groups, we shall no doubt see them develop even more rapidly than
they are now. To refuse to govern these technologies by making self-
conscious policy decisions about the spatio-cultural future we want is to
choose by default the continuation of current trends.

Some Caveats, Spatial and Other

Communications media are powerful and thus potentially dangerous tools. One of the hazards inherent in minicommunications media is
the complete disappearance of a broader cultural and political consensus.

> *There is a growing ease of creating groups having access to distinctly
> differing models of reality*, without overlap. . . . *Imagine a world in which
> there is a sufficient number of TV channels to keep each group, and in
> particular the less literate and tolerant members of the groups, wholly
> occupied. Will members of such groups ever again be able to talk
> meaningfully to one another? Will they ever obtain at least some
> information through the same filters so that their images of reality will
> overlap to some degree?*[25]

Small groups or even individuals could withdraw from all human
contact except that which can be achieved through electronic media.
Bradbury's *Fahrenheit 451* is a chilling fictional description of such a
society.[26] It would be particularly ironic if *communications* media become

the technology that creates a haunting, hollow isolation of tiny groups of individuals.

It should also be obvious that increased cultural diversity, whether place-based or not, carries with it an enormous potential for conflict. Human beings will apparently discriminate against one another over almost any perceived difference, no matter how artificial.[27] People are currently killing one another over race, language, religion, politics, economics, and often, it seems, out of sheer human cussedness. Increased differentiation will enrich the world immensely, but it will also create new distinctions that a species with our casual attitude toward fratricide might seize upon to make life miserable for every disparate group.

There exists a regrettable tendency to view communications as panacea. If only conflicting groups will communicate with each other, many say, they will surely resolve their differences. Such a view is naïve at best, and is more likely absolutely disastrous. We must confront the largely unexplored, but very real possibility that information flows among groups promote as much hatred as understanding. Communications are powerful social, political, and cultural forces, and it is wishful to think that they will not cause great local, regional, national, and international tensions.

Thus, others might profit from the experience of American cities. According to the Kerner Commission, "the communications media, ironically, have failed to communicate," leading to fractionalization of the urban polity and to civil strife.[28] And to the extent that the metropolis itself is a specialized communications medium,[29] it too has failed to generate the information flows necessary to create viable metropolitan communities. The failures of the media and the American metropolis have serious global implications. Metropolitan communications systems are good spatial analogs of national and international conditions some decades later. If the American metropolis is a good spatial model of the future, we face serious problems. We can expect Brzezinski's global city to be composed of many antagonistic global ghettos created by minicommunications.

References

1. Wilbur Zelinsky, "Notes on Some of the Spatial Characteristics of Cultural Systems," mimeographed (University Park, Pennsylvania: The Pennsylvania State University, 1970).

2. John F. Szwed, "Africa Lies Just Off Georgia," *Africa Report*, 15 (October, 1970): 29—31.

3. Zbigniew Brzezinski, *Between Two Ages: America's Role in the Technetronic Era*, (New York: Viking, 1970), p. 19.

4. Alvin Toffler, *Future Shock*, (New York: Random House, 1970), p. 84.

5. Brzezinski, *op. cit.*, p. 35.

6. Toffler, *op. cit.*, p. 252.

7. "Talking Like a Native," *Newsweek*, March 9, 1970.

8. John McHale, *The Future of the Future* (New York: Braziller, 1969), p. 270.

9. Gary Gumpert, "The Rise of Mini-Comm," *Journal of Communications* 20 (1970): 280—290.

10. Billy Rojas, "The Textbook of the Future," *School and Society* 99 (1971): 315-317.

11. *Broadcasting Yearbook/Markets, 1956 and 1965: Spot Radio Rates and Data*, October 1, 1970.

12. *Newsweek*, March 29, 1971, p. 91

13. E. Stratford Smith, "The Emergence of CATV: A Look at the Evolution of a Revolution," *Proceedings of the I.E.E.E.* 58 (1970): 967—982.

14. Nicholas Johnson, *How to Talk Back to Your Television Set*, (New York: Bantam, 1970), p. 144.

15. *Ibid.*, p. 145.

16. Herbert E. Alexander, "Communications and Politics: The Media and the Message," *Law and Contemporary Problems* 34 (1969): 176—277.

17. Ithiel de Sola Pool, "Social Trends," *Science and Technology* 76: (1968) 87—101.

18. Gumpert, *op. cit.*, pp. 284—285.

19. Vine Deloria, Jr., *Custer Died for Your Sins: An Indian Manifesto* (New York: Avon, 1969), p. 230.

20. James E. Vance, Jr., "Land Assignment in the Precapitalist, Capitalist and Post Capitalist City," *Economic Geography* 42 (1971): 119; Stewart Alsop, "It Would Not Be Fun," *Newsweek*, May 17, 1971, p. 116.

21. Melvin M. Webber and Carolyn C. Webber, "Culture, Territoriality and the Elastic Mile," in *Taming Megalopolis*, ed. H. Wentworth Eldredge (New York: Doubleday, 1967), pp. 35—53.

22. Eugene Jennings, "Mobicentric Man," *Psychology Today* 4 (1970): 34—36.

23. Thomas Grubisich, "Reston to Begin Cable TV," *Washington Post*, June 18, 1970.

24. "O.E.O. Rejects Cable TV Pleas for Kansas City, Mo.," *Telephony*, June 6, 1970, p. 59.

25. Paul Baran, "On the Impact of the New Communications Media upon Social Values," *Law and Contemporary Problems* 34 (1969): 249.

26. Ray Bradbury, *Fahrenheit 451 (New York: Ballantine, 1953)*.

27. Henri Tajfel, "Experiments in Intergroup Discrimination," *Scientific American* (November 1970), pp. 96—102.

28. *Report of the National Advisory Commission on Civil Disorder* (New York: Bantam, 1968), p. 383.

29. Richard L. Meier, *A Communications Theory of Urban Growth* (Cambridge, Mass.: M.I.T. Press, 1962).

Chapter   11

Fat City and Hedonopolis: The American Urban Future?

John W. Sommer
Dartmouth College

ABSTRACT: *Among the possible futures of urban America, hedonism (ego-satisfaction) is the most likely. The search for recreational space is becoming a major aspect of human relations and urban and exurban land use as a greater proportion of personal discretionary time is devoted to recreation. Two emerging urban types can be discerned: Hedonopoli are places where there is heavy investment in elaborate and complex leisure-pleasure personal services. Hedonopoli are formed by the coalescence of "fat cities," whose changing land use reflects the shift from production to ego-satisfaction. Mobile parisitopoli are impermanent urban centers exploiting local source materials (such as fishing fleets and towns based upon petroleum, mining, forestry, or military activities). New England is viewed as an area that is becoming a mass commercial playground.*

By looking at the future one can better understand the present, and it is in the present that one will find the seeds of the future. Prediction of the future must be based on analysis of the present. But although we have developed techniques for predicting general trends in human behavior, we remain unable to predict individual behavior or to predict futures at the personal scale. This suggests that we should "think big" and predict at the macro scale. The problem of prediction is rivalled by the problem of language; words and phrases that met past needs may not be appropriate for current concepts.[1] Yet one must not be dissuaded from attempting futuristics, nor from participating in the development of languages capable of expressing forward-looking notions.

As if problems of prediction and language were not enough, futuristic writers must achieve credibility without putting their readers in straitjackets of platitudes and clichés. Stated differently, it is far more important to admit the limits of our "predict-abilities" than to convert readers to a point of view. The essay that follows amply demonstrates that the future is something one may only *surmise* from observation of and reflection on the present.

If (a) predictions at a scale small enough to be personal are not possible; (b) we cannot understand the predictions anyway, because our vocabulary is not up to the task; (c) what follows is really only a consideration of the present; and (d) the research for this essay leans only lightly on scholarly works and heavily on newspapers, might we not forego this exercise in prediction? I think not, for despite such limitations, the future is implicit and discernable in current events as much as it is discernable in scholarly tomes.

Among the possible futures of urban America, hedonism is most likely. Our urban centers are becoming centers of ego-satisfaction, reflecting the intensification of our service-oriented economy. Our society is trimming labor to the point that the search for recreation, rather than for work, is fast becoming the central task of our lives. This search is also becoming the major articulator of human relations and of urban land use.

Our economy demonstrates several tendencies that favor a hedonistic future. First among these is technological change, which allows more and more persons to achieve greater output in fewer working hours than ever before. The result is massive amounts of discretionary time. Second, increasingly refined transportation and communications technologies permit more flexible temporal and spatial utilization of the earth's source materials, which also results in more efficient economic activies. Third, the shift away from flows of materiel toward flows of electronic messages induces a loosening of the actual spatial structure of our cities and spatial reorganization.

Social conditions in America also demonstrate tendencies toward hedonism. First, most Americans with greater discretionary time have utilized it for additional labor (at a second job or in household improvements) or in recreation activities. I contend that an increasing proportion of discretionary time is being devoted to recreation (broadly defined) and that our economic and social structures are adjusting to this value change. Second, there is a growing psychic encapsulation of the individual who focuses on the ego to the detriment of interpersonal or group relations. Instead of an efflorescence of interpersonal relationships, there is a tendency to escape into fantasy worlds of spectatorism, especially through television. Whether this encapsulation is an effect or a cause of increased aggressiveness on the part of urban residents is unclear, but they are surely correlated.[2]

As a geographer, one ponders these tendencies and their spatial implications. As a social scientist, one surveys the situation and sets it in apposition to more general but related systems. As a citizen, one clucks with concern. In the Background section of this essay, urbanization is reviewed as an element of the more general categories of population and settlement. The Foundation section of this chapter defines and describes hedonopolis, fat cities, and mobile parasitopoli. Observations supporting the existence of each of these urban forms are discussed, comments on the spatial implications and their more general societal ramifications are also presented. The Foreground section integrates the three urban types and forecasts the development of hedonopolis in the northeastern United States and in southeastern Canada. There are also comments on possible human responses to hedonopolis.

Background

Human settlement has changed more in the last century and a half than in the previous one and one-half millennia, and equally great changes will occur before the end of this century. World population continues to increase, migration from rural to urban places is unabated, and capital continues to concentrate in cities.

In thirty years the United States could have a population of 300 million that is 90 percent urban. The 270 million U.S. urbanites will be part of an urban population of 3 billion throughout the world. This urban population will include about 45 percent of all humanity (figure 11.1). What a remarkable change from the early days of the industrial revolution, when less than 3 percent of the world's population lived in cities of twenty thousand or more.

Several experts predict a world population within the next one hundred years of 10 or more billion, almost all of whom will be urban. Constantinos Doxiadis and his associates predict a world populated by 12 to 20 billion people who will live in a macro-city Doxiadis calls Ecumenopolis, the city that will span the habitable world by 2100. The extent of Ecumenopolis will be determined by resource availability. According to Doxiadis, Ecumenopolis is as inevitable as it is natural. Rather than wasting effort on forestalling Ecumenopolis, we should instead plan how to make the most of it.[3]

George Macinko rejects Ecumenopolis on principle as well as on faith that world population increase will be slowed.[4] He asserts that man has the ability (and should have the inclination) to avoid Ecumenopolis. One can concur with Macinko that a world so populous should be avoided. At the same time, one can also agree with Doxiadis that planning should take into account the possibility of large population increases. There will be a much larger population in the near future and we should be cognizant of

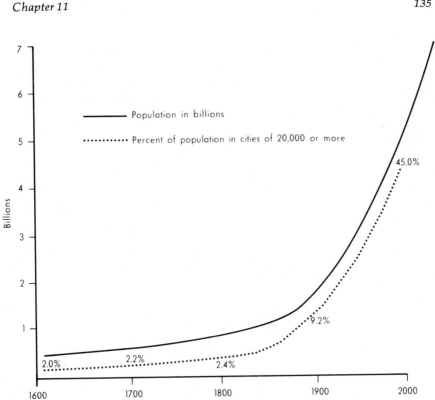

Figure 11.1   Population Increase and City Growth, 1600—2000.
(Sources: D. J. Bogue, *Principles of Democracy*, New York: John Wiley & Sons, 1969, p. 50; K. Davis, "The Origin and Growth of Urbanization in the World," *American Journal of Sociology* 60 (1955): 429—437.

the possibilities and problems it raises.[5]

In the United States rural to urban migration remains an important trend in spite of metropolitan civil disturbances in the past decade, and in spite of popular awareness of the unhealthiness of city air. But there has also been an increasing abandonment of the city core despite massive public expenditures on housing, transportation, and other central city projects. The U.S. Census counts people by their place of residence, and whereas half of the twenty-five largest central cities declined in population, the twenty-five largest metropolitan *areas* increased. Our technical ability to create massive physical mobility has, more than anything else, shaken the city at its base. Further extension of this technical ingenuity in moving people and information will continue to influence human relations and urban land use patterns.

Despite dispersal of residential units and manufacturing plants, there has been no permanent emigration of capital from the center to the periphery. Capital, population, and jobs continue to accumulate in metropolitan areas.

Puritan notions of building character through hard labor have been put aside in the late twentieth century America. Why? Possibly because no one really "enjoyed" sustained hard labor anyway. But more likely because hard, regular tasks are increasingly accomplished by machines. Another possibility is that there is a deep-seated requirement for repose to relieve the increasing stress of modern life. Whatever the cause, people now spend more time trying to satisfy themselves rather than a Supreme Being. Hedonism has displaced Puritanism in modern America, even if some of the discretionary time use has a strained quality.[6] Hedonism is reflected too in employment categories. In effect, we have shifted during the past quarter-century from an industrial society to a service society. No one has argued this change more persuasively than Victor Fuchs, who points out that:

> *The Service sector, also known as the "tertiary" or "residual" sector, has long been the stepchild of economic research. This was unfortunate but tolerable during the 19th and early 20th centuries when the shift from agriculture to industry was in full swing and services were of lesser importance. Since the end of World War II, however, the Service sector has become the largest, and, in many respects, the most dynamic element in the U.S. economy. Furthermore, most of the industrialized nations of the world appear to be following, with some lag, the pattern set by the United States.[7]*

Canada, England, Sweden, and Belgium have become predominantly service oriented. As we would expect, a spatial shift in employment follows such changes in the economy; there is a growing concentration of service functions in the urban centers of these countries.[8]

The above observations on population, technology, and discretionary time disposition are contemporary. What of the future? The evidence at hand can be extrapolated to future conditions.

Population growth rates are unlikely to be checked in this country before the end of this century.[9] Given the numbers of "post-war baby boom" women now at childbearing age, massive acceptance of planned parenthood programs in the United States is necessary even to keep the growth rate down to the level that has prevailed over the past decade. Rates of urbanization must slow because American society is already highly urbanized, but it seems certain that most remaining nonurban Americans will be pulled into the ambits of cities and towns in the next thirty years.[10]

Books on technological forecasting are becoming common, and most of them emphasize developments in transportation and communications—the space-adjusting techniques.[11] Society must ride the crest of communication changes or drown in a sea of information too deep to fathom. Man must transcend information flows through cultural adaptations, and surely these adaptations will have spatial implications. For example, it is conceivable that the "space shrinkage" produced by television is related to aggressive behavior of animals under compressed areal circumstances. Undeniably, it is a long jump from Calhoun's rat experiments and the Sika deer observations of Christian to conclusions about man, but to ignore the warnings implicit in their work would be foolish.[12] Almost everyone has experienced increased adrenal activity at the sight (on television) of urban riots, burning, looting, the events of war, and so on. Television "transports" viewers to a nether world of artificial participation.

Our task is to examine spatial implications of these shifts in population, technology, and human behavior, and to derive useful generalizations for those concerned with the city of the future.

Foundation

Hedonopolis, fat cities, and mobile parasitopoli are conceptions of future urban forms. Three general assumptions underlie these concepts, as well as one or more particular assumptions, all of which must be made explicit. The first general assumption is that mankind will survive. The second is that man will remain a social animal. The third general assumption is that, in the long run, a market economy will persist because such a system optimizes the use of scarce materials, time, and space through the unparalleled flexibility of the market mechanism. I must agree with August Lösch that:

> For me one of the happiest results of my study is to be able to show for the spatial organization of the economy that the free initiative of normal men produces results that in general are wholly desirable, politically as well as economically, provided only that man can build on rational conditions. Because the powerful forces of spontaneity, if rightly guided, are an ally to national economic policy, this [national economic policy] is saved the superhuman task of planning everything down to the very last detail. The mighty elements of spatial discipline tend toward preserving geographical and cultural roots in spite of freedom.[13]

Recently, notions of "satisficing" rather than "optimizing," economic behavior have become fashionable. But the satisficing process should be included within the optimization process, contrary to the suggestions of Wolpert, Morrill, and Hurst and McDaniel.[14] When an individual opts for leisure instead of production, he weighs the utility of leisure against the creation of new goods or services. He opts for recreative activity which, in his evaluation, is necessary to him. Optimization entails satisfaction.

The market mechanism is not a perfect allocator of investment (broadly interpreted). Among other disabilities, there are discontinuities in information that are pertinent to hedonopolis, which is a consequence of our greater desire for leisure-pleasure. Our society is groping because it has not developed an adequate body of information about leisure-pleasure, and, therefore, it has been unable to derive predictable pricing mechanisms to regulate our pursuit of whimsy. Like prospectors in an earlier gold rush, individuals have invested wildly (not necessarily wrongly) in leisure-pleasure projects without wisdom to guide them, and with unknown prospects of return to their investment. New leisure-pleasures are developed monthly—sports, resorts, theaters, drugs, pornography—as a glance at the *Sunday New York Times* will reveal.

Hedonopolis is an urban society in the process of becoming, a society in which there is high investment in elaborate and complex personal services. It is a society in which the marginal utility of investment in goods production is dropping rapidly, while the marginal utility of investment in services is rising as new service functions are articulated.

American society provides the fullest expression of hedonopolitanism, although there are regional differences within America. In general, hedonopolitanism is most evident in the megalopolitan areas of the northeastern United States and southeastern Canada, southern California, London-Liverpool, and Paris-Bonn, but there are many other points where it may be found.

Hedonopolis, in its original form, has found its fullest expression in and around the Northeastern seaboard megalopolis defined by Jean Gottman.[15] There is an enormous concentration of wealth in the great cities of hedonopolis. Hedonopolis is composed of the coalescence of "fat cities,"[16] which, as the term is employed here, are urban centers where land uses reflect society's new-found hedonism and its technical efficiency. A simple land use map of fat city describes it better than many words, and a functional map superimposed on the land use map further enhances one's conception of fat city's structure (figure 11.2). The general land use zones are a core, a ring of residences, and an interurban zone.

Core   How do these structural and functional areas develop? Let us first examine the core. For some years the utility of our city cores has been declining for spatially extensive functions such as manufacturing. This decline has been both absolute and relative. As new, more efficient production methods have required space-extensive horizontal assembly, it has become necessary to move where land is available. Center city is being abandoned by industry. Such moves have been facilitated by improved transport systems, first public then private, which opened up new realms of spatial choice. The automobile was especially important because it allowed for relatively unchanneled movement. Not only did industry move away from the high-rent core, but so did many upper- and middle-income city residents. Office buildings and high-rise residential units bid higher for urban land. Major chunks of land were set aside for transportation facilities, often at public expense.

Other factors promoting dispersal were changes in taste for dwelling units, style or architecture, lot size, method of shopping, and the

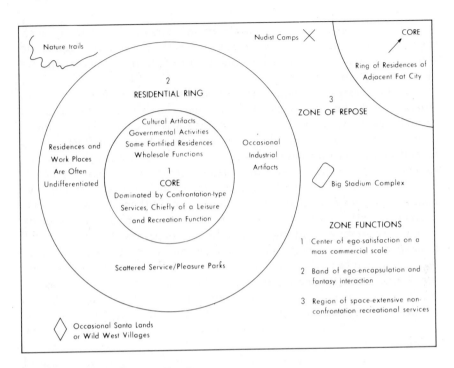

Figure 11.2   Land Use in Fat City.

decay of the central city itself as its tax base dwindled because of out-migration. Americans have chosen to live in single-family dwelling units to escape crowded apartments, and the lots that surround many homes are extensive in their own right (made so in many cases by zoning laws). Suburban shopping centers also contribute to more extensive use of space by providing vast customer parking lots and building horizontal sales space. Unruly low income groups and declining city services have set the city core elements in strange juxtaposition—the stark poverty and violence of the city center's remaining inhabitants contrasts grotesquely with the brightly-lit shops, theaters, and bars that service leisure-pleasure seekers.

This juxtaposition is even more dramatic when one sees the few isolated, plush, "walled cities" of the highly paid workers in the leisure-pleasure industries; apartment buildings with armed guards and elaborate security systems are often surrounded by the ghetto's armed, angry poor.

Existing land use patterns are bound to be ruptured again by our improved technological capability for moving messages and information. As was true of the manufacturing industries that preceded them, many of the service industries in the urban centers will probably migrate outward because of improved mobility and changes in managerial techniques.

Office functions are now performed by massive rows of clerks. Many of these jobs require minimal human interaction. For example, typing bills of lading, writing insurance policies, or computer programming do not require extraordinary contact among personnel. Yet many such functions are conducted on high-rent sites where other kinds of economic activities, those requiring "confrontation-type" human interaction, are bidding to take their places.[17]

Businesses increasingly rely upon telephone messages rather than letters to get their work done. Now that closed-circuit television is commonplace, remote terminal teletype linkages to computers are abundant, and two-way video-telephones are being used experimentally in several cities, existing land use structures may once again be radically shaken. They *must* be shaken if optimization continues to be society's goal.

It will be less costly to business (and to society as a whole) to have many employees remain at their residences rather than journey to work. Secretaries with teletype terminals can work in their homes and thereby save transportation, clothing, and child care expenses. Many men who have spent much of their lives with strangers on commuter trains may soon rediscover their families during the time saved, and increase their recreation possibilities with the money they save. Only those firms that engage in confrontation activities, such as major finance or law firms (where a handshake may be difficult to replace), or those engaged in personal services, especially leisure-pleasure services, will be able to bear central location rents.

Because the core is a central point for the surrounding band of dense population, land use there will be devoted to the most essential societal needs, and non-essential land uses will be excluded. It is highly possible that the city center will be dominated by confrontation leisure-pleasure functions such as theaters, souvenir shops, fancy restaurants, brothels, and so on. For the most part, the core will be a center of ego-satisfaction where individuals can commingle at minimum cost.[18] Commingling is an expression of the deep-rooted gregariousness of the human animal, but it should not be misinterpreted to mean "brotherly love." Nor should the reference to "minimum cost" deceive anyone; this is a relative expression which means that the cost of what is found at the center could not be found so cheaply elsewhere.

Some residual functions may persist in the core. Distribution centers will remain near the core because general distributors require a point central to the mass of population. Goods shopping via television with home delivery service will dictate least-cost transport locations. Such patterns will be reinforced in coastal cities where carriers offload goods at urban focal points for distribution to the residential rings. Ships themselves might become storage places from whence goods are distributed to television shoppers. Fortified dwelling units for the employees of the service industries will dot the core, and the rents for these dwellings will be high.

Public land uses will also occupy the core. The public sector is a major feature of our service-dominated society. It is clear that many government functions will require confrontation. Most legal services require the physical propinquity of the interacting parties, whether for judging other men's actions or for disbursing society's largesse. Courts and museums, albeit superior courts and superior museums, are also likely to be at the core, where they are equally accessible to all members of urban society.

Residential Ring   The residential ring of dense population lies outside the core. Here are the homes and offices of the main body of nonconfrontation service workers, chiefly the clerks and those in middle-management. Upper-management personnel escape the core and the residential ring for the less populated areas beyond, substituting communications and transportation for propinquity.

The industrial parks of today may be replaced by "service parks" which might approximate the "company towns" of the past. Forerunners are the low-rise apartment complexes that are springing up along circumferential highways around North American cities. Such complexes contain highly integrated social and service networks. Individuals who work for the same company often cluster and transact much of their business in the informal confines of their residences over cocktails or a motorized barbecue. Such social and residential units are in symbiosis with regional shopping centers, which are crude forerunners of service parks.

Social relations in the suburban ring are guarded and superficial, making it a zone of ego-deprivation. As more and more business is carried out in the home, and as a great amount of recreation (especially television) is also experienced there, the threat of psychic encapsulation becomes more serious. Spectators often become immersed entirely in their fantasy worlds, waking up only long enough to shut off the late evening news before their "world" is destroyed.[19] Not only are middle- and upper-income people deserting the hazards of center-city living for expeditions to the pleasuring places, they are also deserting the center city psychologically by turning off unpleasant stimuli instead of confronting them.

How will psychic encapsulation and the real physical threats in the core affect progress toward a recreation-based city center? Probably not severely, but this depends upon how severe the threats produced by the urban poor and by criminal elements become. The threat of personal violence has reduced night traffic in American cities to point-to-point movements in the protective confines of automobiles, and has increased urban energy expenditures on elaborate lighting systems. Yet residents of the exurban ring continue to flow to the city in numbers great enough to promote shifts in land use.

Interurban Zones of Repose   Beyond the fringe of the residential ring remain areas of open land such as the Poconos, Adironacks, Appalachia, and northern New England. Such places are vacation areas where residents of fat city seek the unhurried benefits of country life, fresh air, and a different ambiance. They escape the demands of their work and the exhausting demands of their intensive play at the core. The bucolic traditions of America's rural heritage beckon with their symbols of benign leisure. But what futurescape can one find in these regions?

The interurban fringes of our major cities are rapidly being altered to meet the needs of those who seek repose. Fringe land is nibbled away and converted to recreational space for growing hordes of people seeking second, amenity residences. A region now experiencing the outward push of the residential ring is the southern part of northern New England from Ogunquit, Maine, to Bennington, Vermont. Farmlands near major highways are being transformed into housing developments, and highway intersections are becoming service nodes. Vacation homes and resorts dot the landscape, along with boarding schools and lodging for temporary residents. For the most part, industrial sites are absent; the industrial buildings of a previous era are being converted into museums, as sentiment grows to save them from the rubble heaps.

Mobile Parasitopoli   But where are the industrial sites that support fat city? If they have vacated the core, been pushed from the residential ring, and are largely absent from the interurban fringe, where are they? Some linger in each of these land use zones because of inertia, sentiment, and other factors. But most highly generative industrial activities are increasingly found in "mobile parasitopoli." Mobile parasitopoli are impermanent urban centers that exist by exploiting the earth's source materials. Such centers switch to manufacturing as exploitation circuits become established, but mobile parasitopoli may be found anywhere economic source materials are located. The wide-ranging Japanese fishing fleets which conduct highly sophisticated hunts for flesh to feed us are examples. The process has been systematized to the point that one speaks of fish "harvests." Furthermore, these mobile cities of thousands of fishermen have also become modern processing centers with the advent of the "factory" ship and the canning ship. At a slower rate ephemeral "petroleum towns" march over the landscape from one new oil pool to another. More slowly are the mining towns abandoned, with only ghosts of the former structures left behind. The impact of expanding regional and global communications systems has been to facilitate the convertibility of source materials into usable resources, thus accelerating the use of resources, making them scarce and necessitating more frequent moves in search of new source materials.

Foreground

The preceding assessment of the arrangement of urban land uses under hedonopolitan conditions is, in reality, an interpretation of current indicators. These indicators suggest such a powerful thrust that we may be coaxed into believing the future they entail is inevitable. Some will glory that this new day of hedonistic expression, with all of its delicious challenges, is approaching; others will demur. The Foreground section of this chapter treads two paths, one toward acceptance of hedonopolis, the other toward its rejection.

The Achievement of Hedonopolis   There is much to commend the quest for leisure; constructive repose relieves frustration and allows modern man to return to the crucible of stressful optimizing refreshed and renewed. Leisure is not necessarily sybaritic nor is it a random nature walk. Leisure is the attainment of physical or psychic relief from the pressures of daily routine. Some of these "pressures" arise from the dull repetitiveness of a job or a visual landscape. From evidence at hand it appears that this tension between pressure and repose is encouraged by a corporate economy: higher pressure for executives at the top, more of the same routine for clerks at the bottom, and more time for leisure for everyone. Let us consider a specific regional example of hedonopolis.

Northeastern North America   New York City is the vortex of world economic activity. It is also the core of megalopolis and the seat of hedonopolis. Although it is flanked by other vital center such as Boston, Philadelphia, and Washington, it stands alone as the world's foremost purveyor of personal services and pleasure. There is no need to review the array of ego-satisfiers available in New York because most items on the list, such as the Broadway theater district, are well known, and anything else may be invented from the raw ingredients of the city. Other cities are dim in light of New York's variety; that which is "banned in Boston" is a sensation in Gotham. Yet, New York's satellites are fat cities in their own rights; Boston is a center for educational services, Washington for government, and Philadelphia for diverse services. Each of these cities (and others in the Northeast) are service centers with leisure-pleasure cores. Each separately, and all together, exert pressure on surrounding open areas.

The advancing residential edge of the city is familiar to anyone who has toured a metropolitan area. So too are the retirement communities that dot the residential rings around our cities. Beyond these, in the interurban zones, one finds vacation homes and second homes, places where the affluent "get away from it all."

The thrust of the interstate highway system into areas that were previously untrafficked has wrought rapid transitions in land ownership, land values, and land uses. The youth who spent summers at camp in the interurban zone a generation ago is back to purchase a vacation home. Increasingly, however, such purchases are made from large urban-based realty firms rather than from local farmers because realty firms anticipated the demand for private open space. The process is obvious in the South, in the Piedmont to the west of megalopolis, and in northern New England.

This process is particularly acute in northern New England because of the large potential returns to investment in recreational land.

Nowhere on the fringe of megalopolis is the pressure so great. The coast of Maine has long since been purchased by urbanites or by refugees from the cities. Virtually all the north-facing slopes of hills with lengths of more than 4,000 feet and inclines of more than 25 percent have been purchased for ski area speculation. Lakefront property is available only to those with high incomes. Land values at intersections of major roads have skyrocketed and brought in the service plazas that are ubiquitous on the American landscape.

Accessibility has been the forerunner of change throughout New England. Cracker-barrel country stores crumble under competition from corporate chains. Burglary and property damage increase dramatically as urban criminals have access to less suspecting and less protected people. Town meeting government is proving too slow to meet the stepped-up pace of administration and is being replaced by other forms. Local customs and dialects fade as outsiders mix with locals.

Why is northern New England so affected by such trends? A highly generalized map of population density and transportation linkages reveals the answer (figure 11.3). Population increases have been great in megalopolis, particularly in the southern counties of New Hampshire. Growth has also been rapid in the corridor formed by the Hudson River, and the lowlands of Lake Champlain. There is a further extension of population increase in the valley of the St. Lawrence River. The obvious effect of such growth is to surround northern New England (except for northeastern Maine) with a dense band of population. Quebec, Sherbrooke, Montreal, Burlington, Albany, Springfield, Hartford, Worcester, Nashua, Boston, and Portland, each having dense residential rings filled with hedonopolitanites seeking the better life, press inward on northern New England.

Such populations establish potentials for interaction, and interaction demands accessibility. Interstate highways will become increasingly well travelled as contact systems are elaborated. The stark answer to questions about the causes of northern New England's present propensity for rapid change is that it soon will be the least distant location between the encircling fat cities. It will become an "inner urban fringe" subject to economic locational forces similar to those operating in the core of fat city. Land use transition is to be expected, and lifestyles are sure to change.

It is no wonder that the scenic roadsides of New Hampshire and Vermont, formerly part of the interurban region of repose, are becoming sanctuaries for commercialized leisure-pleasure functions heretofore more characteristic of cities. Roadside zoos, fantasy villages featuring anything from Santa and his helpers to Cinderella or the Wild West, and drive-in movies showing X-rated films, compete with quickee golf courses and an array of other exports from fat city.

New England, traditionally a recreation area for a few, is being transformed into a mass commercial playground. The same process is evident on other fringes of megalopolis, but nowhere is it as intense as in

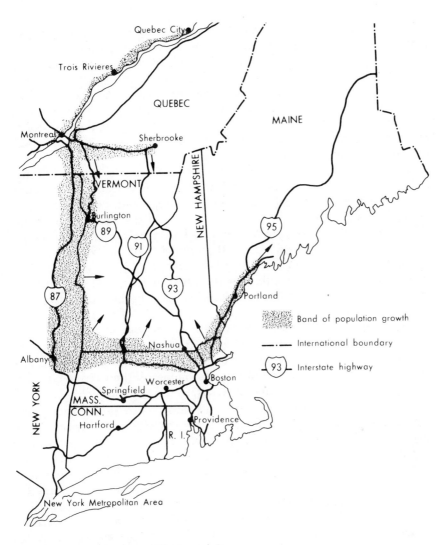

Figure 11.3 Advance of Hedonopolis.

New England. Whether the land use transition in New England will lead to a "folding-in" of the inner urban fringe and a refocussing toward the center of the mass of population, is uncertain. But population is exerting enough pressure to make those concerned with regional development and environmental preservation react to the leading indicators of change. Such reactions buoy the hopes of those who reject hedonopolis and its ethical and geographical implications, and annoy those whose plans for the leisure society are foiled or hindered.

Rejection of Hedonopolis   Countervailing forces are at work that would make the processes described in this chapter merely a passing fancy.

From the inner core of fat city to the wandering parasitopoli there are features that should make one question the future here portrayed.

Fat city, the supposed center for all gratification, is also a source of dissatisfaction. Glaring disparities of wealth and achievement cannot be appeased by a miserable welfare dole, nor by a munificent one. The sheer physical threat to anyone in fat city, rich or poor, could create coercive reaction great enough to destroy the service economy of the core. Some muggings, bombings, or riots may be tolerated by a service economy built on human interaction, but not many.

Another "threat" to the projected land use structure of hedono-polis is moral rejection of hedonism and capitalism. Already, many young people are dropping out of a competitive lifestyle and are subscribing to ecological causes designed to prevent land use change. One might argue that the communes arising in New England are merely another expression of dominant hedonism in which the offspring of the wealthy regale themselves in a prolongation of adolescence by "playing" instead of "working" the land, with subsidies from their parents. Yet there may be more force in their rejection of materialism and hedonopolitanism than they or we realize.

The interurban zone of repose is giving way to intensified use. How many paved Appalachian trails, traffic-jammed state parks, or sewage-filled lakes will be tolerated before this kind of recreation becomes too bleak to attract the hiker, camper, or swimmer? If there are no birds left in this zone because of ecological mistakes, who may bird watch?

At the regional scale, towns and even states are enacting restrictive legislation to thwart the ill effects of increased access. If these measures prevail, the changing land use pattern of the inner urban fringe may never be fully articulated.

At the world scale, mobile parasitopoli are subject to the uncertainty of local nationalisms, and resource acquisition is in jeopardy. Ecuador's seizure of the fishing vessels of other nations, Iraq's seizure of foreign oil holdings, and Chile's seizure of copper mines illustrate the fragile nature of these ephemeral cities. Constant hammering at the developing international economic system and monstrous diseconomies of protracted conflict create circumstances wherein the full use of the earth's source mateials may never be realized. World conflicts are reflections of the tensions within fat city, where rich and poor are also in opposition.

Conclusion

The future is not clearly defined here, nor elsewhere in the book. But here, as elsewhere, we find elemental principles, which, when translated into human actions, produce characteristic spatial forms and patterns at the miniscale of a city core or on a world scale. An examination of contemporary North American society suggests that the strident drive toward self-gratification will generate fat cities, mobile parasitopoli, and hedonopolis itself. Rightly guided, this process need not produce dire anti-social results, even though traditional society may be shaken to its roots.

We may expect optimizing behavior, which includes self-satis-ficing indulgence, to produce the best material state possible. Yet, we would be foolish indeed to imagine that material accretion is the only goal for man, even if it does liberate him for reflective thought. Indeed, we may hope that man will engage in reflective thought and that philosophical and ethical growth will parallel material growth so that "normality," balance, and perspective are restored. Such a restoration of equanimity should provide a rational basis upon which free men, uninhibited by oppressive legalism, may act in their own interest and in their own conscience to produce general conditions that are wholly desirable for all men. The challenge for those who would shape the future lies in the shaping of the conscience of man.

References

1. Thomas Kuhn, *The Structure of Scientific Revolutions* (Chicago: University of Chicago Press, 1970, pp. 147—149.

2. Edward H. Hall, *The Hidden Dimension* (Garden City, N.Y.: Doubleday, 1969), pp. 165—180

3. Constantinos A. Doxiadis, "The City (II): Ecumenopolis, World City of Tomorrow," *Impact of Science on Society* 14 (1969): 179.

4. George Macinko, "Land Use and Urban Development," in *The Subversive Science*, ed. P. Shepard and D. McKinley (Boston: Houghton Mifflin, 1969).

5. It is my opinion that society will be technically capable of feeding such a large population, but it is doubtful that we can generate humanitarian philosophies to cope with such numbers.

6. Herbert York, *Race to Oblivion* (New York: Simon and Schuster, 1970).

7. Victor R. Fuchs, *The Service Economy* (New York: National Bureau of Economic Research, 1968).

8. Leslie J. King, Emilio Casetti, and Douglas Jeffrey, "Differential Rates of Growth in Urban Service Employment," *Proceedings of the Association of American Geographers* 2 (1970): 81—84.

9. Carl Djerassi, "Birth Control After 1984," *Science* 169 (September 4, 1970): 941-951.

10. It is possible that the present United States Census definition for "urban" will have to change as we approach the 100 percent mark in "urbanized population;" otherwise, the categories of "urban" and "rural" will no longer have great meaning. The likely revision of the term "urban" will probably be upwards, or new categories (e.g., suburban, exurban, and so on) will come into being.

11. Edward Ackerman, *Geography as a Fundamental Research Discipline*, Department of Geography Research Paper No. 53 (Chicago: University of Chicago, 1958).

12. John B. Calhoun, "Population Density and Social Pathology," *Scientific American* 206 (1962): 139—148; J. J. Christian, "The Pathology of Over-

population," *Military Medicine* 128 (1963): 571—603.

13. August Loesch, *The Economics of Location* (New York: John Wiley and Sons, 1967).

14. Julian Wolpert, "The Decision Process in Spatial Context," *Annals of the Association of American Geographers* 54: 537—558; Richard Morrill, *The Spatial Organization of Society* (Belmont, Calif.: Wadsworth, 1970); Michael E. E. Hurst and Robert McDaniel, *A Systems Analytic Approach to Economic Geography*, Commission on College Geography Publication No. 8 (Washington: Association of American Geographers, 1968).

15. Jean Gottmann, *Megalopolis: The Urbanized Northeastern Seaboard of the United States* (Cambridge: M.I.T. Press, 1964).

16. Leonard Gardner, *Fat City* (New York: Farrar, Straus, and Giroux, 1969).

17. Confrontation-type interactions are those that require face-to-face contact within the firm or office, and between firms or offices and their customers or clients.

18. Those who have seen Joseph Losey's film *The Tenth Victim* may hesitate to consider the full scope of possible human relations at the core. Losey portrays a society of the future where boredom is staved off by joining in an advanced hunting game wherein humans are victims as well as hunters.

19. The Nielson ratings document the strong trend toward entertaining fantasy and away from "documentary-type" informative programs. *New York Times*, November 11, 1971.

Chapter   12

Detroit Humanly Viewed: The American Urban Present

William Bunge
York University

ABSTRACT: *How can we reconcile the glowing visions of the future presented by some futurists with the far from comfortable realities of current life? Professor Bunge forcefully raises this question in his essay. He characterizes the socioeconomic patterns of the Detroit region as three distinct but functionally interrelated cities: the City of Death; the City of Need; and the City of Superfluity. By describing the evolution of these three cities-within-a-city and the ways the three elements feed upon each other, Bunge reminds us that images of a luscious and opulent future such as those presented by Sommer (chapter 11) are often a refuge for those who cannot or will not confront the enormity of current and short-term problems. The future will perforce be fashioned from the raw materials of the present, and our aspirations for the decades ahead must be tempered by a frank recognition of the obstacles we will encounter in transforming the deadly present into the joyous futures we desire.*

All men are created equal. Any departure in the condition of men from this truth is a measure of the degree of biological breakdown among the species *Homo sapiens*. The extreme irregularity of the income map of Detroit reveals extreme pathology. Rather than reflecting the species natural equality, the map depicts a region of super-abundance adjacent to a region of brutal poverty. Between these two regions is an intermediate zone in constant danger of falling into poverty. Thus Detroit consists of three distinct biological cities: the City of Superfluity, the City of Need, and the City of Death (figure 12.1, A).

This organic instability is a constant source of threatened and actual outbursts of violence. These biological outbursts are commonly attributed to race, religious differences, politics, and even to individual personality disorders. But these factors are not the underlying cause of the animal tension that constantly grips Detroit. Such tensions arise because of the abundance of food that exists in close proximity to regions of near-starvation (figure 12.1, B). The search for food, for life itself, is a ruthless, restless, massive hunt which fills the hungry with a desperate animal combination of hate and hope, while it fills the glutted with a combination of hate and terror as they stand between the warehouses bulging with food and the great masses of the City of Death.

How biologically unnatural the situation. How strange it is that a nation that has starving children has spent five billion dollars a year not to grow food. How strange for a species to permit hungry children to parade past food protected from them by glass. "Overabundant" food is stored in warehouses and is even allowed to rot there, but it is carefully guarded from the hungry children. Only a biological breakdown of the system, such as

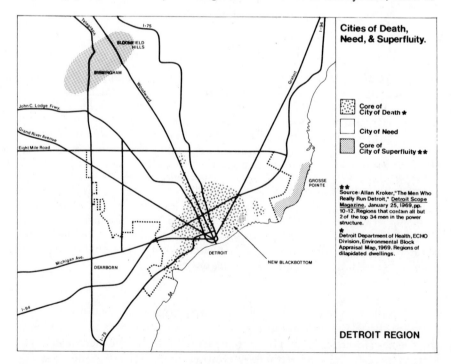

Figure 12.1, A.

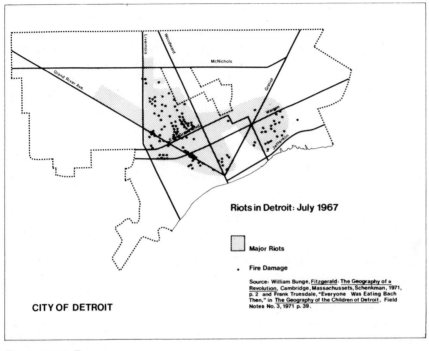

Figure 12.1, B.

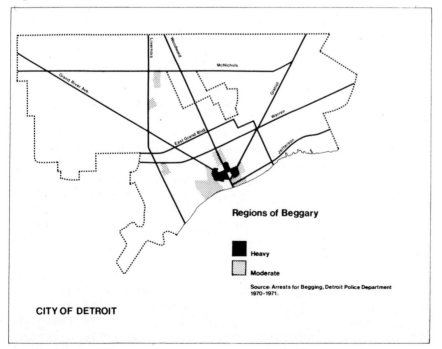

Figure 12.1, C.

the total rebellion of the City of Death in 1967, produces food for everyone. The few days of the riot, when the entire species was well fed, are viewed as a calamity by all except the hungry of the City of Death who remember their brief feast with a wistful smile. Evidently, only when the system collapses can everyone eat (figure 12.1, C).

To be successful, any strategy for self-consciously creating the future must adopt as one of its basic premises the principle that all men are created equal. Similarly, in moving toward the future we must recognize that any departure from equality—such as the existence of Detroit's Cities of Death, Need, and Superfluity—is a measure of biological breakdown that threatens the present as much as the future.

Flows Between the Three Cities

To find Detroit's naturally paid man—the species member receiving his animal worth in the form of "annual income," two criteria must be met: he must not be gaining or losing money to someone else, and he must attain his full natural animal powers as a man. People in the Cities of Need and Death lose money to others by paying a "machine tax" for the privilege of using the machines necessary to life itself. People in the City of Death lose additional money to others because they are often runted in mind and spirit and thus not worth as much as a man raised normally. Men from the City of Death pay the same machine tax as men from the City of Need, but in addition they pay a "death tax" on the weak, the sick, the old, and the children. Thus it is not possible to measure the true worth of a man from the City of Death because of the machine tax and the death tax. Nor is it possible to measure the true worth of a man from the City of Superfluity, for the salary he earns as a skilled administrator is buried in extra money from the other cities.

Highly skilled, self-employed businessmen such as dentists receive their full worth and no more. In the human primate colony of Detroit in the 1970s this true worth is approximately $29,000 per year.[1] Incomes above or below this figure must come from the money flows from one city to another (figure 12.2). Each of the approximately 830,000 workers in the City of Need pays a machine tax to the machine owners in the City of Superfluity equalling $19,000 ($29,000, less their mean wage of $10,000), for a total of $15,770,000,000 per year. Men from the City of Death work side by side at the machines with men from the City of Need and pay the same machine tax of $19,000 per man. But income in the City of Death averages only $5,000 per year. The difference between this $5,000 income and the City of Need's $10,000 income is a death tax, a tax of $5,000.[2] There are approximately 130,000 job holders in the City of Death. Thus their $19,000 machine tax totals $2,470,000,000 and their $5,000 death tax totals

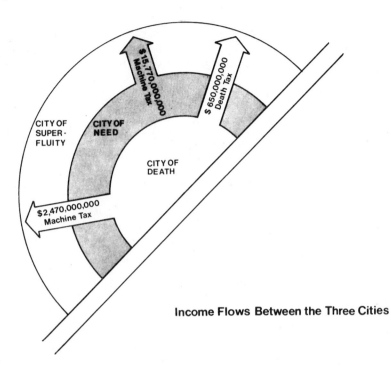

Income Flows Between the Three Cities

Figure 12.2

an additional $650,000,000.[3] The City of Superfluity contains 30,000 job holders who pay no machine or death taxes. They are paid their full earned worth at $29,000 each for a total of $870,000,000. They net an additional $18,890,000,000 from the taxes they levy on the City of Need and the City of Death.

The machine tax is a simple tax, collected by paying people less than their earned worth. But the death tax is subtle and more pernicious. It is collected in various ways, some obvious, some not. Obvious ways include overcharging for food (table 12.1), housing, schooling, street repair and maintenance, clothing, appliances, and loans. Less obvious ways are often equally or more important. Insurance fires raise insurance rates for slum neighborhoods where arsonists burn their businesses in order to build new stores in suburban neighborhoods. Mortgages can last forever. Churches that own their properties will sell to new arrivals, reestablishing the mortgage, and will then use the new income to build a new church in the suburbs. Neighborhoods are penalized for the occurrence of auto accidents by higher insurance rates. If two suburban commuters have an accident, the rate goes up where the accident occurred rather than where both live. "Inconveniences" such as queing for phone calls, waiting for city agents, and waiting for slow buses are serious hidden costs. For instance, a nominal 35 ¢, bus fare might cost a rider as much as $1.50 of extra time because of inconvenient routing or scheduling, for an actual cost of $1.85 per ride.

Table 12.1   Overcharging on Food—A Portion of the Death Tax

	City of Superfluity	City of Death	Percentage Higher for City of Death
Milk, 1/2-gallon container	.51	.64	25%
Crisco Shortening, 3-pound can	.74	1.04	41%
Skippy peanut butter, 12-ounce jar	.40	.51	28%
Pet Milk, 13-ounce can	.16	.21	31%
Sugar, 5-pound sack	.57	.76	33%
Coffee, 1-pound can	.70	.94	34%
Pork and beans, 16-ounce can	.14	.25	79%

Source: "Focus Hope 68", HOPE Food and Drug Survey, 1968

The City of Death is the garbage dump of Detroit. Old cars find their way from the City of Superfluity to the City of Need until they are junked in the City of Death. Junked cars line the streets of the City of Death and junkies line the sidewalks. School books, new and shining, start in "the better neighborhoods," and wend their way year after year toward the human refuse heap of the City of Death. Alcoholics slowly wend their way to the sodden crematorium called "skid row" and from there to inner city medical schools to be chopped up as cadavers.

All dead and dying things drift toward the City of Death. The sick and old from the City of Need are passed from hand-to-hand until they end up in tovernment housing projects. The butchershop leavings, such as the guts of hogs and pig's feet are shipped to the City of Death to appear under pink lights as soul food for blacks or ethnic food for other residents.

The City of Death is besieged. Blockades prevent certain life flows from reaching it. Doctors do not move toward sickness, they flee the City of Death. The blockade excludes materials needed to repair buildings, thus encouraging rats and roaches and producing freezing rooms in the winter.

Not only is the City of Death blockaded, it is also dismantled. When slum dwellers from the City of Death start to penetrate the City of Need, the residents of the City of Need hire hundreds of moving vans and start the dismantling. First, all the furniture is carted off. Junk furniture, old car seats, and orange crates take its place. As the single family homes are converted to multiple dwelling structures, the actual components of the building, including walnut panelling, chandeliers, shrubbery and marble tile, are loaded onto trucks. Some items of value such as copper roofing may remain. These are not dismantled and removed from the City of Death until "urban renewal" tears the whole place to shreds.

People keep drifting downward, heading toward the City of Death. About one-third of the youth from the cities of Superfluity, Need, and Death lose a notch each generation. There is an absolute tendency toward moving down regardless of what happens to the level of living. There is no way to go but down in an unstable system, from riches to need, and from need to death, even as national wealth increases. It is like walking up a down escalator.

Detroit's economic and social geography is dominated by the division of what should be a single human colony into three parts that are fed upon by the destructive parasites in the City of Superfluity. This is the overwhelming reality of Detroit's urban present. Any humane planning for Detroit's future must recognize the existence of the taxes currently levied on the Cities of Death and Need by the City of Superfluity, and such plans must contain strategies and mechanisms for eliminating these parasitical and piratical outward flows. Only by doing so can anyone hope to create a city that is biologically stable over the long-run.

Barriers Between the Three Cities

The three biological cities are separated by various geographical barriers. The most effective cushion between the City of Death and the City of Superfluity is the City of Need which stands between affluence and impoverishment. People from the City of Death search for food in the City of Need, creating tension between the two cities.

Besides this basic buffer, other geographic barriers have been erected. One extremely effective "wall" is nonlocal land use. For instance, a park may or may not be local in use. A small park tends to be a neighborhood focus and is overwhelmingly used by its neighbors. A large park such as a public golf course attracts nonlocal people. It is a geographic barrier. Major thoroughfares, cemeteries, and industrial land act as social walls and make excellent boundaries. The best example in Detroit is the one mile swath of nonlocal land use on the east side that starts at the Detroit River and extends to Eight Mile Road parallel and slightly to the west of

Gratiot. For years this racial barrier (recently breached along the river) defined the eastern boundary of the City of Death.

Where wide swaths of nonlocal land use do not exist, overt walls, complete with barbed wire can be erected if they can be disguised. For instance, expressways aid traffic only along their axes; locally they serve as severe barriers. In Detroit these barriers are ditches with barbed wire fences which lie adjacent to the expressways.

Wherever rich and poor are juxtaposed, walls will be provided. The enclave of superfluity in downtown Detroit is Lafayette Park. To its south is the Detroit River. On the west of Lafayette Park is the Chrysler Expressway, securing that flank. To the east, an old railroad bed in a trench stops people in that direction. Both sides of the track are fenced, and many of the street-level bridges that formerly crossed the railroad trench have been removed or double-fenced. To the north of Lafayette Park lies a series of public and semi-public buildings. The walls around their parking lots seem innocuous, but in other parts of the northern fringe the barriers are naked.

Two streets, Russell and Rivard, head straight south into Lafayette Park from the old slums in the Eastern Market district on the north. By building walls that turn all traffic aside "kitty-corner" across these streets, the streets have been blocked. On the Lafayette Park side the walls are disguised by graceful turns, brick facing, and beautiful shrubbery; people living in the Four Freedoms House immediately adjacent to the wall do not even know the wall exists. The other side of the wall is undisguised. The right angle turn at the intersection is preserved; the wall itself is unfinished concrete block, barren of landscaping. This Detroit Wall does have a small pedestrian opening to enable servants to walk to work from their slum houses.

A species in natural harmony with itself and its environment does not erect such barriers, particularly the kinds of barriers that keep people separate but do not in any way inhibit the flow of death taxes and machine taxes to the City of Superfluity. The Berlin Wall arouses horror and indignation throughout the world and especially in America. Yet the walls between people that we allow the prosperous to build and maintain in our own cities provoke scarcely a murmur except among the unheard people confined in the City of Death. Detroit's future will be a continuation of its Balkanized present unless control over land use is returned to the neighborhoods; only then will nonlocal land uses and naked physical barriers not be used to separate species members.

Characteristics of the Three Cities

The City of Superfluity includes a ring of neighborhoods stretching from Grosse Isle on the south, sweeping over to Ann Arbor and then around to Bloomfield Hills and Birmingham in the northwest, and continuing to the five municipalities that comprise Grosse Pointe in the northeast (figure 12.3, A). The bulk of those high in the power structure live in Grosse Pointe. A Grosse Pointe manufacturer will know far more about these affluent suburbs or, for that matter, more about Hubbard Woods in Northeast Metropolitan Chicago, than he will know about some parts of his own city.

The splendor of the Pointes is unreal, even eerie. Children should be raised in warm, human spaces. The tremendous private parks surrounding the houses are lonely. No child could possibly use that much grass for play. Such estates make children feel apart, distant. A gang of kids would have to be drawn from a square mile of such "homes," and toddlers could never make the distance.

The children of the City of Superfluity want to know why they have so much wealth while other children in Detroit are hungry. Since there is no good explanation, a bad one is provided: they are organically aristocratic by inheritance. In fact, men are as equal and as different as snow flakes. Children of the City of Superfluity are horribly deprived, for they are raised to feel that they are better than others; their deprivation gives that city a bittersweet flavor of happiness.

The City of Superfluity has developed a commuter culture in which the men spend up to four hours a day on an expressway or commuter bus and see their children only on weekends. In extreme cases, men stay in town all week in a downtown hotel, or they work as salesmen and may get home once a week or less. This extreme separation of work from home

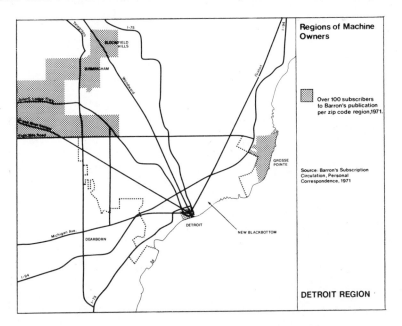

Figure 12.3, A.

alienates the man from his family. Such a man is not only apart from his family but beyond its comprehension, and this produces an agonizing loneliness. No people feel this agony more acutely than the "owners" of the machines. No group of men is less understood; it is their illusion that they own the machinery, when in fact the machinery owns them. Since they are always trying to explain the needs of machinekind to mankind, they are condemned to appear inhuman.

Look at life from the point of view of the men who live in the City of Superfluity. A machine called a wrist watch wields a tyranny over their hours and minutes. The men run themselves on time the better to make the trains work. Unlike industrial workers, who openly hate the drudgery of their work and gladly leave it behind them when they leave the factory, "owners," the most owned of all men, spend sleepless nights in service to "their" machinery. Heart attacks are epidemic among them.

The City of Need stretches in a great arch just inside the affluent suburbs but farther out than the City of Death. This buffer city (figure 12.3, B), includes Southwest Detroit, Melvendale, Redford, Ferndale, Warren, and Northeast Detroit, and is typified by Dearborn. Here are the white workers, the "hard hats," the solid union members of Middle America.

The City of Need shines with hard work. It is the pride of these people and all that they really have to show. It is a neighborhood of "home-owners" (actually mortgage renters) not estate owners. The City is immaculate and superneat but it is not sweeping and free, and the visitor is

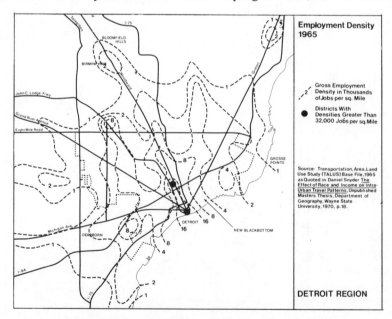

Figure 12.3, B.

compelled to think, "how pinched, how regimented." The City of Need feels and looks hard pressed because it is.

The taxed workers lead an excruciating existence. Unlike humans, machines do not tire. The actual work week for men holding two jobs can be ninety hours (including time spent travelling to and from work). Such men sleep much of the rest of the time. There is little leisure time in the workhouse of the City of Need. A middle-aged automobile worker in Detroit has a certain "look." He is thin, drained, all bones and lean muscle. Machines drain him of calories, and even rob him of fingers, eyes, and arms; every seven thousand automobiles cause an average of one amputation.[4] Dearborn is dominated by the Rouge plant of the Ford Motor Company. On one hand it is a point of pride: "The world's greatest industrial complex." On the other hand the Rouge is a horror, blotting out the sky and clogging the head with its noxious output, and just sitting there, huge and overwhelming, lighting the sky for miles about at night (figures 12.3, C and D).

The children of the City of Need must be prepared to enter the factory. Track education systems slate them as factory fodder before they start school. In school the emphasis is on discipline, punctuality, lining up for bells, and neatness, all in anticipation of later factory life. As the machines increase in complexity, the children who will later operate them must be educated to higher levels. No more is invested in children than is necessary to keep them from falling behind the needs of machines. Thus the City of Need keeps pace with the machines, generation after generation. The machines tax out all the extras, but do not take so much as to kill the goose that lays golden eggs for the owners.

Detroit's inner city slums lie in a small circle starting with Delray on the south, continuing through Bagley, West Side, Cass Corridor, Woodward East, and ending in New Black Bottom. The slums are "another country" from the Cities of Need and Superfluity in more ways than one. Infant mortality in this area matches that in many overseas nations (figure 12.3, E). New Black Bottom has a higher infant mortality rate than thirty-one members of the United Nations. An infant born in Taiwan has a better chance of reaching five years of age than one born in New Black Bottom.

The foreign country that constitutes the City of Death has many features alien to the Cities of Need and Superfluity. The rat region of Detroit (figure 12.3, F) contains an estimated 600,000 rodents, more than one for each small child in the City of Death.[5] Like many foreign nations, much of the region is without doctors. The City of Death is hungry. If children get a quarter, they rush off to buy food. There are almost no movie houses in the City of Death; kids spend their extra money on food. A 1969 Federal survey of 4,000 low income people in Detroit revealed that 40 percent had "serious nutritional deficiencies." Of the children examined, around 30 percent were physically abnormal owing to poor nutrition. Three percent of the poor children showed evidence of rickets. In the City of Death men pick at garbage in alleys, racing rats for what calories and

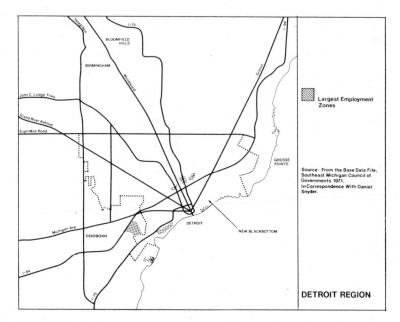

Figure 12.3, C.

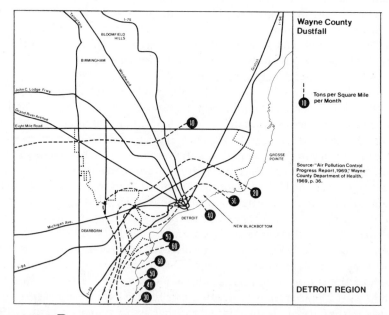

Figure 12.3, D.

proteins might be there. Mothers working as servants in the kitchens of the
rich bring home table scraps for their famished children. In the same way
that less developed nations are falling farther behind the wealthy nations,

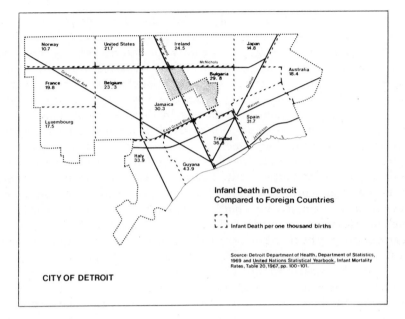

Figure 12.3, E.

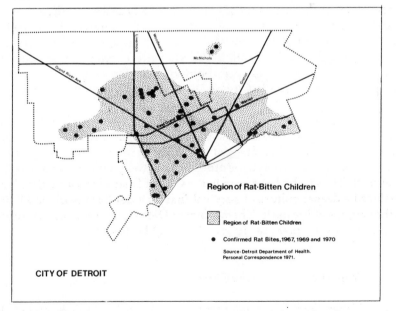

Figure 12.3, F.

the City of Death is a city losing ground, losing the future its children represent. It is a city that may be on its way to annihilation, to extinction, to genocide.

The City of Death is filthy. Abandoned homes punctuate the landscape. Rubbish decorates the berm. Filth is apparent everywhere; garbage is in heaps, street gutters are unswept. But the real tragedy is the extent to which the people complement the refuse. Chronically unemployed slum youth (50 percent and more) populate porches and curbs. Every store has a knot of "useless" young men in its front doorway. Why don't they work? It is not natural for a healthy species member just to "lay on the corner" and the empathetic observer is tormented on seeing the human flotsam of the slum. One also senses the terribly lonely quality of people who do not and cannot care how they look, who are beyond the healthy pain of embarrassment. Toothless old ladies in broken-heeled shoes and sagging print dresses lurch down the sidewalks. Old men sit on a sidewalk door stoop, passing a bottle of wine in a paper sack back and forth. Such people are accustomed to being "invisible" and they have achieved a degree of privacy by living in a world alone, in a counter society where they are no longer picked upon because they have been picked clean.

In the midst of all this death and dying arises a great shout of life. It cries out in the music of the ghetto, whose beat is like a heart pacemaker thumping out "Live! Live! Live!" Life pulsates in the bold colorful dress of the young that shouts "This is me; I'm alive!" Men pushed toward Death reach out for life. Natural animal grace in movement, cool soulful understatement, and a manner of holding the body and wearing clothing as a careful statement of self do not reflect a happy, carefree, irresponsible life—they indicate just the opposite. They are generated by a miserable, grinding struggle against Death itself by a culture that is hungry for life. Detroit's City of Superfluity is notorious for its lack of culture, its tastelessness. But Detroit's City of Death is one of the art centers of the world.

The people of the sheltered city of Superfluity understand little. Those in the City of Need understand that life is hard work, even though they foolishly fear being dragged down by the powerless. The City of Death understands itself and the other cities as well. It understands that life is survival. Those who have been in the City of Death for a long time have developed a deeper culture of survival that includes hard work and living on the margins of life itself. The wisdom of Detroit, now and for the future, lies in its meanest rather than its grandest neighborhoods.

Proportions Among the Three Cities

Understanding the relationships between the interflows and the characteristics of the three cities is a critical prerequisite to designing biologically sound communities. The City of Death is going downhill. Its homes, its streets, its schools, and its children's teeth fall apart as the money is sucked out. The City of Need just manages to keep itself in repair. All things elegant are built in the City of Superfluity by the taxes that flow to that city from the other two. The City of Need improves somewhat each generation as the improved machines insist on more highly skilled men. Thus the city as a whole is improving, with only the permanent slum of the City of Death losing ground. Such average improvement will not avail in the long-run, however, because it is biologically unsound, and built on fear.

Several groups that started outside the slums, such as Chicanos and American Indians, have now been pushed into them. Several groups that were in the slums, such as Italians, Greeks, and Hungarians, could easily return there from the City of Need. Leaving the slums of America may be more a temporary reprieve than an upward-bound, one-way trip to the City of Superfluity. In any case, the threat of the slum is the engine of fear that drives the entire city. Its levels of living set the levels of fear for all people who might return because of prolonged illness or other misfortune.

The proportions of income and people in the three cities are designed to keep the system in precarious balance. The City of Superfluity is small and inconspicuously located. The City of Need is large and it views the smaller City of Death as its antagonist. The City of Death reciprocates; New Black Bottom feels pressured by Dearborn and Dearborn fears New Black Bottom. The City of Need must be larger than the City of Death to keep the latter contained, because the passion of the City of Death is greater than the quiet desperation of the City of Need.

The proportions among the three cities are fixed in a precise but precarious balance that perpetuates the denial of man's natural equality. In all American cities the proportions are the same as they are in Detroit. Small cities have small slums and big cities big ones. This study of Detroit's geography is, in fact, a study of urbanized America and a study of the urbanized world, for the same proportions fulfill the same functions at continental and global scales. If the proportions are upset, especially by relative enlargement or contraction of the City of Death, the disruption of the carefully balanced tensions will destroy the entire biologically unstable system.

Planning Abolition of the City of Death Through Urban Nationalism

There exist two strategies for the elimination of slum conditions. One is to tear down and rebuild the slums in place. The second strategy is to remove the people from the slums. Both strategies, reconstruction and evacuation, should be applied at once. Every improvement of the slums counts. But of the two, the main thrust must be for slum rehabilitation under neighborhood control. Urban nationalism is the means by which slums should be rehabilitated.

Most people conceive of a nation as a land and its people. Land has become magic in our culture. Actually, life is not a search for land but a search for energy. Man spread out across the land to gather the sunlight converted to food through photosynthesis in plants. The concentrated sunlight of coal and oil enabled men to concentrate geographically in cities, but the mystery of land lingered, even though land is everywhere being abandoned. The bulk of Detroit's population is composed of former rural groups, such as southern black farmers and ex-farmers from Appalachia and upstate Michigan. As nations of people abandon their land and move to Detroit their nationhood is trampled because national regions are not taken seriously within a city.

Christaller's central place theory is the proper instrument to use in analyzing urban nationalism.[6] Christaller recognized that a neighborhood's economic and political functions vary in accordance with its size. Thus, it might take two hundred families to support a barber shop. If an ethnic neighborhood has only 60 families, it cannot support its own barber, whereas if the neighborhood has 250 families, it can have its own barber shop. Accordingly, if there are 700 families in the ethnic community, there will be three barber shops. Christaller also argued that the three barber shops will be located so that the trip to the nearest barber shop is minimized; in other words, they will be centrally located. Christaller also postulated a hierarchy of functions. If it takes 1,000 families to support a barber supply house, then a community of 1,300 families will have six barber shops and one barber supply house. Christaller points out that the barber shops will collect at central places with other functions having approximately the same threshold size (such as community shopping centers), while the barber supply house will cluster with a higher order center (perhaps a wholesale supply district). This logic applies as well to such functions as schools—grade schools, junior high schools, high schools, and colleges—and law enforcement—police precincts, police districts, city police, and metropolitan police.

Since a nation is a people, the absolute number of people living contiguously determines the intensity of nationalism that can be attained. The number of people, not the number of square kilometers, determines the degree of nationalism possible. But there are limits to urban nationalism, in that all major cities in the United States are ethnically mixed. Therefore no city or metropolitan region could have an ethnic police force. The ethnic, racial, and cultural groups in America are scattered, and therefore ethnic armies and ethnic police are impossible. Could not all the people be gathered up and re-assembled? Perhaps, but it never has happened. Urban people certainly will not go back to the land because that would mean a terrible drop in economic and cultural standards. You can't keep people down on the farm after they've seen Detroit. Even the more palatable idea of placing all the ethnic groups in separate cities would not work. The apartheid reservation system practiced in South Africa is a brittle and short-sighted policy. Only urban nationalism promises long-term stability.

Does the need for existence as a people, for a means of group expression, mean that Detroiters will never mix? Does this eliminate assimilation into a larger, eventually world culture? Does not urban nationalism intensify differences and raise levels of antagonism in Detroit? Is it not better for all to adopt WASP culture and become one people? No. Differences are beautiful. Variety is the spice of life. Similarity engenders excessive competition for the same niche. Regional injustice, not variety, causes hatred. Without urban nationalism there is no national expression not even for the Detroit Indian, to say nothing of Chicano, Pole, black, Italian, Jewish and Irish. As the people of Poland, Michigan, Tennessee and Alabama moved to Detroit, they lost their cultural identity. Blacks, the one group that cannot pass as Anglos, have developed a distinct Detroit culture based on jazz, dances, plays, and speech idiom that the rest of the culture eventually partially adopts. The way to achieve a rich Detroit culture is not to dilute the non-WASP ones, but to articulate all cultures. Let people decide freely what they will retain. Detroit can maintain an extremely variegated and rich cultural blend of Polish weddings, black music and dance, Irish humor, and English parks.

Urban nationalism is community control and some communities are mixed. Mixed communities also need power to express themselves. There are three definitions of integration. One is change: "integration exists between the time the first black family moves into a neighborhood and the time the last white family moves out." This kind of integration depends on the age of housing. Detroit subdivisions went up quickly and were filled with young couples. While there is movement in and out of a subdivision over the years, a sizable group remains, and they grow older and reach retirement together. They then sell their houses and move to Florida or Arizona, glutting the city with old housing. Young white couples in Detroit now buy new subdivision homes in the suburbs, so real estate agents open the older inner city neighborhood to young black couples. In northwest Detroit the changeover takes about five years. So for five years there is integration, and urban nationalism should reflect the mixture of the old white families and young black families.

A second definition of integration is based on proximity. Proximity varies in integrated neighborhoods. Functions that are personal, such as barber shops and taverns, tend to be segregated. Impersonal functions, such as grocery stores and filling stations, are mixed. Adults tend to remain segregated inside their homes while the children mix on the streets and at school. Scale is everything in defining mixture. If the area examined is big enough, say the planet earth's entire surface, integration is 100 percent. On the other hand, if the area is an individual lot, then only mixed couples' homes are integrated. The face-to-face integration that produces mixed sidewalks occurs where grade schools are mixed. Thus racial data on grade schools provide a good index of face-to-face or "geographic proximity" integration. Today, mixed neighborhoods are extremely painful ones in which to live since they are on their way to becoming slums. Integrated communities have overcrowded schools, deteriorating city services, and declining quality in the shops. Urban nationalism could make these neighborhoods the most exciting places to live, rather than the most depressing.

The third definition of integration is one of attitude. Voting patterns in Detroit reveal that some white neighborhoods will not vote for blacks and others will; all black neighborhoods vote for both races. Again, urban nationalism would allow the fullest articulation of attitudinal integration.

The last two definitions of integration, proximity and attitude, are based on the idea that 50 percent of one group is 100 percent integration. Table 12.2 below shows the relationship. To convert from percentages of minority groups to percentages of integration, just double the percentages of the minority group to arrive at the integration figure (figure 12.4).

Table 12.2.

Percentage One Group:	Percentage Integration:
100	0
75	50
50	100
25	50
0	0

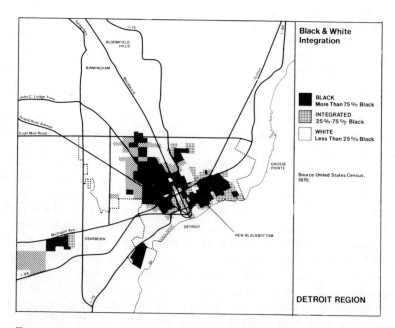

Figure 12.4

Urban nationalism is based on the idea that people should have power in proportion to their numbers. This is the only true test of whether or not they are being gerrymandered. In Detroit in 1969, the School Board decentralized their decision making powers in response to state legislation. In the name of integration the School Board redistricted into equal sized, compact and contiguous units (figure 12.5, B) which appeared fair on the

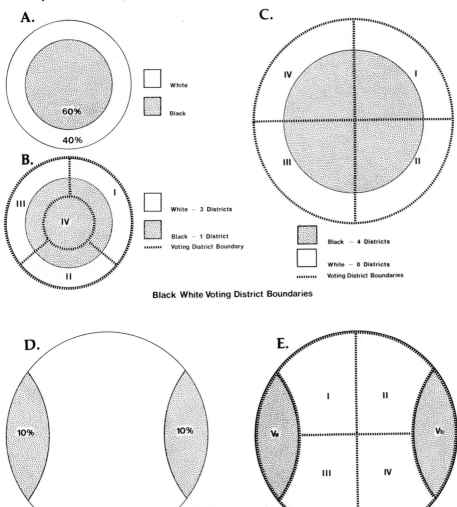

A.

60%

40%

☐ White

▨ Black

B.

III   I

IV

II

☐ White — 3 Districts

▨ Black — 1 District
.... Voting District Boundary

C.

IV   I

III   II

▨ Black — 4 Districts

☐ White — 0 Districts
.... Voting District Boundaries

Black White Voting District Boundaries

D.

10%   10%

▨ Polish — 1 District

☐ Other — 4 Districts
.... Voting District Boundaries

Polish Voting District Boundaries

E.

I   II

Va   Vb

III   IV

**Hypothetical Distribution
of Detroit's Polish Community**

Figure 12.5

surface, given Detroit's racial geography (figure 12.5A). But the arrangement is totally unfair because of the way the voting pattern breaks down (table 12.3). Blacks have 60 percent of the city's population but only 25 percent of the power. They are cheated out of 35 percent of their votes. The ratio of their size to their political power is 60/25 (percent votes/percent power), a gerrymandering of 240 percent. Yet the regions are geographically "standard"; they are not wildly shaped, nor of unequal size.

Table 12.3. Racial Breakdown of Detroit School Board Redistricting
Plan (Fig. 12.5 B)

District	% White	% Black
I	53	47
II	53	47
III	53	47
IV	0	100

The city of Detroit could be gerrymandered another way (figure 12.5, C). Now, power reverses (table 12.4) and 40 percent of the voters get zero vote. The ratio of gerrymandering is 40/0, an infinite number; the gerrymandering is "perfect." But notice again that the districts are "fair." To confirm the contention that gerrymandering is not as much a geographic as it is a numerical process, consider the problem of providing fair representation for noncontiguous Polish neighborhoods (figure 12.5, D). Consider the distribution of voting power (figure 12.5 E, table 12.5).

Table 12.4   Racial Breakdown of Hypothetical Redistricting Plan
(Fig. 12.5 C)

District	% White	% Black
I	40	60
II	40	60
III	40	60
IV	40	60

The noncontiguous district gives the Polish group exactly their just share of power. Contiguous units would be unfair. Similarly, equal area can be unfair. Only where densities of population are uniform throughout the region should the units be of the same areal size. In general, the denser the population, the smaller should be the area of the voting unit.

Richardson's irregular hexagons can vary areal size with population density (figure 12.6, A).[7] If a minority group resides in a contiguous but oddly shaped unit, then the voting district must be oddly shaped. To

Table 12.5   Hypothetical Voting Districts in Detroit

Districts	% Polish	% Other
I	0	100
II	0	100
III	0	100
IV	0	100
V	100	0

prevent gerrymandering people must have voting power proportional to their numbers. The geography that assures this is the fair geography. The bias toward "democratic," geometrically uniform regions is a bias toward simple stuff, in this case the earth's surface without reference to its human content. People must come first. They are the significant geographic element when determining fair voting districts. Geographic analysis starts with a population distribution map of the various cultural groups to be represented.

If white and black neighborhoods are mixed by voting districts they are not being integrated. Mixed voting districts (figure 12.6, B) comply

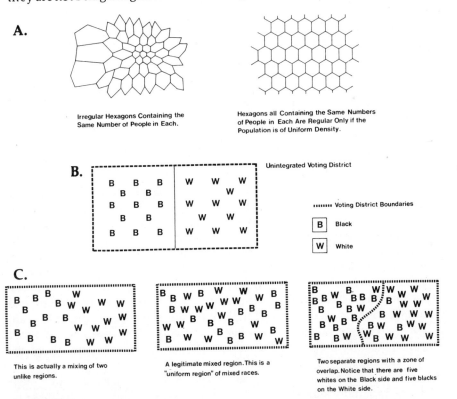

A.

Irregular Hexagons Containing the
Same Number of People in Each.

Hexagons all Containing the Same Numbers
of People in Each Are Regular Only if the
Population is of Uniform Density.

B.

Unintegrated Voting District

.... Voting District Boundaries

B   Black

W   White

C.

This is actually a mixing of two
unlike regions.

A legitimate mixed region. This is a
"uniform region" of mixed races.

Two separate regions with a zone of
overlap. Notice that there are five
whites on the Black side and five blacks
on the White side.

Figure 12.6

with none of the three definitions (change, proximity, attitude) of integration. Does not mixing wealthy and poor school districts assure that the poor district will get some money? No. What does General Motors, the world's largest corporation, do for its neighbor, Black Northern High School? Nothing. Banks in poor neighborhoods pump money out of the area, not into it. Slum dwellers save at the neighborhood bank, but the City of Death is a "high risk" region so no one in the City of Death can borrow the money back. The City of Superfluity is a low risk region, however, so people there can borrow the money deposited in the City of Death. Instruments of wealth remove money from the slums, they do not pump it in.

"Community control" (a weak version of urban nationalism) is a move toward democracy and urban nationalism. It returns the lower half of government to the city. Control over lower governmental functions is sought by units composed of approximately 20,000 people living in an area about one square mile in size; Jane Jacobs calls these units "districts."[8] In Detroit they are known as "community councils" or "homeowners" groups which are in turn composed of "block clubs" (table 12.6).

Table 12.6

Rural:	City of Death:	City of Superfluity:
State	Metropolitan Region	Metropolitan Region
Counties	City Proper	
Counties	Community Councils	Suburbs
Townships	Block Clubs	
Homes	Homes	Homes

A homeowner in the suburb has more rights than one in a slum. For instance, no expressway has ever "renewed" a suburb in the City of Superfluity. "Sub-urbs," that is, sub-urban divisions of the City of Detroit are nonexistent. Those living in the City of Superfluity have suburban divisions, but if city boundaries, garbage collection regions, library districts, school system boundaries, and police districts are mapped suburbs such as Grosse Pointe have numerous boundaries superimposed on one another to reinforce the unity of the area. But the mixed and unmixed ethnic neighborhoods in the city proper have no boundaries at all. Each governmental subdivision maps randomly with respect to any other governmental subdivision. But urban nationalism can solve such problems of hierarchy.

To be democratic, the boundaries must be "natural;" they must define internally similar sets. The boundaries of voting districts must be drawn so that they coincide with ethnic group boundaries. Power would then be proportional to numbers, even for scattered groups with small geographic cores, such as Detroit's Irish (figure 12.6, C). Gerrymandering denies a group its legitimate, proportional power. If voting districts are made larger and larger, the Polish and blacks can be kept a minority with zero voting power. During World War I, wards on the east side of Detroit began to fill up with black and Polish people. Suddenly the council went to city-wide elections, thwarting black and Polish representation on the Common Council. Today, as the City of Detroit is approaching a black majority, the Southeast Michigan Council of Governments suggests a metropolitan police force, which would deny Detroit residents control over their police.

Applying Christaller's hierarchical central place theory can prevent gerrymandering of all kinds. It ensures that ethnic and racial groups enjoy the amount of autonomy and neighborhood control their population size entitles them to. At the same time, it allows truly mixed groups to have proportionate shares of power. When applied to urban regions, Christaller's central place theory is the operational cutting edge of urban nationalism that can help guarantee that Detroit's urban future is more humane than its past and present. Urban nationalism will also restore the territorial integrity of Detroit's communities. All mammals have a biological sense of territory and man is no exception. Outsiders who are paid more than $10,000 per year, such as police, school teachers, merchants, and skilled craftsmen violate neighborhood territories in the Cities of Death and Need. This biological occupation of territories by "foreigners" can also be eliminated by returning community control to the neighborhoods.

The Role of Technical Planning in Urban Nationalism Urban nationalism sets the standards for planning work and for the planners' own conduct. An essential feature of democratic urban planning is close geographic proximity to the people for whom plans are being drawn. If community planning is done under community control—especially in its urban nationalism form defined as "all power short of sovereignty proportionate to the people living in each metroplitan area," planning abuses of the kind perpetuated under the "urban renewal" programs of the 1960s can be eliminated.

Local control of planning is absolutely essential for neighborhood identity. If there were a planning office in each square mile of a city, the plans would take on the distinct flavor of community taste. Everything can be mass-produced except identity. By definition, each region will be unique in some easily identifiable way. Democratic planning through urban nationalism is far superior to the bureaucratic planning which has historically produced alpine ways, autobahns, and expressways. With a wave of the hand, bureaucratic planners sweep away people and communities to make way for monuments and squares.

There are theories and techniques to support democratic planning for the future. The von Thunen rent model proves that it is impossible to move downtown from downtown. In Detroit, as in other cities, men from the City of Superfluity keep thinking that it would be nice to move downtown nearer the suburbs to shorten commuting time and to eliminate the hazards of driving through slums. In the 1920s a "new center" was constructed 4 miles north-northeast of downtown Detroit. The new center has never grown from its initial size. Subsequent downtown growth remained downtown, and the isolation of the new center is a major problem. Planners keep trying to solve it by clearing out all residences between downtown and the "new center." In the 1950s corporate managers applied the suburban shopping center notion to complexes of insurance companies and similar office buildings in attempts to reduce long-haul commuting. But the pull of downtown reasserted itself in the 1960s and most office construction in Detroit is now downtown. The CBD cannot be moved, as the von Thunen model makes absolutely clear.

In the von Thunen rent model, competing areas are placed as near to a central point as possible, producing concentric land use circles of varying width. In the urban application, the central point is the central business district, and the circles of residential land use are the city's three regions, the Cities of Death, Need, and Superfluity. Why is the most powerful city the greatest distance from the center? If the rich are so powerful, why do they spend so much of their lives commuting? How does it happen that the powerless people of the City of Death are located on the most convenient land, often within walking distance of downtown?

The answers to these questions are related to population density per square mile of housing. Slum dwellers spend the least money per person but the most money per square mile for rent. Similarly, slum dwellers pay the lowest transportation costs individually but the most per square mile since there are so many slum dwellers per square mile. The geographic formula is as follows:

$$R = A(P-C) - ATD \cdot 30$$

where,

R = rent (ground rent) per square mile
A = amount of people per square mile
P = price (individual rent) of average dwelling unit per month
C = cost of upkeep of average dwelling unit per month
T = transport cost per mile
D = distance (round trip) from downtown and back.

Daily transportation costs are multiplied by 30 because trips are computed on a daily basis, while rents are on a monthly basis.

The boundaries between the Cities are located at the distances where one form of rent is higher than the other (figure 12.7, A). The highest paying geographic unit, the slums, dominates the center and crowds the other Cities out. But the transport costs per square mile for slums are heavier than for any other group. So the slums are rapidly replaced by the

middle class City of Need. Farther out the City of Superfluity out-competes
the City of Need. By swinging the radii of the three cities about, we can
produce the basic circular pattern of Detroit. These circles explain the basic
geography of Detroit; they also explain why downtown cannot be moved
out of downtown (even by its "owners.") If men attempt to transform "new

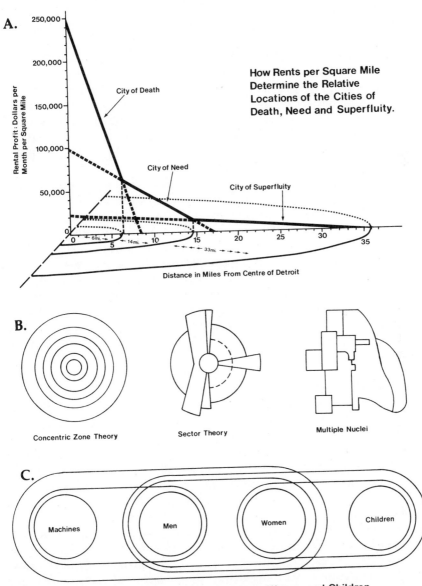

A. How Rents per Square Mile Determine the Relative Locations of the Cities of Death, Need and Superfluity.

Concentric Zone Theory   Sector Theory   Multiple Nuclei

Venn Diagram of Spaces of Men, Machines, Women and Children.

Figure 12.7

centers" or suburban offices into a new central business district they will generate tremendous transportation costs which must be reflected in higher rents. If a new suburban center is built, all major transportation routes must converge there, not at the old center. Then, according to von Thunen's law, the area around the new center will become slum. The ultimate cost of moving the central business district is the cost of moving the entire city from the old center to the new. There is no change at all in the relative locations of the internal city: the new center becomes the new center of the slums and all commuter distances shift to the same range as before. For Detroit's "new center" of the 1920s to work, the "owners" would have had to move all of Detroit 4 miles north-northeast. People can no more repeal the laws of geography than they can repeal the laws of physics.

All cities are the same shape; only their sizes vary.[9] Small cities have small slums and big cities have big slums. Detroit's slums keep growing because the city of Detroit grows. Growing slum neighborhoods can hardly be stopped by homeowner groups or by any other limited remedy.

The overall shape of the city appears to be a star-shaped, modified circle. Stars can be made to converge to circles as the points become less pointed and more numerous. The von Thunen principles suggest circularity, but centrifugal forces pushing salients of the city into the countryside also are at work, and a compromise shape results.[10] The two extreme shapes are: a perfect circle representing compactness, and a star with an infinite number of points demonstrating anti-compactness. The edge of a city enjoys both worlds, rural open green space and urban excitement and accessibility. So from time to time planners try to increase the length of the boundary relative to the area of the city by planting "new towns." Such satellite towns are rapidly absorbed into the main city as it grows to form one huge roundish blob again.

In geographic literature, the city is mapped according to three patterns: rings, sectors, and multiple nuclei (figure 12.7, B). In recent years research has suggested that these patterns stem from different characteristics; rings from family structure, sectors from economic structure, and multiple nuclei from ethnic structure.[11] Unfortunately, there has been little progress in relating the three patterns. They are presented as if three thoroughly independent spatial forces get all mixed up in producing the pattern of the city. This is needlessly primitive, for all three patterns are related to near circularity. The radii of the sectors are approximately the same length, and thus the overall shape of the sector pattern approximates the ring pattern in its circularity. Similarly, though multiple nuclei are scattered randomly, the overall shape is quite compact. All three patterns have an approximately circular overall shape. No mandates from the power structure or from town hall can change the shape of cities, decentralize downtown, move it or abolish it.

There are other technical subjects in which geographers excel that can be used to create a humane urban future. For example, the boundaries of the regions of the city can be drawn objectively by computers. The anti-gerrymandering principles of urban nationalism can be programmed. Such technical approaches must not be rejected as undemocratic. Science is democratic or despotic only in terms of the uses to which it is put.

One democratic feedback in science is to teach it in schools to young children so that the level of competent popular understanding is raised. Geographers can begin to shape a humane urban future by teaching their trade to children at a much earlier age than present curricula allow. Kindergarten children can be taught city planning techniques.[12] If democratic planning is taught in elementary schools, technical arguments will not be beyond the competence of the average voter.

Human Versus Property Planning

The most intriguing of present-day land uses are the distributions and combinations of machines, men, women, and children (figure 12.7, C). We find machines with men, but they are found less often with woman, and never with children. The pairs that are seen most often are machines and men, men and women, and women and children. The triplets that are most prevalent are machines, men and women; or men, women and children. The progression in these linkages from machines at one extreme to children at the other is most instructive, for it describes the way we organize our world.

What is so intriguing about these spaces is their relationship with safety. The unsafe spaces are those where men and machines are together. These spaces include logging camps, cowboy ranches, factories, and prisons. Machine and men spaces are unsafe microspaces where men challenge each other in duels, often employing the machines called weapons. Planning to eliminate or reduce them is more than amenity planning. It is survival planning. Male and female micro-spaces reverse all of this. Women will join defensive armies to protect their homes and children, and this suggests that the deadly spaces called war zones could be eliminated by thoroughly integrating women into the combat corps. In forestry, ranching, and industrial work, men defeat safety by refusing to use "unmasculine" safety equipment. All-male mountain-climbing teams and all-male high-steel construction workers are always plunging to their deaths. Heterosexual mountain-climbing teams are much safer since the men have a good reason not to take too much risk. Factories will be unsafe until they are made into heterosexual micro-spaces, and "prison reform" requires conjugal visits, that is, elimination of the all-male micro-spaces.

Men and children rarely meet in the same place. It is rare throughout the mammalian order. Indeed, perhaps the spaces described here represent not only "human geographic nature" but "mammalian geographic nature." Perhaps zoologists will find these geographic spaces pertaining among other animals.

An especially deadly space is one occupied by children and machines. The automobile has been placed too close to the children on residential streets that have been converted to commuter streets (figure 12.8, A). The parking lanes are cleared making three or four traffic lanes, one-way traffic is established, and a *de facto* 50 to 60 mile an hour speed limit is encouraged. Children tumble into the traffic as they run down their front steps and across "the curb" which curbs everything but the children.

The home, the nest where the child is raised, is a space for men, women, and children, and is relatively free of machines. Factories should become a space for men, women, and machines, for if women were present, the men would use safety equipment and the management would be forced to humanize the production lines.

In urban planning that is directed to the fulfillment of human needs, land is mapped according to present or desired human land use with no necessary reference to property. Since it is humans that interest us, we should start all planning by making maps of existing human spaces and maps of the human spaces we wish to achieve. The property maps should be arranged to produce the desired result; property is to be treated with contempt relative to human conditions and human needs.

Geographers must start where men are, in cities, and apply themselves directly to human survival needs. Geomorphologists have always been interested in "surface material" such as ice on the polar glaciers. But geomorphologists have no interest in the surface material

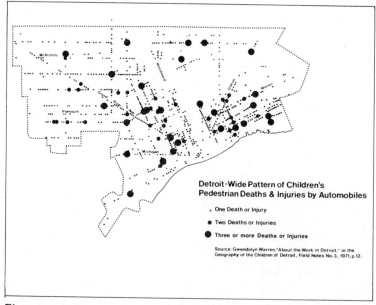

**Detroit-Wide Pattern of Children's
Pedestrian Deaths & Injuries by Automobiles**

. One Death or Injury

● Two Deaths or Injuries

● Three or more Deaths or Injuries

Source: Gwendolyn Warren,"About the Work in Detroit," in the
Geography of the Children of Detroit, Field Notes No. 3, 1971, p.12.

Figure 12.8, A.

called "city." Cities are some sort of thin but highly impermeable crust. This "hard pan" produces a desert, for although rainfall remains the same as before the crust of the city was laid down, much of the purpose of this crust is to whisk the rain away into the urban rivers called sewers. Thus the surface is turned into a true desert. Interaction between surface material and climate is profound. The geographer-climatologist Bryson measured the urban temperature increase caused by furnaces and automobiles. He found that the increased temperature caused peculiar inrushing winds that accentuated smog and he noted that the city had far fewer sunny days than did the surrounding countryside.[13] But Bryson and other physical geographers do not plumb the full depth of the problem.

What has been the criterion of "significance" traditionally used by physical geographers? Geographers do not care about terrain from the point of view of ants, but from the point of view of men. How flat must terrain be to be usable as flooded irrigated land? At what slope is the land too steep to plow? What slope can an army tank climb? Climatology employs similar human criteria to determine what is worth studying. Vegetation, with obvious implications for agricultural crops, is often the test of climatological significance. In physical geography, only that which has effect on mankind is studied. Now that men are much less dependent on the countryside than on cities, why have geographers not followed mankind? Why have geographers left their minds back on the farm? Today, regions of cities are far more in need of study than regions of increasingly depopulated farm land. The human usage of urban space is more relevant to human survival than is property land use. Economic geographers should not map the world production of hemp, slate, or even oil. They should map income levels in the cities that produce rickets in children. Of all the geographers guilty of not following the logic of mankind, none are guiltier than physical geographers. Again, what of the "surface materials" of the city? For instance, can a small child put his tender rump down all over the city with equal safety and comfort? Where has man created regions of glass, gravel, and garbage? Where has man created regions of green grass for the child's posterior? Where is the climate a desert for children, devoid of water, swimming holes, swimming pools, wading pools, sprinklers, lawns, boulevards, and grass on the berm? Is not "desert" the accurate climatological description of a slum? The climate and landforms of cities are not amusing subjects. "Changing the climate of Detroit" may sound like a political matter but it is a physical, even mechanical, human problem.

Men and machines are changing more and more rivers around Detroit and other large cities into concrete tubes. Should not a geomorphologist study the spread of sewers, the laws that govern the interaction between sewers and the land, and the way such interactions predict the future shape of the earth? The bulldozer is becoming a serious "agent of erosion," but because it is not "natural," geomorphologists ignore it. Many geomorphological features are possible. For example, if the hydrogen bombs go off, how pitted will the earth's surface be? Will each city become a huge pit, like craters on the moon? If a hydrogen bomb cut backward into the geomorphologically fragile Niagara Escarpment at Niagara Falls, what would happen to the Great Lakes? When will Lake Erie drain? How will the landscape look? How will Lake Detroit look?

The major thrust of geographical futuristics must be to move the missile death traps, the potential Graveyards that Detroit and other cities have become, toward a natural state, a survival state. No literary license is being taken in referring to Detroit as a graveyard, because if mankind kills himself off, he will die in place, in the cities where he now barely lives.

Detroit Guilt

The machines are not yet tamed. The cities of the world have been created essentially for machinekind, not mankind. The only animal not caged at the zoo is man, which makes him the most dangerous animal of all. But there exists one other uncaged creature, the machines called automobiles. The automobile is given more and more freedom to roam over Detroit and the children less and less. The fencing put up to "protect" children from the expressway traffic, the fences along arterial streets, and the fences around parking lots, are caging the children. Only the sidewalks are theirs. All other space is off limits to them. "Private property, keep out!" "No ball playing." Yet machines are welcomed all over the landscape. "Free Parking," "Drive-in Movie," "Motel." In Detroit there is even a drive-in funeral parlor where one can view the deceased from the comfort of one's car. Airplanes fill the air with noise and fumes. An index of the increasingly unbridled strength of the machines is the noise they produce. Each decade they are noticeably louder and more powerful. More and more, they drown out the animal sounds of children.

Which individuals or groups are to blame for this situation? Easy answers come to mind. The rich people in the City of Superfluity have the power and therefore the responsibility. They are overwhelmingly white Anglo-Saxon Protestant, and would appear to be the cultural and racial oppressors of the rest of Detroit. But evidence contradicts this. The commuter culture is miserable and artificial. Businessmen have epidemic high blood pressure, a disease of tension. Suicides are undifferentiated by income, race, class, or culture (figure 12.8, B). Suicide indicates uniform misery, the ultimate misery.

What is the cause of all the misery? It is no accident that Detroit's nickname is "Mo Town," meaning "Motor Town." Detroit has the highest ratio of machines to men in the world. Moreover, the machines are worshipped more ardently and given more of the physical space there than in any other city. Machine spaces of all kinds dominate the center of the city whereas the child spaces are extremely pinched. The machines have become wild animals. Do they not move with more and more freedom over the earth's surface? The Rouge plant in Dearborn still needs human pilots to deliver raw materials to it, but the internal conveyor systems and the potential for fully-automated assembly lines approach self-reproducing assembly lines—factories that produce other factories. Reproduction is not that far away. It is man's great conceit that he, rather than the machines, is evolving.

In Detroit machinekind has run amuck. It is unbridled, wild, and out of control. If the automobiles demand more expressways to move over the surface, people's homes come down. And in the face of this apparent-when-thought-about danger, mankind is divided into those who think they own the machines and those who think other men, not the untamed machines, are their enemy. Yet members of the so-called power structure are as much entrapped by machinekind as anyone else, because the machines own them. Mankind and machinekind coexist in Detroit, but mankind is in service to the machines there and elsewhere and he will remain enslaved to machines in the future unless self-conscious strategies for freeing him are instituted.

Geography is a marvelous means for teaching our fellow men about the real nature of the crisis of Detroit, about America's urban present. We need maps of all kinds of human spaces, but we are especially in need of maps of machine spaces and child spaces, maps that will make the rich realize how much they have to gain by giving up their "ownership" and uniting with the poor. We need advocate plans that cage the machines, that liberate our children, and that liberate all of us in doing so. Only by taming the machines can we hope to make Detroit a human city.

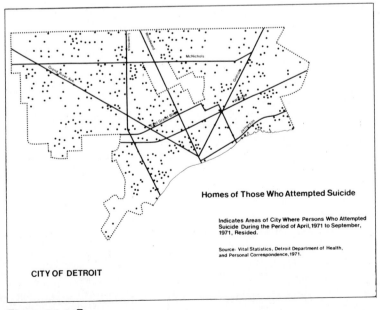

Homes of Those Who Attempted Suicide

Indicates Areas of City Where Persons Who Attempted Suicide During the Period of April, 1971 to September, 1971, Resided.

Source: Vital Statistics, Detroit Department of Health, and Personal Correspondence, 1971.

CITY OF DETROIT

Figure 12.8, B.

References

1. American Dental Association, *The 1968 Survey of Dental Practice* (1969), p. 12.

2. $10,000 is inflated slightly above the approximate wage of an automobile worker. Research Department, Solidarity House, United Auto Workers International, Detroit, 1971, in conversation.

3. The work force of Detroit consists of about as many jobholders as households. While some households have two jobholders, others have none. According to the U.S. Census of 1970, the Standard Metropolitan Statistical Area (SMSA) of Detroit contains 1,039,000 households. The 1965 Transportation Area Land Use Study (TALUS) shows that 13.4 percent of the households in the SMSA were receiving incomes below $3,000, 83.3 percent had incomes between $3,000 and $20,000 and 3.3 percent were receiving incomes above $20,000. At inflated 1972 figures, income flows should approximate the levels in the table below:

Estimated 1970 Money Flows to the City of Superfluity

	Job Holders	Average Salary	Machine Tax	Death Tax	Flows
City of Need	830,000	$10,000	$15,770 M	0	-$15,770M
City of Death	130,000	$ 5,000	$ 2,470 M	$650 M	-$ 3,120 M
City of Super- fluity	30,000	$29,000	0	0	+$18,890 M

4. Workmen's Compensation Department, Michigan Department of Labor, *Annual Report, January 1, 1967 - December 31, 1967*, p. 17.

5. In John B. Calhoun's classic work, "Ecology and Sociology of the Norway Rat," *United States Public Health Service Bulletin*, December, 1963, is a map entitled "Typical Baltimore 'Row House' Block-Number 14-1: 34, 35 Survey July 9, 1947." Calhoun mapped the locations of 148 rats. If we use the results of the Detroit Department of Health's city-wide survey (Question: "Do you have any trouble with rats?") and if we assume that the worst of Detroit was as bad as Calhoun's Baltimore block, we can give fractions to Detroit neighborhoods reporting lighter trouble with rats and we can multiply these figures of rat population density times the number of blocks in the rat region of Detroit. The resulting estimate of Detroit's rat population is approximately 600,000.

6. Walter Christaller, *Central Places in Southern Germany* (Englewood Cliffs, N.J.: Prentice-Hall, 1966).

7. Lewis F. Richardson, "The Problem of Contiguity," *General Systems Yearbook* 6: 139-187.

8. Jane Jacobs, *Death and Life of Great American Cities* (New York: Random House, 1963).

9. Stig Norbeck, *The Law of Allometric Growth*, Discussion Paper No. 7, Michigan Inter-University Community of Mathematical Geographers, 1965.

10. Charles C. Colby, "Centrifugal and Centripetal Forces in Urban Geography," *Annals of the Association of American Geographers* 23: 1-21.

11.   Robert A. Murdie, "The Social Geography of the City: Theoretical and
      Empirical Background," in *Factorial Ecology of Metropolitan Toronto, 1951-
      1961*, Department of Geography, University of Chicago Research Paper No.
      116 (Chicago: University of Chicago Press, 1962), pp. 9-26.

12.   In the early 1960s the author taught kindergarten children in Livonia, a Detroit
      suburb, many urban planning techniques by having the children arrange toy
      houses, streets, people and so forth on a blank map. The children invariably
      located the school centrally using topological measures of distance (the
      number of blocks) rather than metric measures (the total length of trips in feet
      or miles). Invariably they would not locate the church near the railroad as they
      followed a strict regime of zoning their land use.

13.   Dr. Reid Bryson, then Chairman of the Department of Meteorology at the
      University of Wisconsin, was studying the urban pollution and micro-
      climatology of Madison, Wisconsin in the late 1950s.

Part III: Approaches and Alternatives

Chapter 13

Escaping From Paradox:
Some Possible Paths

The Editors

It is appropriate to examine the course of our journey and to determine where we have yet to go. In Part II we looked at some implications of the new spatial conditions. We steeped ourselves in the difficulties inherent in the present paradoxes of stress and disengagement; adhocracy and bureaucracy; and the overloads of alienation and resource exhaustion. We now sense the need to escape from paradox. We seek a high road toward more positive and potentially comforting subjects, toward "alternative desirable futures" (figure 1.1).

Doing anything seems preferable to inaction in the face of the contradictions of the present, even if that anything is only proposing a set of alternative futures. Mapping out alternative futures is the first step in building regions for the future

Elements of Forecast-Oriented Chapters

The chapters of Part III are possible maps or forecasts of the future. Forecasting implies scientific prediction as well as educated intuitive speculation. Geographical forecasting involves the use of scale, viewpoints, techniques, and data. The chapters of Part III may be classified most usefully according to the forecasting techniques they use, but before they are discussed in that respect, a few words concerning scale and viewpoints are necessary.

Scale   Fundamentally, forecasting is extrapolation in one form or another. Regardless of changes in scale, an extrapolation will remain valid if the internal relationships or basic characteristics of the data remain the same. Unfortunately, by the nature of things, scale changes are associated with changes in characteristics. Size (and therefore scale) is related to form.[1] Consequently, forecasting by extrapolation requires a change from one statistical universe to another.

If one interpolates beyond the end of the numerical sequence one, five, ten at the same rate, one expects to find the value fifteen as far beyond ten as ten was beyond five. Such "extra" or outside-the-limits "interpolation" is called extrapolation. The key terms in extrapolation are "the same distance, at the same rate," or "in the same proportion." In geographical forecasting, "scale" can be substituted for such phrases. At a given scale, proportion, or rate, we have what is called a common "statistical universe" in terms of characteristics of the data sets appropriate to a given set of circumstances.

A major change in scale may present a new set of internal relationships representing a significantly different set of circumstances. Extrapolation across such a scale boundary will most surely produce errors in forecasting. On the scale of tensions in baseball, a bases-loaded, late-in-the-game home run is entirely different from a routine long fly in a bases-empty early inning. The differences in the distances the ball travels may be trivial; but the differences in terms of tension in the game and in effects on the outcome of the game are of an entirely different magnitude. It is this hidden paradox that baseball fans appreciate and that those who are bored by the game do not understand.

Simple extrapolation is limited in that the forecaster is generally unaware of changes of circumstance that are bringing about a new statistical universe. Forecasts based on seemingly logical extrapolation can be invalidated by any changes in circumstances. Extrapolations based on an assumed constant statistical universe might be called first-order forecasts. Similarly, forecasts across an anticipated future scale boundary into a significantly different statistical universe might be called higher-order forecasts. The forecasts presented in Part III fall primarily (but not wholly) within the more constant statistical universe of presently perceived circumstances.

Viewpoint   Viewpoints may be classified according to the individuals or groups holding them. Different interest groups, social classes, and cultures possess varied viewpoints. Subjective qualities of mind and differential experience produce a wide range of reactions to environmental stimuli. Differences in perception, belief, and attitude are subsumed under the rubric of viewpoint. As order-seeking social scientists, we attempt to classify viewpoints; we recognize the inevitable presence of individual points of view. The simple classification into individuals, interest groups, social classes, and cultures is a useful one. The viewpoint of an interest group is explored in Wolfe's chapter on tourism, which forecasts the behavior resulting from the viewpoint of a particular type of resource user. Differences between class points of view were certainly evident in the descriptions of Fat City and the City of Death. And on a still larger scale, the great schism revealed by Warntz's world potential maps (chapter 6) mirrors the traditional dichotomy between so-called Western and non-western cultures. Viewpoint is an organizing theme for classifying the previous chapters as well as those that lie ahead.

Technique   It is by the techniques used in them that the chapters in Part III may be most usefully and consistently classified. Chapters 14 through 19 represent four principal techniques of forecasting: 1) simple extrapolation, 2) scenario, 3) simulation, and 4) Delphi. Although the range of techniques used is by no means exhaustive, the following chapters will establish the *direction* of our escape from present paradox.

Janelle (chapter 15) is concerned with dimensional guidelines for forecasting. His extrapolations are first-order. Carol and Wolfe cast their chapters (16 and 17) in the scenario format. Wolfe's is generally first-order, whereas Carol varies the fundamental conditions of Africa to produce second-order forecasts. Millward (chapter 18) simulates the future growth of cities, and Smil (chapter 19) employs the Delphi technique to forecast the future arrival of energy resource innovations. Interestingly, Smil's forecasts with respect to fusion power are similar to Philbrick's speculations in chapter 2.

Data Versus Speculation   We must take into consideration the difference between speculative and empirically-based works. In Part II Zelinsky posited the emergence of a new type of cultural region, that is, the "voluntary region." Such regions are probable "aggregations of like-minded, mobile, atomistic individuals" coming together (regionalizing) "on the basis of personal predilections." His imaginative suggestions are speculative; he describes his work as a "plunge into *terra incognita*." By contrast, Wolfe's "Recreation Scenario for the Province of Ontario, Canada" is based on empirical data inventory. Without the initial step of data collection, no policy formulation could occur. Zelinsky's speculations do not depend for their viability on follow-through in the subsequently analyzed data sources. Wolfe, on the other hand, has a specific commitment. He needs to know, with respect to accepted terms of reference in an established bureaucracy, the best way to answer specific questions that underlie policy decisions.

We may escape from paradox through action, using the forecasting techniques presented in Part III as well as others. Forecasting techniques, however, do not guarantee insight. Understanding of changes in the tensions and scales of the "game" is of fundamental importance. Our plans and actions for the future must not be based on blind extrapolations of our incomplete understanding of the present.

Futurism and "The Plan"

As we migrate from the past and its tyranny of place, we discover in the present new elements: tyranny of freedom in communication and information overloads. We lose our local self-reliance as we become part of an increasingly interdependent, "time-space-convergent," global community. These, as we saw in chapter 5, are the "Implications of the Present." Leaving the present behind, we hope to formulate new "Approaches and Alternatives" that are desirable futures.

If we distinguish between futuristics and plans we will keep our options open and should avoid falling into undesirable futures. The future is an open system with an almost infinite set of alternatives. A plan is inviting because it is definite and it promises perfection through the application of rules. But such plans also lock us into "best" solutions and severely limit our options. Too late we recognize that this was not the alternative desirable future of which we dreamed.

A *dynamic* plan is a present base from which an almost infinite set of desirable futures leads into still more paths, unexplored, strange, and different. We might identify futuristics with adaptive planning, which can claim to be dynamic if it provides—inherently—for the infinite variety of real futures. Even with this qualification, however, futuristics may not be *equated* with any kind of planning, even adaptive planning. For a plan is a constraining set of edicts that intones what must and must not be done. It is precisely the kind of prescriptive intonation that is at the root of the present paradoxes from which we seek to escape.

References

1. D'Arcy Thompson, *On Growth and Form* (1917; abridged and reprinted, Cambridge: The University Press, 1966).

Chapter   14

Geography and Futurology

Bruce Ryan
University of Cincinnati

ABSTRACT: *Futurology welds the past, present, and future into a rational and coherent structure. Its forerunners, its relation to the social sciences, and its potential relationships to geography are important considerations in developing a geographical futuristics. What changes in scale and emphasis might geographical research undergo? What methodological issues arise in geographical forecasting and planning? What geographical subfields will emerge as geographers begin to forecast the evolving spatial organization of the earth? Ryan suggests that studies of population redistribution, concern for the future quality of the environment, and study of the impact of urban congestion on open space are immediate and important issues for geographical futurology. In all cases, forecasting discontinuities in the direction and rate of change is the key to valid and productive trend projections.*

"*Après nous le déluge,*" Madame de Pompadour is supposed to have said in 1757, after the Battle of Rossbach, with a whiff of the Revolution in her nostrils. She might have spoken for all those who flinch from contemplating the future from the vantage point of "these most brisk and giddy-paced times." "I never think of the future," said Einstein in 1930. "It comes soon enough." So, too, Sir Cyril Hinshelwood, FRS, addressing the Royal Society on its tercentenary in 1960:

Reprinted with permission from *The Australian Geographer*, 11 (1971): 510—521.

> *The literary basis of so much history can easily falsify the perspective....*
> *A few dramatists can characterize a whole period as licentious; even*
> *resolutions of undergraduate debating societies, if they catch the fancy of*
> *the journalists, may help to fix a label on an age. But the future germinates*
> *unknown and silently.*[1]

Given the uncertain prospects that cloud academic life in the 1970s, it is little wonder that geographers have largely turned their backs—sometimes in despair, often cynically—on the think tanks and scenario-composing, the normative statements of alternatives, the guiding predictions and their canonic variations, that now fascinate the futurologists. But in neglecting the future, geographers have been intimidated by the dimensions of time as they have never been by the dimensions of space. What follows is nothing more than a modest plea for the calculated meshing together of geography and futurology.

If one searches the recent geographical literature for what H. G. Wells called "the shape of things to come,"[2] one may find instead that, as a small profession, we have scarcely described the shape of the present. Why, then, should our efforts be dissipated still further by joining forces with those sociologists, economists, and political scientists whose concerted efforts to brainstorm the next thirty years have created futurology?

There are three justifications for doing so. Firstly, the future deserves more scholarly and intrinsically analytic attention than journalists, politicians, and the dreamers of science fiction can reasonably provide. Secondly, geographers have a distinctive contribution to make, without which futurology can only suffer. Thirdly, attention to the future could bring into a common focus much of the presently unrelated work in empirical and theoretical geography, thereby rewarding the discipline itself handsomely. This essay simply tries to amplify these arguments.

Forerunners of Futurology

According to the philsopher John Wilkinson,[3] the term "futurology" was coined in 1949 by the historian Ossip Flechtheim to classify those contemporary studies which try "to put all temporal species [past, present *and* future] together in a rational and coherent structure." Since the future appears to be "fully available," what matters is "its growth, its rootedness in past and present, its potential being."[4] Futurology may be distinguished from such free-floating enterprises as science fiction and Utopian design by its explicit insistence on relating the future to both past and present.

Not that futurology has no past. In *The Future In America*, H. G. Wells himself finds his own "prophetic habit of mind" anticipated in the Heraclitian maxim: *There is no Being but Becoming.* "This habit of mind," he wrote, "confronts and perplexes my sense of things that simply *are*, with my brooding preoccupation with how they will shape presently, what they will lead to, what seed they will sow and how they will wear."[5] The skyscrapers of lower Manhattan reminded him "quite irresistably of piled-up packing cases outside a warehouse," out of which would come "the real thing, palaces and noble places, free, high circumstances, and space and leisure, light and fine living for the sons of men. . . ."[6]

The Wellsian enchantment with technological change also foreshadowed the futurologists. In 1936, for example, C. C. Furnas published *The Next Hundred Years*, which he subtitled "The Unfinished Business of Science."[7] In scope and single-minded intent, this work surpasses even *The World in 1984*, an anthology of some hundred medium-range forecasts edited by Nigel Calder from the pages of the *New Scientist*.[8] Calder's collaborators, celebrated and level-headed specialists almost to a man, seldom resort to the pentecostal sermons that pepper Furnas' work. For them, the future is no longer charged so emotionally with uncertainty, and its planned determination is clearly within their capabilities. Whereas Calder is cautiously optimistic, Furnas cannot forget the human casualties of scientific progress, even at the occasional risk of resembling a latter-day Luddite: "If it were not for dangers of plagiarism this book should be named The Shape of Things Yet to Be Done, for it deals not only with the things that should be but must be done before we can rightfully use the word Progress."[9]

This contrast in attitudes between Calder and Furnas, so far as monitoring the social consequences of scientific research is concerned, calls into question a caustic view of futurology advanced by Donald G. MacRae, the British sociologist. With an asperity commonly found in review articles he observes that we live "in an age obsessed by our anxieties and therefore by the desire to fix and reify tomorrow that we may at least behave more practically today." He further contends that "such anxieties are particularly to be found in rich and bloated eras, in societies at once learned and cruel,"[10] whether in ancient Rome or neo-Christendom. Whether the black arts of futurology are more symptomatic of today's troubles may well be doubted. Not only has "future-writing" enjoyed a long and uninterrupted vogue, but if the same black arts are conjured up by Furnas and Calder out of such dissimilar contexts as the Great Depression and the advent of Sputnik, what becomes of MacRae's analogy? Regardless of historical context, practical Utopians have found in it the need for enlightened change, not bored inaction.

Futurology and the Social Sciences

More acceptable schemata of Utopian activity have been devised by W. H. G. Armytage[11] and Frank Manuel[12] in their historical studies. Both writers expose the roots of the all too bewildering jungle that now flourishes in the glasshouse of futurology. Manuel traces a succession of new themes and fashions in the "utopian dreaming" (or "waking-dreams") of each period since Sir Thomas More published his prototype in 1516: the earliest are the "utopias of calm felicity," where an "Epicurian-Stoic" might find his self-fulfillment; next, the "open-ended" Utopias of the nineteenth century which, following the French Revolution, recast Utopia in a much more dynamic, socialist, and externally-determined mould; and most recently, the "contemporary eupsychias" in which psychological and philosophical problems overshadow the economic. Like Manuel, Armytage also correlates Utopian fads with the historical episodes that spawn them, but his matrix is a finer and more subtle mesh, and there is more than a hint of the teleological fallacy in his announced theme: "the rise of . . . 'conflict models' of prediction out of what might otherwise be regarded as a welter of futuristic fantasies."[13]

Even so, Armytage does explain how "a constructive debate about tomorrow is emerging, providing us with operational models of what tomorrow could, or should, be," thereby enabling modern man "to maintain his equilibrium." The principal vehicle of this debate is what he calls the "surmising forum,"[14] a "sodality" of scientists, intellectuals, national advisory commissions, and assorted futurologists. Among the better known of these are the *Commission on the Year 2000*, established in 1965 by the American Academy of Arts and Sciences and funded by the Carnegie Corporation;[15] and Bertrand de Jouvenel's *Futuribles*, "a research organization formed in Paris [in 1961], thanks to the aid of the Ford Foundation, by a small group presenting a wide range of nationalities and specialities, brought together by a common conviction that the social sciences should orient themselves toward the future."[16]

Confining futurology to the social sciences, of course, is to jettison much of the baggage on the bandwagon. Should it really exclude the engineer's contribution to technological forecasting, except when it has some social impact? Should it ignore the creative artist's vision of the future, even in the genres of science fiction and such films as Stanley Kubrick's *2001: A Space Odyssey*, or his earlier *Dr. Strangelove?* If the biomedical sciences are omitted, or communications technology, who then will begin to comprehend what Marshall McLuhan and others are saying about the role of the mass media in alienating youth, creating the generation gap, glorifying psychedelic freak-outs, or, to take another tack, disseminating propaganda during democratic election campaigns?[17]

Geographers, in particular, may wonder how their traditional notions of space can cope with the diffusion of ideas and images by the mass media, when the diffusion itself is aimed at (and swallowed by) *age*-specific sections of the population that are not segregated *spatially* from the remainder. Conversely, to consider cases where such sections *have* been isolated physically, an important geographical study remains to be done of those drop-out hideaways in the American West, where hippie communities have fled to avoid cultural assimilation in the great melting pot of modern times.[18] In Dennis Hopper's film, *Easy Rider*, these opposing social forces of inclusion and exclusion clash with devastating mutual intolerance, yet are conveyed spatially in picaresque form as the travels of a latter-day Don Quixote, with Sancho Panza in tow. Surely, if this is how the younger generation perceives "the spatial organization of society," á la Morrill,[19] geographers should watch futurology like hawks. Despite academic appearances, it is no longer a non-subject propped up by non-books.[20]

Often quite explicitly, the other social sciences have already come to terms with futurology. In a wide-ranging survey of how sociologists are responding to the study of the future,[21] Henry Winthrop asks his colleagues to choose consciously which values their research will serve. He dismisses as complacent self-deception the pursuit of *value-free* conjectures about the future, despite the "psychic investments" already made by sociologists in such a quest, but willingly admits the relevance of science and technology, from which he contends most social change now derives. Not surprisingly, he casts sociologists, for all their lassitude, as the fuglemen of the future.

More reassuredly at home with futurology, however, are the economists, whose self-confidence—stemming from decades in the hot seats of decision making—is exemplified in Andrew Shonfield's "Thinking About the Future."[22] Although Shonfield casts his net well beyond conventional market economics, his central concern is the reappraisals economists must make if their methods and concepts are to serve futurology. Like Winthrop, he advocates taking a long and flexible view of shifting social goals, especially by way of cross-national comparisons, and pleads for an appreciation that social investment programmes (like R&D in business) require a long lead-time, a minimum critical size, and a trade-off between such incompatibles as the wishes of private consumers and the collective amenity rights of society. To counteract "the primacy accorded to statistics based on the long-term projection of national income figures" (in a specific comment on Herman Kahn and Anthony J. Wiener's *The Year 2000*[23]), Shonfield also exhorts non-economists to engage in forecasting—so that "futurology remains allied to fantasy."

Allied to history, however, futurology has only aggravated certain open wounds inflicted on that field by its professional practitioners—if their own testimony is to be believed. The logic of the situation is such that most historians would absolutely deny the propriety of their studying the future. Paradoxically, however, this may well be one way around the impasse several contemporary historians believe themselves to be in—an impasse described by Carl Bridenbaugh as "The Great Mutation,"[24] and by J. H. Plumb as "The Death of the Past."[25] Both historians were referring to the way in which modern men have increasingly discarded the lessons of history, have cut themselves adrift from the past, finding it almost completely irrelevant to the modern world of science and unprecedented change. In Bridenbaugh's words, we have witnessed "the inexorable substitution of an artificial environment and a materialistic outlook on life for the old natural environment and spiritual world view that linked us so irrevocably to the Recent and Distant Pasts."

Severed from the past by what Sir Keith Hancock calls "our theorizing . . . our affluence, our gadgetry, our urbanization, [and] our secularization,"[26] future historians may be unable to recapture those dear, dead days, beyond recall. But if history may be defined as the study of "other times than the present," historians could become brilliant futurologists. In Cincinnati, my own graduate seminar in historical geography compares two transitions—that of rural America into urban America during the period after 1880, and that of the present into the future, into Daniel Bell's "Post-Industrial Society."[27] This latter transition, if monitored and analysed by historians as meticulously and exhaustively as their discipline dictates, could provide the intellectual bridge that connects us all with the past—if only historians will redefine their field to encompass "other times than the past." Many already do,[28] and may yet prove Plumb and Bridenbaugh to have been mistaken.

Futurology and Geography

Where, amidst the confusion summarized above, does geography fit? The remainder of this essay consists of conjecture about its potential relationships with futurology. Four parts of the interface are considered: (i) changes in scale and emphasis that geographical research may undergo in the next decade or so; (ii) strategies for the geographical study of the future; (iii) geographical forecasting and planning; and (iv) subfields of geography likely to achieve prominence if futurology bursts upon us.

That the scale and emphasis of geographical research are affected profoundly by changes in research methods is surely a platitude—witness the outgrowth of computer mapping from electronic data processing, or the easy accommodation of both the older "aerial photography" and the newer "hyperaltitude (satellite) photography"[29] within the ambit of "remote sensing." It is equally certain that geographers, like the rest of mankind, are seduced by fads: if one post-graduate student doodles with SYMAP, the others must, and the only theses worth attempting become those that employ the latest techniques, or those "instant exercises" for which pre-digested, computer-packaged data are immediately available. For such geographers, the future may look more like a barrel of molasses than an isarithmic surface.

This convergence of methods and topics encourages us to confuse the present topic, the "geography of the future," with "the future of geography."[30] Obviously if more geographers do study the future, geography itself cannot help but change. After all, it can only be what geographers do. Assuming, then, that new techniques are developed and disseminated, on what dance will they lead geography—as a substantive field?

To be rash and superficial, it might be argued that improvements in research techniques extend either the detail attainable or the capacity to process data. The first favors "micro-studies," the second "macro-studies," if one may resurrect two Aunt Sallies buried ages ago by O. H. K. Spate.[31] That is, to some extent, one development runs counter to the other, so that particularity is sacrificed to generality, or vice versa. Greater detail, which Haggett terms "fidelity"[32] and novelists used to call "veri-similitude," also favours attention to individual cases or people, whereas enhanced data-handling capacity tends to inspire the study of aggregates. Within geography, both these contrasting tendencies are at work. The first is to be seen in studies of consumer behavior, locational decision making, and of ways in which individuals perceive their spatial environment.[33] The second has enlisted systems analysis—with its ramifications into linear and heuristic programming, game theory, and other cybernetic models[34]—as an aid to comprehending the interrelated processes at work within large and complex "functional entities." Between these ever-widening extremes of scale, geographers are free to emphasize certain human groups, and certain "spatial contexts" (or "regions," in a broad sense), much more frequently in the future.

To take one example, those whose focal interest Ullman has called "a perception-behaviour assessment often of irrational activities affecting space"[35] have already begun to share with psychologists and urban designers a concern for human idiosyncracies which was quite foreign to geography until fairly recently. Sonnenfeld, for example, has not only calibrated levels of human interaction with the "behavioural environment,"[36] but has categorized the "environmental personality" of individuals—their "predisposition to behave [in a certain way] within the context of . . . the geographic environment of space, resources, and landscape."[37] Such studies may betray a growing concern with *enclosed* space, with the urban setting and interiors of buildings where we are living so much more of our lives. Indeed, the emerging "classics" may be Kevin Lynch's *The Image of the City*,[38] or Robert Sommer's *Personal Space*[39] (with its analyses of places for refuge, learning, drinking, and dreaming), or Gordon Cullen's *Townscape*.[40] As an antithesis, is it fanciful to detect an "agrarian" outlook and a scale of investigation more appropriate to the "open frontier" in the regional studies produced by geographers during the first half of this century?

New research emphases may also lend greater prominence to studies of certain population groups; not the immigrants and ethnic minorities who have received what may be a disproportionate share of geographical attention in the past, but the new "problem" groups—the alienated young, the drop-outs, the radicals, the "loners," the drug addicts, the elderly and superannuated, those trapped in poverty, and those with leisure to burn. If gigantic "intellectual communities" gather together in Clark Kerr's "multiversities,"[41] as a logical outcome of Michael Young's "Rise of the Meritocracy,"[42] and if theoretical knowledge does become *the* growth industry, as so many expect, geographers might want to devote more attention to the spatial ordering peculiar to such communities. Students themselves are eager to understand their campuses, not to mention the adjacent communities where their own impact is paramount, and might be enlisted more often in research projects of this kind.[43]

In wider perspective, these concerns are strands in a web of "action-orientation" that has entangled the social sciences in recent years, and threatens to make "contemporary relevance" the main criterion for the allocation of research funds. Many geographers share Raymond A. Bauer's dissatisfaction with the statistical "social indicators" now used by governments "to assess where we stand and are going with respect to our values and goals."[44] Many are committed to Peace Research, to resource management and public policy, to planning, area development, and applied geography generally. In 1969, at the Annual Business Meeting of the Association of American Geographers in Ann Arbor, Michigan, many of these concerns were consolidated in the unprecedented and successful "Resolution on National Priorities."[45] Only an incorrigible cynic could read into this resolution the beatification of an interest group within the profession, and only the valiant and venerable could "note with sadness" the political activism it implied, reminding us that "the business of geography is geography, not politics."[46]

Strategies for Studying the Future

Quite unsympathetic to this reaction are those whose futurology is too complex and urgent to be left to scholars working in self-imposed (and even self-indulgent) isolation. They see big business and big government controlling the infrastructure of the economy, rendering the study of the individual product, of "local" government, or even individual enterprise, at worst antiquarian and at best marginal to understanding of the sort that affects big decisions. The planner must do more than recommend change. In Leonard J. Duhl's views, "he must know how to guide change as the therapist guides his patient." In "our system," therefore, he must be "an astute politican [engaged in the] process of conciliation and reconciliation, of accommodation between competing interests."[47]

What strategies, then, are appropriate for studying the future if the goal is effective and timely intervention in the course of events, or, to use Edmund Leach's phrase, to bring our "runaway world" under human control?[48] For without question, futurology has boomed largely because a glut of unexpected and incomprehensible changes has left bewilderment in its wake, and because "the pace with which such changes are taking place has reduced the reliability of practical experience as a guide to public policy and has diminished the usefulness of conventional judgment in dealing with social problems."[49]

Paralysed as individuals, those who might be regarded as futurologists have joined forces in the "surmising forums" mentioned above. In one way, these may be interpreted as formal outgrowths of the "invisible colleges" of individuals who have communicated with one another over the years, and whose personal correspondence has fashioned an informal network of scientific communication complementary to that of the journals, congresses, and institutes which serve the larger scientific establishment. Thus constituted, surmising forums obviously tend to be inter-disciplinary teams of intellectuals whose bent is mainly towards application, innovation, and almost stream-of-consciousness creativity. The "working parties" of the American Academy's *Commission on the Year 2000* are good examples, organized as they are around such sweeping themes as "the life cycle of the individual," "the social impact of the computer," and "intellectual institutions."[50]

Within the whole spectrum of surmising forums, however, the Commission represents only the middle ground, where concern with the future is spasmodic but protracted. Other forums lay claim to larger or lesser interests, Samuel Z. Klausner's symposium on *The Study of Total Societies* signalling one extreme.[51] No less alert to the untidy altogetherness of things, but focused more narrowly, are such research organizations as Resources for the Future (RFF), whose 1970 "Conference on Research Possibilities on Nonmetropolitan Problems and Prospects" brought together a typical complement of seventeen spare-time futurologists—a demographer, political scientist, historian, rural sociologist, several economists (regional, theoretical, and agricultural), representatives from the Farm Foundation and the Ford Foundation, three research directors from RFF, and two geographers—both of us from Cincinnati.[52] Our discussions were expected to transcend the exchange of anecdotes about previous research on nonmetropolitan problems; indeed, our proclaimed purpose was "to consider together what research ought to be undertaken, where it might best be done, by whom, and where the money might come from."[53]

One proposal[54] was to segregate studies administratively according to institutions, so that empirical work was undertaken primarily in the land grant colleges, where state investment funds were already appropriated for such purposes, while theoretical studies of nonmetropolitan America were concentrated in the *non*-land grant colleges. Foundations, it was suggested, might abide by some such rule of thumb in deciding which research proposals to finance. Even so, universities are inevitably encumbered by their teaching programmes, and those located in metropolitan areas find increasingly that strained relations with local communities demand an urban involvement that deflects research away from rural problems or foreign areas. Instead, the luxury of contemplating the future, unobstructed by "disgruntled stockholders or rebellious students or disenfranchised voters," has been cornered by the "think tanks."[55]

These "private problem-solving organizations," idolized by the popular press for "thinking the unthinkable" with such megalomaniac distinction, began in many instances as adjuncts to government agencies, largely for policy research and military planning, but have since branched into predicting the stock market, the appearance of new consumer durables, and the incidence of violence. The Hudson Institute and the RAND Corporation are among the best known. Unlike universities, where common humanity is much too firmly entrenched, think tanks hark back to the shrines of oracles whose prophetic powers were in part magic, in part their seclusion from the society which consulted them. In the long run, it seems unlikely that think tanks will become the cathedrals of futurology.

Theory or Imagination

No matter where it is undertaken, the study of the future poses some nice methodological issues, many of them (to judge by the last four paragraphs) regaled in the Emperor's new clothes. For many geographers, Holy Writ states that prediction depends on the generation of sound theory, and geographers will cope with the future only when their theoreticians return from the deserts of quantification. My only comments are skeptical and suggestive of alternative approaches, although I hesitate (half-heartedly) to agree with de Jouvenel that "it is utterly implausible that a mathematical formula should make the future known to us, and those who think it can would once have believed in witchcraft."[56]

"In the long run the quality of geography in this century will be judged less by its sophisticated techniques or its exhaustive detail, than by the strength of its logical reasoning." Thus Peter Haggett, winding up *Locational Analysis in Human Geography.*[57] G. H. Dury also finds our best hope for the progress of geography in those "well-known and well-tried methods of scientific controversy," where colliding evidence and contrasted views may be resolved, and geographical judgements crystallized, through the orderly conflict of rival hypotheses.[58] Daniel Bell sums up the prevailing view:

> *What has now become decisive for the organization of decisions and the control of change is the centrality of theoretical knowledge—the primacy of the theory over empiricism, and the codification of knowledge into abstract systems of symbols that can be utilized to illuminate many different and varied circumstances.*[59]

Out of theoretical knowledge come innovation and policy analysis, as attested by the ever-expanding role of basic science in applied technology, and of economic theory in economic policy. Indeed, the sociologists Glaser and Strauss have reacted in such dismay to the everlasting verification of *existing* theory by empiricists (when the generation of *new* theory seems so imperative), that they have produced a manual on how to dredge theory directly from data.[60]

Nothing kills theories like data, of course, and a few cautionary fellows persist in claiming a place for empirical studies, even if data for the year 2000 have to be found in a crystal ball. However, despite very reassuring advances in electronic data processing, some futurologists fear a public backlash if further invasions of "privacy" are mounted by census collectors, market analysts, and other survey teams, and despair that starving data banks may cripple research. If they are right, more frequent recourse may have to be had to unobtrusive, non-reactive measures,[61] to surrogate indices of indeterminable authenticity, and to remote sensing.

Before turning to geographical forecasting—the real nub of the matter—the probable format of published futurology deserves a passing note, since hard-nosed geographers have been trained like racehorses to write up their work in a rut of hypotheses, conceptual frameworks, and inductive or deductive principles, building only out of verifiable facts. Being different, even letterwriting is a difficult genre for some geographers, let alone the dream-like fantasies that pass for portraits of the future. Fortunately, the perception school of behavioural geographers has now restored the respectability of imaginative writing, once almost exclusively the handmaiden of historical geography. Yet the reverence for neither more nor less than the indestructible facts dies tediously. As exemplary an historian as George F. Kennan has confessed how he stewed inwardly over adding "a tethered nanny goat" to his description of the railway bridge spanning a border stream between Finland and the Soviet Union, not knowing whether a goat was actually there in 1918, but never having seen similar Russian settings without one.[62]

One model for writing about the future is the "scenario"—a hypothetical sequence of events that could lead plausibly to one of several "alternative futures." Kahn and Wiener have popularized this model by simulating how the escalation of international conflict through certain stages might trigger off nuclear war.[63] They claim that, by focusing attention on "causal processes and decision-points," scenarios help the analyst (or Duhl's "therapist-planner") to get a "gut-feel" for the cocoon of interwoven events that constitutes an "alternative future," and for the "branching points dependent upon critical choices" along the way. That is, they oblige a writer to relate events to one another in narrative form. Scenarios also stimulate and discipline the imagination, dampen out unconscious "carry-over thinking" from irrelevant previous experiences, and force a novice at futurology "to plunge into the unfamiliar and rapidly changing world" of the future. Lending itself as it does to exaggeration, parody, satire, and the dramatic or casual introduction of paranoid personalities, the scenario is already represented by some truly galvanic essays, among them Harold Orlans' "Between Fragmentation and Cohesion,"[64] a macabre perversion of America in the year 2000, and Randolph

Churchill's "The Queendom of the United States"[65]—women's liberation run riot following the coronation of Her Federal Majesty Miss Marlene Dietrich, the first American monarch (or rather, matriarch), in 1960.

Among geographical scenarios, O. H. K. Spate's "Progress at Mbananakoro"[66] is an early classic, but how many other geographers have the temerity, wit, or sense of priorities to put their own reputations on the firing line and devise others? How many of us are capable of cooking up "alternative spatial or ecological futures" for some familiar nation or region or city, or even for an isotropic plane that cannot snap back? Geographers who engage in the profession and practice of futurology may well have to seek their paragons outside the discipline, or else, like Daedalus, spread the wings of their own self-assuredness and tackle really wide-ranging analyses of complicated issues, as the economists and sociologists have done for years. Is there a geographer alive who could probe the "transitory and permanent factors" responsible for "Unstable America" with quite the same credibility, insight, and audacity as Daniel Bell?[67]

Geographical Forecasting

Geographers might protest, of course, that they should be no more expected to contemplate the whole universe than a butcher should—that their job, like his, is restricted by convention (and reinforced by training) to one part of the universe, or to one way of exploring it. Their forecasts, unlike Bell's, should focus upon neither the individual human condition nor the stresses within society, but rather, to paraphrase Taafe, upon the evolving spatial organization of the earth as expressed in patterns and processes.[68] That is, a geographical forecast for 1980, say, would refer to a particular part of the earth's surface, and might indicate the probable distribution of its population and resources, the circulation of people and commodities (possibly in some cycle of production and consumption, or in a migration manifold), and various kinds of spatial interaction and areal association.

To many geographers, such an exercise will seem insufficiently dynamic and unduly concerned with pattern. They will inquire by what processes and stages, and through what intervening patterns, is the present spatial organization of the region expected to become that of 1980? Or if this earth-bound horoscope for 1980 is really an expression of local goals, they will want to know (being practical futurologists) what plans, policies, legislation, resource deployment, readjustments, and hardships will be necessary to attain these. In short, they will demand a trajectory, not simply a target—however independently difficult to determine the latter may prove to be.

Studies of spatial diffusion, if projected into the future, have an obvious place in such geographical forecasting, whether in the empirical identification of leading and lagging sub-regions within the zone of diffusion, or as simulations of innovation waves.[69] Diffusion studies also have the virtue of grafting a spatial dimension to the larger field of technological forecasting. Indeed, if technological change proceeds through the three stages of invention, innovation, and diffusion,[70] and if its translation into social change is accomplished mainly through the diffusion of existing techniques and "privileges" from only a few centres of invention, rather than through ubiquitous innovation, geographical forecasting deserves a much more exalted role in futurology than it presently enjoys.

How else might geographers attempt to predict the "evolving spatial organization of the earth?" A random selection of potentially useful approaches, at least in the "spatial tradition" of geography, may be illustrated by current research at the University of Cincinnati. Wolf, for example, has harnessed together two vintage ideas—demographic trend analysis and Blumenfeld's concept of the metropolitan tidal wave—to produce a graphic and persuasive account of population redistribution in Ohio for the entire twentieth century.[71] His study is not only rich with planning implications, but exemplifies the complementarity of empiricism and theory in discerning the future. In another study which tries to ascertain where specific types of manufacturing plants might be sited, Stafford has turned from the traditional theories of industrial location to the simulation of managerial decision making, and is testing what he terms a "Location Decision Discrimination Net"—a filtering system which screens out all but the "correct locations."[72] My own Appalachian research is an evaluation of the future central place system envisaged by one regional planning commission.[73] Like Stafford's work (although here the resemblance ends), it is addressed, in muted tones, to those potent but unknown gentlemen who will make the next decisions, and thereby discipline the future.

Beyond Cincinnati, certainly, and probably beyond any precedent in the history of the field, new life has also been discovered in the ecological, or man-land tradition of geography. This vitality and urgency, underwritten by the currently ecumenical "environmental crisis,"[74] seems likely to arouse in many geographers a lively and perhaps abiding concern for the future impact of technology and human population growth on the delicate and destructable environment that sustains life on earth. A curious consortium of interests has congregated under this umbrella. As usual, there are opportunists, publicists, and composers of such programmatic agenda as the present essay, some of whom see another golden moment for redefining geography nearer their heart's desire.[75] Nevertheless, several salient directions in geographical scholarship appear to be converging on a common concern for the future quality of the environment. By good fortune, however, neither the call for applied geography in a technical sense, nor that for geographical contributions to the formulation of planning policy, has gone unheeded.[76]

What interests have bought stock in this consortium? Understandably, conservationists and those eager to improve resource management have been among the first to commit themselves.[77] Recreational geography, too, has found an almost conciliatory role in assessing, predicting, and even moderating the impact of urban congestion on open space. As Ullman points out, such novelty attaches to certain recreational schemes that the extrapolation of trends to predict their effects is simply out of the question; instead, forecasts must be based upon "geographical analogs," that is, upon studies of "comparable" projects elsewhere.[78] Nor is it surprising that the perceptionist/behaviourist school of geographers is also well represented, since values, habits, and attitudes underpin the urge to flee from polluted, crime-saturated surroundings into the feral wilderness, where the "quest for purity and virtue in the outdoors" can be indulged more leniently, as David Lowenthal has noted, amidst the "luxuries of camping."[79] And what premonitions should we see in Lionel Tiger's lament at the continued training of "biologically ignorant social scientists,"[80] now that Robert Ardrey's *The Territorial Imperative* and similar works persuasively convey the importance of ethology (the study of animal behaviour) to an understanding of "the naked ape" himself? Are we to anticipate some new synthesis of human and physical geography founded upon a universal concern for the future quality of the environment?

Conclusion

If those of us in the "spatial or geometrical tradition" of geography can reorient our research toward the future in the practical ways suggested above, and if those of us in the "ecological or man-milieu tradition" can tolerate such strange bedfellows when survival is imperilled, is there no futurology for regional geographers of the maligned "antimacassar school of thought?"[81] Here, perhaps, one interface with futurology is the study and attempted resolution, *by some future date*, of problems presently confined to specific regions—to coastlines, or the Scottish Highlands,[82] or depopulating rural areas beyond the effective service hinterlands of metropolitan cities,[83] or the "hollows" and "ghettos" shut off from the mainstream of society. Another possibility is to invent regional geographies of the future—"new maps of hell," so to speak. *London 2000* has already been tried,[84] but a regional geographer steeped in historiography might reflect upon the global patterns implicit in Kahn and Wiener's *The Year 2000*, or Orwell's *1984*. To such work, Brian Goodey's recent cartographic reconstruction of Sir Thomas More's "Utopia" is a neat antithesis.[85] In fact, one might plead that historical geographers experienced in "retrodiction" (Gilbert Ryle's term for "establishing what the past must have been like on the basis of present evidence") should occasionally turn their thoughts, skills, and sensibilities through 180 degrees, towards "prediction."

In all these prospects, however, there lurks an ever-present danger in the facile projection of past trends. As Peter F. Drucker argues, the unsuspected and apparently insignificant *discontinuities* in development, rather than "the massive momentum of apparent trends, are likely to shape and mould our tomorrow."[86] The real trick is to forecast discontinuities in the direction and rate of change, to anticipate the "demographic inflection" on the logistic curve (where growth rates start to dwindle), to understand how the attainment of certain thresholds or saturation limits or densities effects a discontinuity in the evolving spatial organization of the earth.

David Lodge has written "that there have been two major, sustained attempts to create Utopia in modern history. . . . The first was America, and the second the Soviet Union."[87] I think also of Australia, that third modern Utopia, whose geographers could brainstorm its future so profitably and profoundly. For where else in the world does the future germinate quite so silently and quite so unknown?

References

1. Sir C. Hinshelwood, "The Royal Society after 300 Years," *The Listener* 64 (1960): 81.

2. The title of one of his books, published in 1933 by Macmillan, New York.

3. J. Wilkinson, "Futuribles: Innovation vs. Stability," *Center Diary* 17: (1967) 25.

4. O. K. Flechtheim, *History and Futurology* (Verlag Anton Hain K. G., 1966).

5. H. G. Wells, *The Future of America* (New York: Harper and Brothers, 1906), p. 4.

6. *Ibid.*, p. 258.

7. C. C. Furnas, *The Next Hundred Years* (New York: Reynel and Hitchcock, 1936).

8. 2 vols. (London: Penguin Ltd., 1965).

9. Furnas, *op. cit.*, p. 5.

10. D. G. MacRae, "The Futurity Play," *Encounter* 34 (1970): 90.

11. W. H. G. Armytage, *Yesterday's Tomorrows—A Historical Study of Future Societies* (London: Routledge & Kegan, 1968).

12. F. Manuel, "Toward a Psychological History of Utopias," *Daedalus* 94 (1965): 293—322.

13. Armytage, *op. cit.*, p. x.

14. *Ibid.*, pp. 170—201.

15. See "Toward the Year 2000—Work in Progress," *Daedalus* 96 (1967) especially the essays by Daniel Bell.

16. B. de Jouvenel, *The Art of Conjecture*, trans. N. Lary (New York: Basic Books, 1967), p. viii. De Jouvenel prefers the term "conjecture" to "futurology."

17. J. G. Blumler and D. McQuail, *Television in Politics* (London: Faber & Faber, 1969).

18. A. Carter, "Stealing is Bad Karma," *The Listener* 83 (1970): 855—858.

19. R. L. Morrill, *The Spatial Organization of Society* (Belmont, Calif.: Wadsworth Publishing Co., 1970).

20. An orientation course is provided by J. McHale, *The Future of the Future* (New York: Braziller, 1969).

21. H. Winthrop, "The Sociologist and the Study of the Future," *American Sociologist* 3 (1968): 136—45.

22. A. Shonfield, "Thinking About the Future," *Encounter* 32 (1969): 15—26.

23. H. Kahn and A. J. Wiener, *The Year 2000—A Framework for Speculation on the Next Thirty-Three Years* (New York: Macmillan, 1967).

24. C. Bridenbaugh, "The Great Mutation," *American Historical Review* 68 (1963): 316.

25. J. H. Plumb, *The Death of the Past* (London: Macmillan, 1970).

26. Sir K. Hancock, "Ordeal by Thesis," *Australian Humanities Research Council Annual Report, 1965-66* (Sydney: Sydney University Press, 1966), pp. 25—36.

27. Our texts are W. C. Rohrer and L. H. Douglas, *The Agrarian Transition in America* (Indianapolis: Bobbs-Merrill, 1969); and "Toward the Year 2000—Work in Progress," *Daedalus* 96 (1967).

28. R. L. Heilbroner, *The Future as History* (New York: Harper & Row, 1959).

29. N. J. W. Thrower, "Annals Map Supplement Number Twelve: Land Use in the Southwestern United States—From Gemini and Apollo Imagery," *Annals of the Association of American Geographers* 60 (1970): 208—9.

30. H. Carol, "Geography of the Future," *Professional Geographer* 13 (1961): 14—18.

31. O. H. K. Spate, "Quantity and Quality in Geography" *Annals of the Association of American Geographers* 50 (1960): 390.

32. P. Haggett, "Models in Geography," (Seminar Paper, University of Cincinnati).

33. E. J. Taffe, ed., *Geography—The Behavioral and Social Sciences Survey* (Englewood Cliffs, N. J.: Prentice-Hall, 1970), pp. 89—98.

34. R. Boguslaw, *The New Utopians—A Study of System Design and Social Change* (Englewood Cliffs, N. J.: Prentice-Hall, 1965).

35. E. L. Ullman, in *Problems and Trends in American Geography*, ed. S. B. Cohen (New York: Basic Books, 1967), p. 127.

36. T. F. Saarinen, *Perception of Environment*, Resource Paper No. 5, Commission on College Geography (Washington, D. C.: Association of American Geographers, 1969), pp. 5—6.

37. J. Sonnenfeld, "Personality and Behaviour in Environment," *Proceedings of the Association of American Geographers* 1 (1969): 136—40.

38. K. Lynch, *The Image of the City* (Cambridge, Mass.: MIT Press, 1960).

39. R. Sommer, *Personal Space—The Behavioral Basis of Design* (Englewood Cliffs, N. J.: Prentice-Hall, 1969).

40. G. Cullen, *Townscape* (London: Architectural Press, 1969).

41. C. Kerr, *The Uses of the University* (Cambridge, Mass.: Harvard University Press, 1964).

42. M. Young, *The Rise of the Meritocracy* (London: Thames & Hudson, 1958).

43. One such attempt is described in B. Ryan, D. Cooke, and C. Neale, "Project Cincinnati Campus," *Journal of Higher Education* (1971).

44. R. A. Bauer, ed., *Social Indicators* (Cambridge, Mass.: MIT Press, 1967).

45. W. C. Calef, "Annual Business Meeting. Ann Arbor, August, 1969," *Professional Geographer* 21 (1969): 413—15.

46. G. F. Carter to the Editors, *Professional Geographer* 22 (1970): 100.

47. L. J. Duhl, "Planning and Predicting: or What To Do When You Don't Know the Names of the Variables," *Daedalus* 96 (1967): 782.

48. E. Leach, "A Runaway World? Men and Nature," *The Listener* 78 (1967): 621—4.

49. Kahn and Wiener, *op. cit.*, p. 3.

50. *Daedalus* 96 (1967): 979—84.

51. S. Z. Klausner, ed., *The Study of Total Societies* (New York: Doubleday, 1967).

52. M. Clawson and J. A. Schnittker, "Nonmetropolitan America: Problems and Prospects," paper delivered at Conference on Research Possibilities on Nonmetropolitan Problems and Prospects, Resources for the Future, Washington, D.C., May, 1970.

53. M. Clawson to Resources for the Future Conference participants, February 2, 1970.

54. By J. R. Hildreth, Managing Director of The Farm Foundation, Chicago.

55. The Twentieth Century Fund, *Annual Report* (New York: 1968) pp. 16—17.

56. B. de Jouvenel, *op. cit.*, p. 173.

57. P. Haggett, *Locational Analysis in Human Geography* (New York: St. Martin's Press), p. 310.

58. G. H. Dury, "Rival Hypotheses—Some Aspects of Geographical Judgement-Forming," *Australian Journal of Science* 30 (1968): 357—62.

59. D. Bell, "The Measurement of Knowledge and Technology," in *Indicators of Social Change*, ed. E. B. Sheldon and W. E. Moore (New York: Russell Sage Foundation, 1968) pp. 155—6.

60. B. G. Glaser and A. L. Strauss, *The Discovery of Grounded Theory—Strategies for Qualitative Research* (Chicago: Aldine, 1967).

61. E. J. Webb et al., *Unobtrusive Measures—Nonreactive Research in the Social Sciences* (Chicago: Rand McNally, 1968).

62. G. F. Kennan, "History as Literature," *Encounter* 12 (1959): 13—14.

63. Kahn and Wiener, *op. cit.*, p. 6: pp. 262—4.

64. H. Orlans, "Between Fragmentation and Cohesion—En Route to the Year 2000 A.D.," *Encounter* 34 (1970): 11—21.

65. R. S. Churchill III, "The Queendom of the United States—Royal Celebrations in Olde York. An Englishman's Reflections on the American Monarchy," *Encounter* 9 (1957): 19—25.

66. O. H. K. Spate, *Let Me Enjoy* (Canberra: Australian National University Press, 1965), pp. 66—87.

67. D. Bell, "Unstable America," *Encounter* 34 (1970): 11—26.

68. E. J. Taffe, ed., *op. cit.*, pp. 5—6.

69. P. R. Gould, *Spatial Diffusion*, Resource Paper No. 4, Commission on College Geography (Washington, D. C.: Association of American Geographers, 1969).

70. D. A. Schon, "Forecasting and Technological Forecasting," *Daedalus* 96 (1967): 759—70.

71. L. G. Wolf, "The Metropolitan Tidal Wave in Ohio, 1900-2000," *Economic Geography* 45 (1969): 138—54.

72. H. A. Stafford, "An Industrial Decision Location Model," *Proceedings of the Association of American Geographers* 1 (1969): 141—5.

73. B. Ryan, "The Criteria for Selecting Growth Centers in Appalachia," *Proceedings of the Association of American Geographers* 2 (1970): 118—23.

74. H. W. Helfrich, ed., *The Environmental Crisis* (New Haven: Yale University Press, 1970).

75. E. Waddell, "Methodology and Explanation in Cultural Geography, or, The Quest for an Interface in Man-Milieu Relationships," in *New Directions in Theoretical Cultural Geography*, papers prepared for the 60th Annual Meeting of the Association of American Geographers, San Francisco, 1970.

76. E. Darling and J. P. Milton, eds., *Future Environments of North America* (New York: Natural History Press, 1966).

77. P. Shepard and D. McKinley, eds., *The Subservise Science—Essays Toward an Ecology of Man* (Boston: Houghton Mifflin, 1969).

78. E. L. Ullman, *loc. cit.*

79. D. Lowenthal, "Recreational Habits and Values: Implications for Landscape Quality," in *Challenge for Survival*, ed. P. Dansereau, (New York: Columbia University Press, 1970), pp. 103—17.

80. L. Tiger, "The Dangers of Finding Something Out," *Encounter* 33 (1969): 59—63.

81. J. H. Paterson, *North America*, 4th ed. (New York: Oxford University Press, 1970), p. iv.

82. D. S. Thomson and I. Grimble, eds., *The Future of the Highlands* (London: Routledge & Kegan Paul, 1968).

83. B. Ryan, "Metropolitan Growth," in *Contemporary Australia*, ed. R. Preston (Durham, N. C.: Duke University Press, 1969), pp. 196—225.

84. P. Hall, *London 2000* (London: Faber & Faber, 1963).

85. B. R. Goodey, "Mapping 'Utopia'—A comment on the geography of Sir Thomas More," *Geographical Review* 60 (1970): 15—30.

86. P. F. Drucker, *The Age of Discontinuity* (New York: Harper & Row, 1968), p. ix.

87. D. Lodge, "Utopia and Criticism—The Radical Longing for Paradise," *Encounter* 33 (1969): 74.

Chapter 15

Predicting Urban Spatial Change

Donald G. Janelle
University of Western Ontario

ABSTRACT: *Spatial and temporal results of aggregate behavior provide a means of forecasting emergent patterns of urban land use. It is necessary to develop additional means of identifying social and technological innovations and techniques for monitoring the spatial responses to such innovations. But how can the geographical importance of a specific innovation be assessed, and what spatial changes can be attributed ot it? A model of spatial transformation that uses a dimensional approach (points, lines, surfaces, volumes, and motions) offers some help in analyzing the spatial impact of innovations. The time lag between invention and innovation seems to offer an opportunity for the application of the model and its future refinements. Should this be the case, future innovations may not catch us as unprepared as have previous changes.*

The prediction that 1 million new housing units will be required by 1980 to shelter the population of the Province of Ontario conjures an image of extensive physical changes within urban areas. In addition to housing and jobs, public and commercial services must be provided for the anticipated population. These new facilities must be superimposed upon, incorporated within, or added to existing cities. To this extent, parts of the present cities foretell the nature of the future whole.

Empirical evidence leads some to suggest that urban change is orderly; perceiving such order as geographic pattern is the basis of many conceptual models of urban growth and organization.[1] The crucial test of these and other models rests upon the logical extension of this reasoning—do these perceived patterns permit prediction? Given the pattern perceived or deduced from incomplete evidence, is it feasible to predict events in current or future blank spaces for which empirical data are lacking?

Approaches to Time-Spatial Change

Recent social science analysis of behavior and decision making focuses largely on individual actors. However, space-time manifestations of aggregate behavior should also be studied, for they may provide new insights for predicting the emergent pattern of cities. In fact, this approach may offer an expedient (though not necessarily sufficient) means for measuring man's space-time responses to technological and social innovations.

Changes in urban land use clearly illustrate the complex behavioral forces that shape the city. According to Chapin, land use patterns show "... the cumulative effect of myriad decisions and actions by households, institutions, corporate interests, and government stemming from profit making, livability and culturally rooted values."[2] Such combinations of policy-directed levers (taxation, land use controls, and so forth) and functionally competitive forces of market expansion and consumer preference preclude easy explanation of the patterns they produce. Ultimately, explanation of individual decision making will be essential, and current efforts in this direction should be extended. But meanwhile, tools for interpreting changes in aggregate behavior which enable us to derive process-oriented models of urban land use change will yield helpful intermediate results.

Deterministic models have been useful as an expedient, though not completely adequate, approach to explaining and predicting urban growth. In one of the more exhaustive of such studies, Milgram used a multiple regression analysis of land transactions in investigating urban expansion into northeastern Philadelphia from 1945 to 1962, and thereby identified factors relevant in the determination of land prices.[3] Such research provides empirical raw material that can be incorporated into deterministic as well as stochastic approaches to urban growth modelling. The approaches suggested by Garrison, Morrill, and Chapin are particularly worthy of study.[4] Bourne's studies of Toronto have made good use of land use transition probabilities in identifying regularities in the reorganization of inner-city areas.[5]

Further efforts at predicting the transformation of urban space will draw heavily upon such pioneering studies. However, progress toward comprehending current structural changes in our cities would be achieved if systematic attempts were made to identify and measure the geographical impacts of technological and social innovations.

Spatial Response to Innovation

Technological innovation involves channeling our understanding of nature into new human capacity. Social innovation is "... the diagnosis of social needs and opportunities and the development of concepts and institutions to satisfy them."[6] Technological and social innovation is always risky, because "present resources are committed to future, highly uncertain results. Present action and behavior are subordinated to the potential of an as yet unknown and uncomprehended future reality."[7] Social and technological innovations continually alter the choices open to urban planners. In this sense, planning innovations involve substantial risk, because damage frequently results from failure to adequately anticipate the future. To reduce the likelihood of such mistakes, means for measuring the spatial and social impacts of innovative forces are needed. To be more precise, answers to the following questions are needed:

> *How can the degree (or intensity) of innovation and the spatial responses to innovation be measured?*
>
> *What regularities of spatial development are associated with given technological and social innovations?*

Since answers to these questions concern predictability, it is necessary to specify the time-spatial context, the duration of time intervals and geographical scales which will be most revealing of relationships between innovations and spatial organization. If answers to these questions are found, it will then be possible competently to consider answers to socially relevant questions such as the following:

> *How can innovative forces be manipulated to yield the desired response in land use allocation and in other areas of spatial concern?*
>
> *Given an acceptable plan for a city, what combinations of social and technological innovations are necessary to carry it out?*

Given the state of the art, it is presumptuous to offer precise answers to questions of such complexity. At best, this discussion may suggest useful guidelines for seeking such answers.

Identification and Measurement of Spatially Relevant Innovation

Innovations are spatially relevant to the extent that they are space/linkage consuming, space/linkage adjusting, and space/linkage intensity-modifying. Suggested measures of consumption include number of units of area occupied, units of area occupied as a proportion of total area, and flow (for example, traffic) as a proportion of linkage capacity. Space/linkage adjustment represents the departure of patterns from previous and current trends. Adjustment processes include those which are space/linkage creating and space/linkage destroying. Thus, the construction of an expressway through a residential neighborhood produces new patterns of residential land use. Similarly, the interaction or linkage patterns of the area are likely to change in response to both the barrier effects of the expressway and the increased accessibility provided between certain areas of the urban environment. Space/linkage adjustment is measurable as a time-dependent rate of change in the ratio of phenomena per unit area or per unit distance. The space/linkage intensity-modifying characteristics of innovation are related to adjustment and consumption. They may be measured as rates of change in activity per unit area or as changes in the levels of interaction per unit of distance.

According to these definitions, all innovations have spatial relevance. Does this mean that it is necessary to specify and measure all innovations to understand spatial processes? Not necessarily. Transport improvements are especially significant geographically, but it is not essential to identify and comprehend *all* transportation innovations to understand their spatial implications; a few measurable and partially predictable characteristics of transport improvement are sufficient. For instance, travel time, travel cost, volume of traffic per unit of time, cost, or distance, frequency and regularity of service, and the route flexibility of vehicles are all spatially important. None requires the expertise of a traffic engineer or a transportation technologist to use in geographical analysis. And, given the high intercorrelation of these measures, one or two of them can serve to monitor changes in a transport system. In essence, efforts must be made to simplify identification of innovative forces and the measures thereof which are most diagnostic of emergent spatial systems.

Identifying and Measuring Spatial Responses

A general approach based on the identification of geostatistical measures is presented as one possible procedure for monitoring spatial development over time. Although this approach ignores the complex interplay of all the decision making forces contributing to the changing spatial pattern, it does yield measures of structure through time.

Industrial land in London, Ontario for each of four selected years between 1850 and 1960 was graphically collapsed to a circle proportional to occupied area about the mean position of the distribution (figure 15.1). The movement of the geometric center through time can be expressed as a linear measure of velocity as follows:

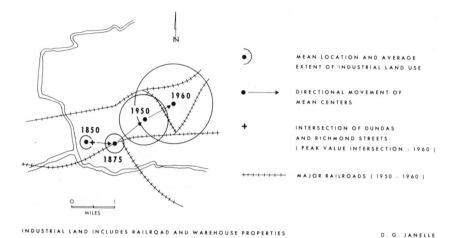

Figure 15.1 Mass Movement and Areal Expansion of Industrial Land: London, Ontario (1850–1960).

$$\text{where:} \qquad m = \frac{d_1 - d_0}{y_1 - y_0}$$

m is the average annual distance of movement, $d_1 - d_0$ is the distance separating the geometric centers of a given distribution in the initial year of measurement y_0 and its geometric center in some subsequent year y_1, and $y_1 - y_0$ is the interval of years from the initial y_0 to year y_1.

The spatial reorganization of industrial land use in London can be described by the directional and linear shifts of its geometric mean position (figure 15.1) and by its areal expansion (table 15.1). These measures are also expressed as rates of movement and expansion over time. When applied to several different land uses, these measures are means of determining the ratios of expansion between uses, the relative locational stability or mobility of land occupance systems, and the tendency of different land uses to approach spatial concordance or divergence. These statistics are adaptable to a wide range of geographic problems other than those related to urban physical structure. Problems related to social and cultural space can be considered in this framework. Deskins, for example, studied the changing positions of mean centers for residences and workplaces of blacks and whites in Detroit from 1953 and 1965 to determine what social and technological innovations led to the dispersal of job opportunities, concentration of the black population, and the consequent increase in the distances separating blacks from jobs.[8]

It is possible to measure innovation by defining useful surrogates (for instance, travel time as a measure of innovation in transportation) and it is possible to monitor the spatial responses to innovations by measuring changing geographic patterns. But it is not always possible to identify the specific innovations responsible for specific measurable spatial changes. Therein lies a need for a major research effort. How can the degree of spatial relevance of specific innovations be measured, and what regularities in spatial change can be attributed to particular innovations?

Table 15.1   Geostatistical Measures of Change in Industrial Land
Use: London, Ontario (1850-1960)

Time Period	Linear Shifts in Mean Position (in feet)	Annual Rate of Linear Shift (feet per year)	Direction of Linear Shift (Azimuth)	Surface Area Expansion (square feet)	Annual Rate of Surface Area Expansion (sq. ft/year)
1850-1875	3,170	127	89° E	853,630	34,145
1875-1950	4,520	60	51° E	26,488,139	353,175
1950-1960	3,620	362	60° E	33,234,882	3,323,488

A Dimensional Approach Spatial Impact of Innovations

Geographers have traditionally abstracted space and spatial phenomena into four basic dimensions—*points, lines, surfaces* and *volumes*[9].Philbrick, Bunge, and Warntz have suggested that the edge of a line is a point, the edge of a surface is a line, and the edge of a volume is a surface.[10] Time is generally treated as a separate dimension. Philbrick however, considers time within the more general framework of *motion* and defines the edge of motion as a volume.

Motion can be considered an inherent attribute of the four spatial dimensions. Thus, industrial land in London, Ontario was viewed as a state of motion at the surface level of dimension, where motion was defined both as a rate of change of position with time in a specified direction (velocity) and as a rate of change in areal extent. The motions of points, lines, and volumes could be similarly considered. Since any of the four space dimensions is conceptually reducible to any of the other three, this view is not incompatible with Philbrick's recognition of volumes forming the edges of motions. Depending on the study's objective, industrial land could be viewed under any of the four basic dimensions—points, lines, surface, or volumes. Two principal advantages of studying dimensional motion in this way are: (1) The space and time attributes of phenomena are combined in a single space-time measure (for example, velocity) in accord with the accepted notion of their inseparability; and (2) Once spatial phenomena are rigorously defined according to appropriate scales and dimensions, it is possible to monitor their changes through time.

Spatial change is a response to innovation, and the ultimate objective of futuristic geography is to determine the precise spatial result of any innovation(s). Although this ultimate goal is beyond the scope of this discussion, the general model described below might be a stimulus to development of more sensitive indicators of the spatial repercussions of new ideas and technologies.

A Model of Innovation-Induced Spatial Transformation

Any innovation will result in the *transformation* or reorganization of existing spatial patterns. Such transformations take the forms of *origination* (the development of new points, lines, surfaces, volumes and motions), *elimination* (eradication of spatial precedent), *positation* (intensification of existing pattern through increasing rates of growth, areal expansion and so forth) and *negation* (decline in intensity or extent of spatial phenomena and pattern). The basic assumptions incorporated in this model (figure 15.2) include the following:

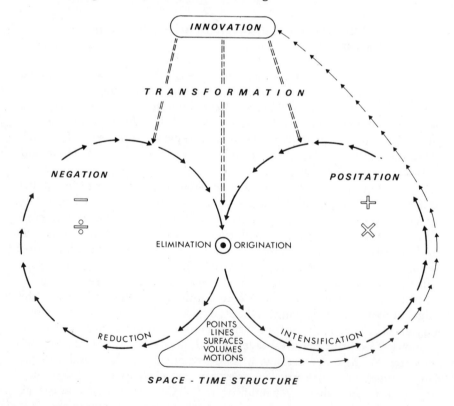

Figure 15.2   A Model of Innovation-Induced Spatial Transformation.

(1)   *All geographic phenomena are causally linked with all other
        geographic phenomena.*

(2)   *Spatial change at the earth-scale takes place in a system of fixed
        energy supply. At larger scales of analysis (that is, at local or
        regional scales) it is possible to consider exogenous inputs.*

(3)   *Matter can neither be created nor destroyed.*

(4)   *Therefore, the continual operation of the innovative
        forces—positation and negation, origination and
        elimination—represent transformations of existing patterns into new
        spatial forms. Thus, as the cycles of positation and negation feed
        each other, elimination and origination occur at the same point.*

(5)   *Any innovation may simultaneously result in spatial responses of
        negation and positation. For example, the consolidation of school
        districts yields functional decline for some communities and gain for
        others.*

(6)   *Any state of spatial organization will, through a positive feedback
        process, affect future innovation (the feedback loop from space-
        time structure to innovation in figure 15.2). For example, congested
        flows along a highway may generate a multitude of technological
        and behavioral responses either to eliminate or avoid the congestion.*

The prime requirement for improvement of this model is the
specification of sophisticated measurement strategies for detecting precise
impacts (rates of change in negation and positation) of innovations upon
specific land uses. In using and refining such a model, it is essential to
specify dimensions. At the *line* level, one would examine the impact of
innovations on linkages, on flows, and upon the points that form the edges
of lines. The elimination and creation of routes and the reallocation of flows
over various linkages and among establishments are results of innovations
that affect linear features. At higher dimensional levels such as surfaces or
volumes, linear components may restrain surface motions, leading to
accelerated or decelerated movements of surface edges along prescribed
paths. The easterly shift of industrial land use in London, Ontario, for
example, illustrates the significance of linear orientations of transport
facilities (figure 15.1). In the case of a surface having a less rigid linear
substructure, surface motions may have multiple degrees of internal-
external freedom; thus, a multitude of complexly related innovative forces
would be required to control its motions. Refractory situations of this type
might suggest, as a possible innovation, increasing the rigidity of underlying linear components. Similarly, governing volumetric motions must be
done in terms of the rigidities imposed by their component surfaces and
surface motions. Needless to say, these are just a few of the complexities
which might be incorporated into a sophisticated system for measuring the
spatial repercussions of innovations.

Lead-Times for Decisions and the Directed Future of Urban Spatial Structures

Associated with the need to measure and predict spatial change resulting from given innovations is our increasing need to forecast inventions and innovations before they occur. The general decrease in the time interval between invention and innovation allows us less opportunity to assess the potential developments associated with either accepting or rejecting the innovations. As Lynn notes: ". . . the over-all lapsed time for technological development has declined during the last sixty to seventy years, from a mean of thirty-seven years in the early twentieth-century period, to twenty-four years during the post-World War I period, to fourteen years during the post-World War II period."[11] Planners and others in positions to direct urban spatial development do not have ready access to information on new inventions. Given our present levels of understanding, it is unlikely that such information could be used effectively were it available. Nonetheless, this critical lead-time should be used for evaluating potential long-and short-term impacts of inventions upon urban spatial structure.

Technological change is at the root of many urban and other problems. The speed of technological change is faster than the rate of change in society, and lead-times are inadequate for effective prediction of spatial equilibrium disruptions arising from innovation. Certainly innovations such as the automobile have upset the early twentieth century conditions of location, transport costs, and spatial organization. However, there is evidence that fears provoked by cultural lags are becoming less warranted:

(1)   *After an exhaustive study, Jacob Schmookler concluded that variations in social demand are far more significant to the invention-innovation process than are changes in the conditions of supply.*[12] *This finding tends to weaken the arguments of social or cultural lag which have been advanced as explanations for many of our social ills. It also suggests that if society can identify its goals and establish its demands, inventive effort may assuredly be oriented toward their fulfillment.*

(2)   *Findings by John Platt indicate that our concepts of social lag are misleading.*[13] *For example, he notes that since 1940 more than half of all major social inventions, such as the credit card, the Peace Corps, the Antarctic Treaty, and others were adopted within two to twelve years of their initial proposal. The time-lag to their introduction was, on the average, no longer than for major technological innovations. Thus, it seems that social invention and innovation can be every bit as responsive to identified needs and demands as technology. Social innovation need not necessarily be a reaction to technological innovation. To date, however, differences*

in volumes of technological and social innovations have fostered persistent gaps.

(3)   The time-lag from invention to innovation represents an opportunity that is not being exploited; this is particularly so in planning for the development and redevelopment of our cities. Current information on social and technological invention should be made available to specialists for analyzing potential impacts of new ideas and technologies upon the spatial structure of our cities. Such evaluations must be based on well-articulated public goals, and on reliable forecasts of trends in public thinking. Such efforts at technological forecasting are underway,[14] and they should extend the opportunity-time available for evaluating innovations. Man may be able to direct his future with more precision than he has done in the past, at least with respect to finding solutions to urban problems.

Conclusion

The guidelines for spatial prediction suggested herein are tentative and need considerable refinement. Although procedures for measuring both the degree of spatially relevant innovation and the spatial result of combined innovative forces have been suggested, difficult problems remain. These include the need to improve the precision of such measures and the overriding need to identify the specific spatial implications of specific innovations.

The model of spatial transformation proposed here lays bare the essential framework in which innovative forces transform phenomena abstracted into spatial dimensions (points, lines, surfaces, volumes) into new patterns. But for the most part the questions that evoked the guidelines presented here remain. Can pattern be predicted? What innovative forces lie behind spatial land use changes? Can innovations and the spatial responses to them be measured? How can the time-lag between invention and innovation be exploited for the evaluation of spatial implications? How can the application of innovative forces be manipulated to yield desired spatial responses? The answers to these questions remain incomplete, and further exploration is needed.

References

1. A brief description of these concepts is presented in Chauncy D. Harris and Edward L. Ullman, "The Nature of Cities," *Annals of The American Academy of Political and Social Science* 242 (November, 1945): 7—17.

2. F. Stuart Chapin, Jr. and S. F. Weiss, eds., *Urban Growth Dynamics* (New York: John Wiley & Sons, 1962).

3. Grace Milgram, *The City Expands, A Study of the Conversion of Land From Rural to Urban Use, Philadelphia, 1945-62,* (Philadelphia: Institute for Environmental Studies, University of Pennsylvania, 1967).

4. See the following: William L. Garrison, "Toward Simulation Models of Urban Growth and Development," in *Proceedings of the I.G.U. Symposium in Urban Geography, Lund, 1960,* ed. Knut Norberg (Lund, Sweden: Gleerup, 1962), pp. 91—108; Richard L. Morrill, "Expansion of the Urban Fringe: A Simulation Experiment," *Papers, The Regional Science Association* 15 (1965): 185—199; F. S. Chapin, "A Model for Simulating Residential Development in Urban Development Models: New Tools in Planning," *Journal of American Institute of Planners* 32 (1965): 120—125.

5. See Larry S. Bourne, "A Spatial Allocation-Land Use Conversion Model of Urban Growth," *Journal of Regional Science* 9 (August, 1969): 261—272. In addition, Bourne has employed a markov chain model in extrapolating the conversion probabilities through four time periods to the year 2002. See L. S. Bourne, *Forecasting Land Occupancy Changes Through Markovian Probability Matrices: A Central City Example,* Research Report No. 14 (Toronto: Department of Geography, The University of Toronto, August, 1969).

6. Peter F. Drucker, *Landmarks of Tomorrow* (New York: Harper and Brothers, 1957), p. 32.

7. *Ibid.,* pp. 45—46.

8. Donald R. Deskins, Jr., "Residence-Workplace Interaction Vectors for the Detroit Metropolitan Area: 1953 to 1965," in *Special Publication No. 3, Interaction Patterns and the Spatial Form of the Ghetto* (Evanston, Ill.: Department of Geography, Northwestern University, 1970), pp. 1—23.

9. John P. Cole and Cuchlaine A. M. King, *Quantitative Geography* (New York: John Wiley & Sons, 1963).

10. Allen K. Philbrick, "Geographical Measures of Dimensional Diversity" (Paper presented before the 21st International Geographical Congress in New Delhi, India, in 1968); William Bunge and William Warntz, *Geography, The Innocent Science,* to be published.

11. Frank Lynn, "The Rate of Development and Diffusion of Technology," in *Automation and Economic Progress,* edited by Howard R. Bowen and Garth L. Mangum, (Englewood Cliffs, N.J.: Prentice Hall, Inc., 1966), p. 105.

12. Jacob Schmookler, *Invention and Economic Growth* (Cambridge, Mass.: Harvard University Press, 1966).

13. John Platt, "What We Must Do," *Science* 166 (November 28, 1969), pp. 1115—1121. See also Karl W. Deutsch, John Platt and Dieter Senghass, "Conditions Favoring Major Advances in Social Science," *Science* 171 (February 5, 1971): 450—459.

14. See Erich Jantsch, *Technological Forecasting in Perspective* (Paris: Organization for Economic Co-operation and Development, 1966) and Robert Ayres, *Technological Forecasting and Long-Range Planning* (New York: McGraw-Hill, 1969).

Chapter   16

Geographical Scenarios for an Underdeveloped Area: Alternative Futures for Tropical Africa[1]

Hans Carol
York University

ABSTRACT: *A scenario is not a prediction. It is the end result of a scientific simulation game. Three geographic scenarios are developed for tropical Africa over the next century. Scenario A is evolutionary: the present thirty-four countries merge into ten larger states, governments are democratic, and modernization is based upon diffusion of industrial technology and capital from advanced nations; the future is progressive and open-ended. Scenario B is revolutionary: all countries are fused into one large state based upon Marxist-Leninist-Maoist principles, modernization is based upon diffusion from communist countries, and the economy is centrally planned; the future is progressive, predetermined. Scenario C is reactionary. Modernization ceases in the reversion to hundreds of tribes and kingdoms; the future is static and predictable. Population, feeding capacity, agriculture, mining, urbanization, transportation, economic achievements, and ecological considerations are discussed for each of the three scenarios.*

This chapter is concerned with the problem of extending geogra-

Editor's Note: This chapter is a preliminary part of a larger research project Professor Carol was pursuing at the time of his death.

phic studies from past periods to the long-range future. Figuratively speaking, we attempt to push intellectual antennas into the void of a distant future. In doing so, geographers have to borrow heavily from viewpoints and techniques developed by those in other fields, particularly the futurists.

From Jeremiah to Buckminster Fuller, men have been interested in the future. The philosopher Mario Bunge lists expectation, guessing, prophecy, and prognosis among the nonscientific approaches to the future.[2] Among the scientific approaches, Bunge distinguishes strict scientific prediction (in which the initial state of the system as well as the laws which govern it are known) from lax scientific prediction (in which the initial state of a system and laws governing it are not precisely known). In geography, studies of short-range trends are lax predictions.

Scenarios arise from a somewhat different concern with the future. According to Helmer, scenario-writing involves constructive, scientifically controlled imagination. ". . . an operations-analytical scenario starts with the present state of the world and shows how, step by step, a future state might evolve in a plausible fashion out of the present one. Thus, though the purpose of such a scenario is not to predict the future, it nevertheless sets out to demonstrate the possibility of a certain future state of affairs by exhibiting a reasonable chain of events that might lead to it."[3]

It is important to bear in mind the difference between prediction and scenario-writing. Long-range scenario-writing does not attempt to predict a future state; it merely develops intellectually interesting alternatives, one or none of which may come true in a distant future. Long-range scenario-writing is like a scientific simulation game. One shows how certain currently known processes may operate over a period of time and how they will produce certain results. Simulation of the future is all that science is capable of doing if we consider the human future as open-ended. Scenarios may fuse with short-range extrapolation and predictions of the type presented in *The Year 2000* by Kahn and Wiener.[4] Thus, scientific scenarios and science fiction are similar in scope, though different in method.

In 1969, while working on a human geography of Africa, I decided that it would be fascinating to extend the time span from the past millennia (particularly the past century) into the next century. Thus I could use the knowledge of processes gained through study of past development to elaborate a long-range view of future possibilities. Would it be possible to construct alternative geographies ranging over a century? Would such an effort extend meaningfully the geographer's traditional concern with man-environment relations, with human ecology? I am fully aware of the preliminary nature of this first attempt, but I envisage a great potential for refinement. The scenario technique may be applied to shorter periods, to smaller areas such as single countries, or to specific topics such as urbanization.

Rules for the Game

There is an essential difference between exploring the future in the technologically more developed nations[5] and in the less developed nations. The former change primarily by innovation, whereas the latter change primarily by diffusion. The advanced nations have no model to follow; the less advanced develop mainly by transfer of known science and technology. The basic assumption is that tropical Africa as a huge underdeveloped area may, in a modified form, follow the path of the developed countries. This parallel approach may be oversimplified, but it allows us to postulate the transfer of known processes of change that have occurred over the last two centuries among the industrial nations.

Several rules must be laid down in order to play the game of futuristic geography: (1) Cultural values and social goals implied in the three alternatives to be put forth are considered to remain constant over the decades. Thus, changes in the assumed trajectory through resistance, sabotage, rebellion, and wars are ruled out. Likewise, external influences are assumed to remain persistent and act solely on demand by African governments. The impact of charismatic personalities, as important as it is in reality, is not taken into account. (2) Only currently known science and technology are taken into account; unknown inventions of the future may have a great influence, but they will have to be disregarded here. One must work with present scientific viewpoints and known methodology. Surely, far more sophisticated techniques of research will be developed in the future; but these too cannot be considered. (3) The natural resource base is evaluated under currently known technologies. Since resources are culturally determined, we cannot know what substances and processes of the natural environment will be considered valuable and usable in a distant future.

Such assumptions constitute the rules under which this game is played. With the help of flow charts, systems diagrams, and various models, three geographic scenarios have been developed.

Because there is no predictive value in scenarios, some readers may consider a simulation approach irrelevant. However, beyond the scientific fascination of plumbing the future, there are practical benefits to be derived. Planners, politicians, and society at large may become aware of the long-range consequences of their decisions. In a refined form, the technique of alternative scenario-writing may be applied to various time sequences, including the short-range five-, ten-, or twenty-year phases. The most promising short-range alternatives could be chosen and their consequences evaluated in terms of desirable long-range scenarios. Thus, more than in the past, the future may be consciously chosen by society rather than passively endured. By extending our concern from the past and present into the future, by blazing exploratory trails into the unknown, we stretch our minds, become future-conscious, and consider current decisions in terms of their possible long-range consequences.

Scenarios for Tropical Africa

The area selected includes all of tropical Africa, and excludes northern and southern Africa. This area comprised 8.2 million square miles and 235 million people in the 1960s; it approximates the size of the United States and Canada in area and population. In terms of economic-technological development however, it is one of the least developed areas of the world with a Gross National Product (GNP) per capita of approximately U.S. $100 compared to over $3000 for Anglo-America; tropical Africa comprises not two but thirty-six political territories.

A futuristic study of this huge underdeveloped area must ask such questions as: Will it be possible for the peoples of tropical Africa to raise their standard of living considerably? Is the agricultural resource base (traditionally considered far inferior to that of the mid-latitude lands) an insurmountable obstacle to improved food supply for a rapidly growing population? Is the largely tribal or recently detribalized African society able and willing to modernize rapidly? There is no way of predicting how African (or any other) society is going to change over the span of a century. But we may write scenarios based on certain assumptions; we recognize possible trajectories, develop alternative strategies, and map alternative futures.

Four time phases are distinguished: the period of the 1970s and early 1980s; a crisis by the mid-1980s from which three alternative scenarios emerge; the initial phase of the three scenarios extending to the end of this century; and a long phase of persistent development during the first half of the twenty-first century.

The rate of modernization in tropical Africa during the 1970s and early 1980s is assumed to be considerable, measured by the Gross National Product, which will increase by 1 to 10 percent annually for the various countries. Population will increase according to·the United Nations' high prediction of a 3 percent annual growth rate.

In the 1980s a major crisis is assumed, caused directly by a slump in world markets and indirectly by an unstable social structure in most countries; prices of African raw materials will fall. The assumed crisis marks the take-off for major changes. Of the many possibilities that could come about, only three radically different alternatives are explored: Scenario A—Evolution; Scenario B—Revolution; and Scenario C—Reaction. Evolution assumes intensification of current relations between Africa and the industrial nations; Revolution assumes a Maoist strategy of development for all of tropical Africa; Reaction assumes a return to tribal values and ways of life.

In *scenario A* (evolution) society seeks to strike a balance between the needs of the individual and the requirements of society in local, state, and worldwide communities. The thirty-four countries of tropical Africa, some of which are barely viable, strive to consolidate into fewer, viable units and they eventually merge into ten large states. The nations are governed by democratic principles, stressing consent rather than force. All countries are members of the Organization of African Unity and the United Nations. Modernization is brought about by diffusion of know-how and capital from the more advanced nations; worldwide socioeconomic inter-dependence is stressed. The national economies are based on mixtures of private and social enterprises, and the major economic goal is to raise the living standard for all sectors of the population. The future is progressive and open-ended.

In *scenario B* (revolution) the values of society are determined by Marxist-Leninist-Maoist principles. The individual's happiness is a con-sequence of his willing acceptance of correct party principles. All thirty-four countries are fused into one large state, the United People's Republic of Africa (UPRA) after protracted revolutionary wars. Strong political ties are maintained with China and other communist revolutionary regimes. Modernization is brought about by diffusion of know-how from these countries, though with far less capital investment than in scenario A. Self-reliance and economic self-sufficiency are stressed in the centrally planned economy. The UPRA aims at a rapid buildup of economic and military strength. Massive population growth is encouraged and individual con-sumption is low but egalitarian. The future is progressive and pre-determined.

In *scenario C* (reaction) traditional values of small groups deter-mine individual and social behavior. Hundreds of tribes and kingdoms form dozens of ill-defined federations. Relations with the outside world are minimal. Modernization ceases and people revert to traditional ways of life with low standards of living. The future is static and predictable.

Mapping the Cultural Landscape of the Mid-Twenty-First Century

Both the evolutionary and the revolutionary scenarios are based on the assumption of massive modernization. Modernization of tropical Africa is guided by simulation models of industrialization and urbaniza-tion. The theory and data used to construct such models are derived from nineteenth and twentieth century European experience, and I have used such macro-variables as: population, types of resource systems, agricul-tural resource base, theoretical feeding capacity, urbanization, and gross national product. In the construction of future environments, the inter-relations among these variables are critical (figure 16.1)

The compatibility of the development process with the basic

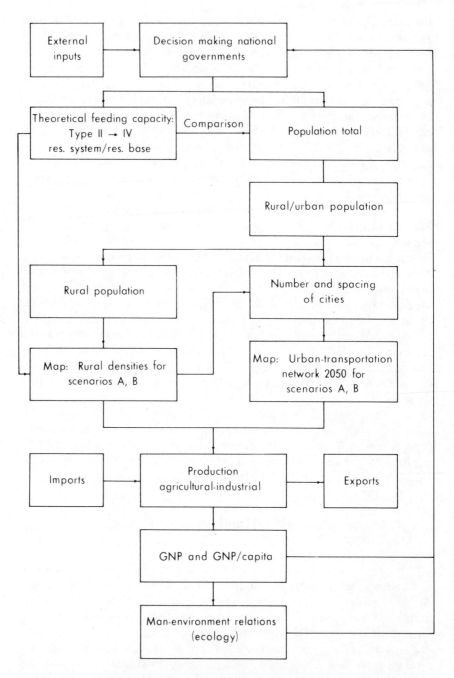

Figure 16.1 Systems Diagram Showing Interrelatedness of Major Elements Taken into Consideration for Scenarios A and B.

sociopolitical values of the three scenarios is kept in mind. The limitations imposed by the format of this chapter demand a rather condensed verbal discourse with brief interpretations of models and final results expressed in maps. The present study must be judged as technically crude, compared to Forrester's elegantly computerized extrapolations over a long span of time. However, as Forrester writes, "the model is only as good as the expertise which lies behind its formulation."[6]

Modernization, the motor of change in scenarios A and B, requires the changing of resource systems from traditional to industrial types. The concept of "types of resource system" becomes one of the key terms in this study.[7] This concept can be broadened and merged with the concept of "states of technology" to create a global classification called Types of Resource Systems:

Type I: hunting and gathering society

Type II: agricultural society

Type III: urban-rural (preindustrial) society

Type IV: industrial society

Type V: affluent (postindustrial) society

Tropical Africa can largely be characterized as having emerged from nineteenth century Type II and (in part) low Type III resource systems through partial modernization into various intermediate phases of Type IV.

The discussion of the simulation processes is organized under the following headings: population, feeding capacity, agriculture, mining, urbanization and transportation, economic achievement, and ecological considerations.

Population   The total population curves reflect the general values embedded in the three alternatives (figure 16.2). In scenario A, in which emphasis is on the well-being of the individual, population growth follows the low prediction (2 percent annual growth rate) of the United Nations to the year 2000, when total population will have increased to 500 million. Population control, stressed from the outset, will become effective during the first half of the twenty-first century. By the middle of the century zero growth rate is achieved—and the total population is stabilized at 650 million.

In scenario B, the UPRA initially demands a massive labor force in order to achieve development goals. Population growth follows approximately the United Nation's high prediction (3 percent annual growth rate) to the year 2000. Subsequently, the growth rate is slowed through birth control to 1 percent per year by the year 2050. The result is a very high total of 1.45 billion people.

Scenario C assumes retribalization. Cutting off relations with the outside world brings about catastrophic deterioration in supplies of water, food, and medical care. The consequences are epidemics and mass

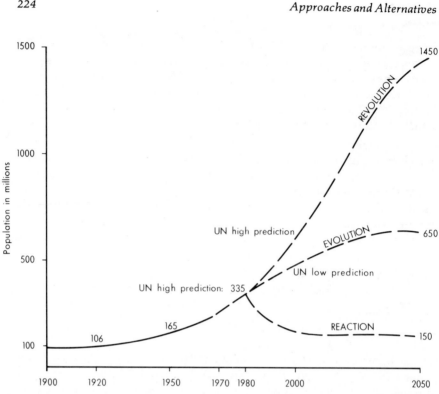

Figure 16.2 Population in Tropical Africa (1900—2050) According to Three Scenarios: A—Evolution; B—Revolution; C—Reaction.

starvation. Within two decades, the population is reduced to 150 million, a major "culture catastrophe" rather than an "eco-catastrophe". Through adjustment to subsistence agriculture, this population level is maintained at a zero growth rate through the first half of the next century.

The proportion of population in urban areas is of crucial importance, since it is a prime indicator of the degree of modernization. In Type I and II resource systems, the entire population is engaged in food production; in a Type III preindustrial resource system a substantial minority of 10 to 20 percent is released from agricultural activities, engages in manufacturing and service activities, and creates urban settlements. In a Type IV resource system, the urban segment of the population increases to more than one-half and perhaps to as much as 80 percent of the total, while the rural segment decreases accordingly (figure 16.3). This changing relationship recapitulates earlier European experience.[8]

The process of industrialization as experienced by the Western world over the past two centuries probably will be emulated in abbreviated and strongly modified form in Africa. Achievement of industrialization (Type IV resource system) requires a half and half split between rural and urban population. For scenario A, the process of industrialization will be

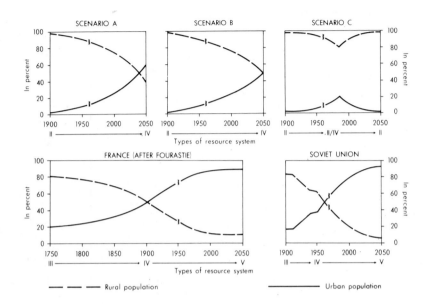

Figure 16.3 Model of Rural-Urban Proportions of Population for Scenarios A, B, and C. For Comparison, France and the Soviet Union Are Presented.

faster than in B because of massive inputs from the outside world and slower population growth. By the mid-twenty-first century, rural population will be down to 40 percent and the urban population up to 60 percent. This is a proportion roughly equivalent to that of the Soviet Union in 1967, when the proportions reached 45 and 55 percent respectively.[9] For scenario B, with its very large total population and slower industrialization (in favor of self-reliance), the proportion of rural to urban population is pegged at a half-and-half mark in 2050. For scenario C, owing to decline of modernization, a reverse occurs: the proportion that is rural reverts to almost 100 percent by 2050 (figure 16.3).

Feeding Capacity From the foregoing, disquieting questions arise: could Africa supply adequate food for large numbers of people, particularly the hundreds of millions of urban dwellers assumed in scenarios A and B? Is tropical Africa not notorious for its poor agricultural resource base, for the meager food supply of its present population of only 235 million?

An answer to this question requires studies of food production in relation to types of resource systems and the agricultural resource base. This relationship is summarized in a model of Theoretical Feeding Capacity (T.F.C.) based on empirical data collected from many sources in tropical

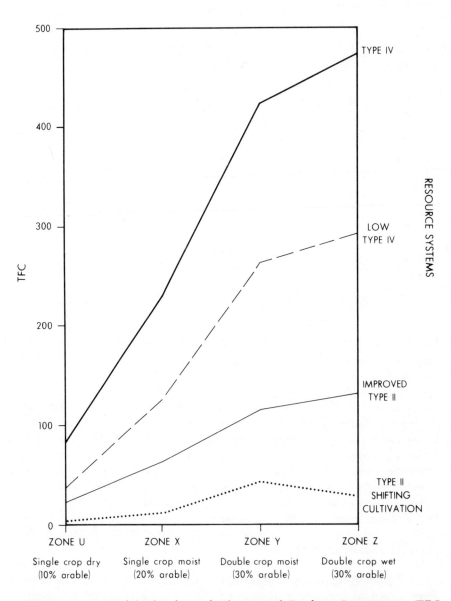

Figure 16.4 Model of Adjusted Theoretical Feeding Capacity (in TFC units) by Resource Systems and Agro-Climatic Resource Zones of Tropical Africa.

Africa.[10] The theoretical feeding capacity estimates the number of people that can be fed on a diet of 1,000,000 calories per year on 1 square kilometer. T.F.C. values were calculated for Resource Systems II, IV, and transitional levels between II and IV as measured within broad climatic agricultural resource zones:[11] single-crop dry (U), single-crop moist (X), double-crop moist (Y), and double-crop wet (Z). The estimates were adjusted for the estimated percentages of land that can be put to cultivation: 10 percent for zone U, 20 percent for zone X, and 30 percent for zones Y and Z (figure 16.4). The low proportions of cultivated land allow utilization of only the most suitable areas and tend to ensure ecological diversity and stability.

This model produces the following calculations of the "adjusted feeding capacity." It is assumed that modernization of agriculture in scenarios A and B yields a "medium" Type IV agricultural resource system. The calculation of the adjusted feeding capacity under such utilization is surprising: by modernizing Africa's agriculture to the level of a medium Type IV resource system, the agricultural productivity could be raised many times above the present level; theoretically 1,000,000 calories per year could be provided for about 4 billion people (figure 16.4). This stunning figure, which surpasses present world population, represents no maximum; the resource system could become still more productive. The resource base (calculated solely on rain-fed agriculture) could be vastly improved by irrigation and drainage and the low proportion of cultivated land could be increased. On the other hand, the feeding capacity of 4 billion is based on a diet of only 1,000,000 calories per year (2740 per day) including only basic requirements of proteins, minerals, and vitamins.[12] This diet, based on customary food habits, will certainly be improved toward greater variety of foodstuffs with greater emphasis on animal proteins with rising standards of living. Also, nonfood crops will take up a significant portion of the total crop area. Export and import of foodstuffs are not considered; they would be insignificant, however, in the case of scenario B. The map in the upper right corner of figure 16.5 indicates the adjusted feeding capacity related to the four agro-climatic zones.

The answer to the questions posed above can now be given: The huge population figure of 1.45 billion, as assumed in scenario B for the year 2050, compares with a theoretical feeding capacity of 4 billion, thus leaving a healthy safety margin of 2.7 billion. For scenario A, with a population of 650 million, the safety margin would be six times the theoretical feeding capacity. But is it possible to feed the 150 million people postulated in scenario C on the basis of a Type II resource system? The feeding capacity under shifting cultivation amounts to 280 million persons (figure 16.4), suggesting a safety margin of 1.8. Thus, the populations of all three scenarios would have safe amounts of food.

These figures indicate clearly that tropical Africa's low agricultural productivity is not the result of a poor and unchanging natural resource base (as has been often stated), but rather of low levels of human input. Through modernization of the resource system, the agricultural productivity of tropical Africa may surpass the productivity of the highly developed mid-latitudes.

Agriculture   In scenarios A and B, modernization of agriculture is recognized as a primary economic goal. Traditional shifting cultivation is

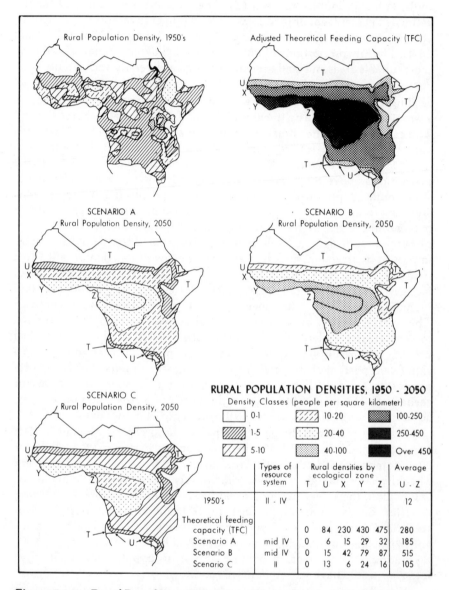

Figure 16.5   Rural Population Densities of Scenarios A, B, and C for Agro-Climatic Zones by Mid-Twenty-First Century.

gradually replaced by permanent cultivation through the use of chemical fertilizer. Vast stretches of currently unused or underused lands are brought under cultivation, partly by eradication of the tse-tse fly. Subsistence crop production shifts to market-oriented production, thus allowing best use of the agricultural potential for each resource zone. This trend is reflected in the density of the rural population, which is distributed according to the qualities of the agricultural resource base (figure 16.5).

For scenario A the basic unit is the individually operated farm. Cooperatives make marketing of products and purchase of seeds, fertilizers, pesticides, and machinery more economical. Development depends on the diffusion of knowledge from research stations, experimental farms, and efficient government extension services. Heavy emphasis is put on export crops such as coffee, cocoa, cotton, tropical fruit, and forest products, which produce much of the farmers' income and the nation's foreign exchange. The calculated rural population densities increase from six persons per square kilometer in the dry single-crop zone to thirty-two persons per square kilometer in the permanent cultivation zone in the rain forest area.

In scenario B, reliance is placed on collective farming with communes of tens of thousands of people. Production goals for the communes shift, as the transport network improves, from subsistence to market-oriented regional specialization. This allows optimization of the varied natural resources and a better food supply for the rapidly growing population of the UPRA. Export of agricultural crops is minimal. Massive human labor inputs (available from rapid population increases) make up for the short supply of mechanical equipment. This pattern changes toward the middle of the twenty-first century when manufacturing industry reaches full scale and the population growth rate slows. Rural densities are far higher than in scenario A; they vary from fifteen to eighty-seven persons per square kilometer from the least to the most productive zone (figure 16.5). Such rural densities approximate those in the more intensively cultivated areas of Western Europe. They are far higher than rural densities on the best lands in North America, but far lower than present rural densities in the best agricultural areas of Africa and China.

In scenario C, the trend toward agricultural modernization is reversed in favor of traditional resource systems. Coupled with this trend is the replacement of export crops with subsistence crops. In the search for survival, vast stretches of formerly unused lands are brought under shifting cultivation. Thus, the current uneven population distribution adjusts to the agro-ecological zones, although the densities are low. The highest rural densities (with twenty-four people per square kilometer) occur in the moist double-crop zone.

Mining Mineral production differs widely among the three scenarios. For scenario A, with its principle of interdependence, the countries of tropical Africa make maximal use of their mineral resources. The large imports of capital goods are acquired through exports of minerals. To an increasing degree, however, minerals are consumed in African factories. In scenario B, with its policy of severing relations with the industrial nations, mineral output declines greatly at first but later increases with growing industrialization. For scenario C, mining rapidly ceases to exist except perhaps for easily accessible and transportable precious metals and stones. The population employed in mining activities in scenarios A and B is included in the urban sector.

Urbanization and Transportation   In scenario A, the urban population increases during the period 1985—2050 from 20 to 60 percent or to 390 million (figure 16.3); in scenario B the equivalent figures are 50 percent and 725 million. In scenario C the percentage declines to 1 percent or 1.5 million. This small urban population is located in the remnants of previously established cities.

How will the urban population of scenarios A and B be distributed? Since we have assumed that by the mid-twenty-first century tropical Africa would approximate the degree of urbanization achieved by the Soviet Union in 1967 (45 percent rural, 55 percent urban), it might be appropriate to take the size classes of cities of the USSR as a model. But because of the small maps presented here (figures 16.6 and 16.7), cities were classified into only two functional classes: metropolitan cities of one-quarter to one million people and super-metropolitan cities of over one million. These two types contain about 40 percent of the total urban population, whereas 60 percent live in smaller cities and towns.

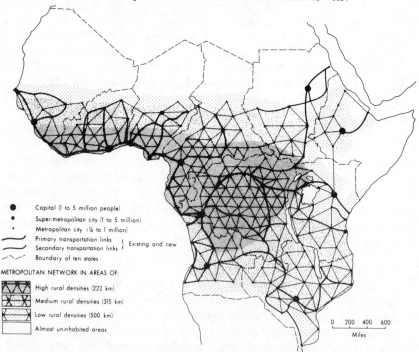

Figure 16.6   Scenario A—Evolution: Metropolitan Hierarchy and Transportation Network by Mid-Twenty-First Century.

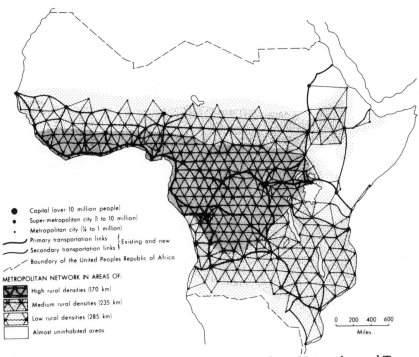

Figure 16.7   Scenario B—Revolution: Metropolitan Hierarchy and Transportation Network by Mid-Twenty-First Century.

The cities fulfill central functions (including administration) and manufacturing functions. Manufacturing includes processing plants for regional raw materials and footloose industries that can be located at the central places. Since the cities are primarily located according to their service functions for both the surrounding rural population and the people of smaller cities, a regular triangular network, which follows central place principles, should evolve. Accordingly, the number of cities was allocated for each rural density zone and the spacing between them was calculated. The results indicate, in highly generalized form, essential elements of the cultural landscape of the year 2050. In scenario B, (figure 16.7) a planned urban network covers all settled lands of the United Peoples' Republic of Africa. The metropolitan centers are spaced 170 kilometers apart in zones of dense rural population, increasing to 235 kilometers for the medium rural density zones. The transportation network has primary and secondary transport links (representing rails, roads, and waterways) and a tertiary network that links all cities with a straight-line grid. Irregularities in the spacing of cities and networks occur because of the specific locations of nineteenth and twentieth century cities and transport lines, because of thinly populated areas, and as a result of natural obstacles. Other irregularities occur owing to the industrial satellite cities surrounding some major cities of 5 to 10 million people. An example is the Kisangani and

Kinshasa-Brazzaville complex, the foremost industrial region (based on an abundance of hydroelectric power) of some 15 to 20 million people.

The urban and transportation pattern of scenario A (figure 16.6) is far less regular and dense. The spacing of metropolitan cities is 222 kilometers in the densest rural zone and 315 kilometers in the zone of medium rural density. In addition to the irregularities noted in scenario B, a major difference occurs through the division of tropical Africa into ten national states, each one emphasizing its own functional integration and oriented toward its own capital city. Consequently fewer connections occur across the borderlands, although most countries are interconnected through primary transport links.

Economic Achievement   In both scenarios A and B the major national goal is to achieve development of the economy by means of changing to a Type IV resource system. In scenario A this is done to maximize the material well-being of individuals and of society as a whole; in scenario B the purpose is to increase the economic (and military) power of the UPRA by holding back production of consumer goods. Growth is achieved by massive transfers of science and technology from advanced nations in scenario A, by self-reliance, economic self-sufficiency, and rapid growth of the labor force in scenario B.

Economic growth can be measured by the two well-known yardsticks: GNP and GNP per capita. How can we derive these measures for the far-distant year 2050? One way is to simulate the actual economic growth in agriculture, mining, and industry in several five- or ten-year plans. The other is the macro-economic approach which appears to be easier. A suitable model of economic development, that is, the Soviet Union, is adopted, and its essential features are transferred to tropical Africa.

For the early 1960s, the GNP per capita of the U.S.S.R. was reported by the World Bank to be $890. With a population of 228 million, the GNP of the Soviet Union would be on the order of $203 billion. If in the year 2050 scenario A would have achieved a GNP per capita equal to that of the Soviet Union in the early 1960s, the GNP for all countries (with a total population of 650 million) would amount to $578 billion.[13] The initial per capita income of the mid-1980s (crisis point) would possibly climb to a projected $150, yielding a total GNP of fifty billion dollars for a population of 335 million. The GNP would double every eighteen years to achieve $578 billion by 2050 and would thus maintain a 3.8 percent annual increase. GNP per capita would double first after twenty-seven years, indicating an annual increase of 2.7 percent. The succeeding doubling times would be twenty-four years; and then twenty-one years with annual increases of GNP per capita of 3.0 and 3.3 percent, respectively.

Scenario B starts from the same platform as scenario A. The low rate of technological input from outside is compensated by a far larger labor force. Thus, it might be possible that the GNP of the U.P.R.A. would, by mid-twenty-first century, reach $578 billion, the same level as in scenario A. However, the GNP per capita would amount to only $398, 45 percent of the value reached in scenario A. In scenario B, the GNP per capita would double first in 2032 and not again until 2076. The average annual increases during the first period would be only 1.5 percent. The major difference between scenarios A and B lies in the control over the GNP. In scenario B, this control is exercised by a single authority which gives it an economic power far in excess of that exercised by any one of the ten states found in scenario A.

The process of industrialization, as anticipated for scenarios A and B, will bring about a remarkable improvement in the standard of living through persistent efforts over decades, rather than through a "great leap forward". For scenario C, the GNP per capita would revert to about $50, a value which was characteristic of the least developed countries of tropical Africa during the 1960s.

Ecological Considerations   Although it was assumed that the development of scenarios A and B would follow approximately the path set forth by the industrial nations, it was also assumed that Africa would learn about the negative side-effects of industrialization. The concern for the man-environment relationship would be built into development plans so. that soil erosion and air and water pollution would be minimized. The quality of life in tropical Africa would be improved by air conditioning of buildings and by pest control. Natural environments would be preserved in large nature parks.

If we should apply the crude yardstick, namely that pollution and environmental problems are related to population numbers, to densities, and particularly to the level of industrialization, it is obvious that the environment would appear least endangered in scenario C and most in scenario B. A closer look, however, may reveal that regular burning under shifting cultivation and widespread burning of savanna grass for grazing may well contribute more to alterations of natural vegetation, to soil erosion, and to pollution of the atmosphere, than "clean" agriculture and manufacturing, the latter being largely based on hydroelectric power.

Conclusions

To develop long-range scenarios through comparative simulation appears to me a genuine and exciting research frontier. The construction of alternative futures necessitates the interplay of empirical knowledge, theory, and imagination. Scenarios make us aware of the future; they provide blueprints of possible developments. They give us some simulated constructs against which actual events and trends can be related and evaluated in their significance to long-range goals.

Scenarios A and B are two theoretical possibilities by which tropical Africa could, with help from outside and determination within, industrialize by the middle of the next century. The standard of living could be raised several times above the present one, thus fulfilling goals aspired to by leaders of African governments. If there should be development along the lines of scenario A, a level of living equal to that of the United States in 1970 could be reached within a century. This would be considered a tremendous achievement by those who measure improvement in absolute terms; for those who measure achievement in relative terms, the remaining (though reduced) gap between tropical Africa and the most advanced industrial nations, would be disappointing. How could we measure the level of achievement of the advanced nations by 2050 in order to assess the gap? To write scenarios for the advanced nations for the next century is entirely different from the task undertaken in this study. There are no models for comparison; scenarios would have to be developed along the lines employed by Kahn and Wiener.

For scenario B, the GNP per capita is thought to be about one-half that of scenario A. Nevertheless, the United Peoples Republic of Africa would emerge as one of the great powers of the twenty-first century. On the other hand, it is possible that Africans will reject the endless struggle for development and will revert to traditional values and ways of life, as suggested in scenario C.

In all probability none of the three alternatives is likely to happen. Only optimists would believe in a rational evolutionary development which would be consistently maintained over a century; only idealists would believe in man's willingness to sacrifice his personal life to benefit the society of a far distant future; only pessimists would believe in the virtues of traditional values at the cost of forsaking the advantages of industrial civilization. Behavior of the individual and society is conditioned not only by a linear pursuit of set goals (as assumed in these scenarios) but also by drives, dreams, fears, hopes, customs, and by the availability of natural resources, a complex mix that changes over time.

It is likely that African nations will find certain features of all three scenarios attractive. Experience from the past seems to indicate that the optimal biosocial climate for human development is achieved when extremes are balanced and when human needs to exist as an individual and as a social being are met.

This preliminary study suggests that three scenarios (selected from an innumerable range of possibilities) could, under certain specified rules, plausibly lead to the three alternative environments postulated for the year 2050. Actually, of course, currently unknown methods of development will be used over the next century; new ideas and inventions will become available and will greatly influence the actual development of tropical Africa. Thus, if the current growth-oriented philosophy should continue, modernization could be more rapid than anticipated for scenarios A and B.

However, should a neo-Malthusian philosophy prevail throughout the globe, growth would be slowed everywhere.[14] A third philosophy might advocate zero growth for the industrial nations and rapid growth for the less developed nations in order to equalize opportunities for all mankind. Whatever philosophies and political pressures come forward, the future remains open-ended.

References

1. The Canada Council supported this study with research grants in 1969 and 1970, and I was aided by three research assistants: Leonard Guelke in 1967, Fridtjof Nolte in 1970, and Victor Konrad in 1971.

2. Mario Bunge, *Scientific Research II: The Search for Truth* (New York: Springer Verlag, 1967).

3. Olof Helmer, *Social Technology* (New York: Basic Books, 1966).

4. Herman Kahn and Anthony J. Wiener, *The Year 2000: A Framework for Speculation on the Next Thirty-Three Years* (New York: Macmillan, 1967).

5. Brian J. L. Berry, "The Geography of the United States in the Year 2000," *Ekistics* 174 (May 1970): 339—351.

6. J. W. Forrester, "Counterintuitive Behavior of Social Systems," *Theory and Discussion* 2 (1971) 109—140.

7. The concept of resource systems was developed by Walter Firey in an agricultural context. The term includes values, technology, and natural resources. W. Firey, *Man, Mind and Land, a Theory of Resource Use,* (Glencoe, Ill.: Free Press of Glencoe, 1960).

8. J. Fourastié, *Le Grand Espoir de XXe Siecle* (Paris: Presses Universitaires de France, 1949).

9. Central Statistical Board under the Council of Ministers of the U.S.S.R., *Soviet Union 50 Year Statistical Returns.* (Moscow: Progress Publishers, 1969), p. 23.

10. The T.F.C. values are calculated according to the following formula:

$$\text{T.F.C.} = \frac{\text{yields (kg/ha)} \times \text{calories (kg)} \times 100\,(\text{ha})}{1,000,000\,(\text{calorie consumption per year}) \times \text{rotation factor}}$$

    The empirical values are based on data gathered for tropical Africa, for food produced under identifiable resource systems and identifiable resource bases. Empirical values of reliable cases are plotted on the T.F.C. model from which the adjusted model (figure 16.4) was derived.

11. M. K. Bennett, "An Agroclimatic Mapping of Africa," *Food Research Institute Studies* (1962): 195—216.

12. A diet of 2,740 calories per day per capita, compares favorably with the present one as reported by F.A.O. for tropical Africa: lowest per capita consumption is reported as 1,870, highest as 2,420 whereas for individual countries the average may be about 2,100 calories per day.

13. Although such an assumption might either prove to be too high or too low, it is within reason due to the diffusion of goods and ideas from the more developed countries of the world.

14. As mentioned above, J. W. Forrester's views on natural resources reflect a neo-

Malthusian philosophy; consequently they lead to the following conclusions: "From the long view of a hundred years hence, the present efforts of underdeveloped countries to industrialize along Western patterns may be unwise. They may now be closer to the ultimate equilibrium with the environment than are the industrialized nations. The present underdeveloped countries may be in a better condition for surviving the forthcoming worldwide environmental and economic pressures than are the advanced countries." J. W. Forrester, *op. cit.*, p. 15.

Chapter   17

A Recreation Scenario for the Province of Ontario, Canada

Roy I. Wolfe
York University

ABSTRACT: *This scenario focuses upon an aspect of outdoor recreation and tourism, the potential demand for summer cottages by the year 2000. Assumptions are made about population, education, occupation and income, family style, the economy, world civilization, urbanization, agricultural land, and standards of land use. The scenario is modified after the effect of second residences upon water bodies and fishing waters, and compatibility with other government plans is considered.*

This scenario was written to discover what sort of information is required for the formulation of rational, defensible assumptions about the future. The final report of the Ontario Recreation Study will present formal, detailed plans for the period up to 1980. Relatively firm predictions will have been made of the demand for recreational opportunities at that date, and planners will take these predictions into account in formulating their proposals. The assumptions for the twenty years following 1980 will also take these predictions into account. An extra burden is therefore placed

Reprinted from *Design for a Province-Wide Tourism and Outdoor Recreation Participation Study* by permission of the Ontario Department of Tourism and Information.

upon systems analysts and model builders, for they will have to build an unusually varied and sophisticated set of feedback devices into their systems and models to make them responsive to interactions among predictions, assumptions, and scenarios.

The scenarios that will appear in the final report will cover all forms of outdoor recreation and tourism, and will be based upon a wide range of assumptions about potential demand and the resulting pressure it will impose on natural resources. The present scenario is not nearly so comprehensive; it is restricted mainly to the potential demand for summer cottages, on the assumption that extreme conditions prevail and the demand for cottage sites is high.

Hypothetical Assumptions for The Year 2000

Population   The population of Canada will increase to about 45 million, and that of Ontario will continue to comprise a little more than one-third of the total, or about 16 million. Growth in the United States will be at a somewhat lower rate; the present 200 million will increase to about 350 million. Even so, if Ontario continues to draw its tourists from approximately the same areas as it does today, the recreational needs of as many as 150 million Americans will have to be considered; pressures on recreational resources in their home regions will have become so great that there will be an enormous spillover into Ontario.

Education, Occupation and Income   The level of educational attainment (as measured by the Education Index devised for the 1966 Park User Survey) will double, as will the level of occupation and income.

Family Style   No assumptions are made about the age-mix of families, the status of the nuclear family, or shifts in fashion likely to affect recreational behavior in the year 2000. The implicit assumption that all these elements will remain unchanged—that there will be as many pre-school children per family as today, that the family unit will adhere in the same way as it does now, and that people will want to continue doing what they are now doing in just about the same proportions—will certainly be found to have been incorrect, but it is retained here for simplicity.

This implicit assumption creates a grave weakness in the present scenario, but it must remain because there is no way to imagine what sort of light the systems models are likely to throw on such variables. Possibly they will throw a very strong light on some of them. The model builders will examine the historical record in general terms from 1871 to 1951 and in considerable detail for the years since 1951. They may establish trend lines for family style of such certainty and clarity that it will prove possible to extend the lines far into the future with reasonable confidence. This is possible, but not probable; and even the final scenarios may well be weak on this point.

The Economy and the World Situation   Another set of assumptions has been implicit in the earlier ones, but these are reasonably tenable. They are that over the long haul there will be no catastrophic economic or political events that will markedly lower populations, destroy natural or manmade resources, check the rise of affluence, or inhibit travel from nation to nation. If Canadian birthrates are lower, immigration from Europe, possibly from Asia and Africa and even from the United States will be great enough to raise population to the expected figure. Canadians will be able to travel unhindered to any country, and tourists from abroad will be able to enter Canada easily.

Greatly expanded economic activity, not only in Ontario but in the contiguous provinces and states as well, will itself put great pressure on natural resources that might otherwise be available for recreational use. Model builders will, therefore, have to incorporate economic indicators into their analyses to provide some idea of the amount of additional land, water, trees, and mineral products that will be required by commerce, industry, agriculture, forestry, and mining by the year 2000. The additional pollution of air, land, and water occasioned by this expanded economic activity will have to be assessed so that the ultimate scenario will contain a realistic set of proposals for combating such undesirable effects.

Urbanization   Fully 90 percent of the people in the study area will live in metropolitan areas or in the fringe areas just beyond them. Whereas today a high proportion of city people are but one or two generations removed from farm or village, by the year 2000 another full generation will have intervened between the rural and the urban experience. This will have to be taken into account by model builders, and it may in a small way help remove the weakness introduced into the scenario by the assumption of unchanged family style described above.

Not only will city people be further removed from the country in time (by a full generation), they will also be farther removed from it in space. There will be twice as many people in the cities of Ontario in the year 2000 as are living in all of Ontario today. Existing cities will spread over large areas of land, and new cities will be built where none exist now.

These changes could, of course, bring opposite effects. Expansion of the existing cities will push the countryside farther away. But if new cities are built in the north among the lakes of Ontario's prime recreational regions, those living in the new northern cities will be much closer to recreational resources than those remaining in the great cities to the south.

Agricultural Land   Expanding cities will put two kinds of pressure on agricultural land: there will be more city people to feed, and less land will be left for growing food. Cities are laid out on precisely those lands that are best for agriculture—lands that are flat, well drained, and usually fertile.

It will not do to say that Ontario will simply have to import such food as it cannot grow, because the same processes will be taking place everywhere else. The agricultural land that remains will have to be cultivated more intensively than ever, and land that is now marginal, and which therefore may have potential recreational uses, will have to be farmed.

The implications seem obvious. The scenario will have to disregard the farm as a recreational resource in the year 2000. Whatever potential still exists for growth in the number of recreational farms will have been long exhausted. Indeed the reverse process may have set in; farmlands now devoted to recreation may be returned to more utilitarian purposes. These assumptions might be tested in systems models, but they should be given a low priority, for there are even more urgent matters to be taken in hand. Certain principles must be formulated for taking inventories.

Inventories

We are obliged to ask: Why do we take inventories in the first place? Then follows the further question: Once we have them, what do we do with them? It is not enough to answer that the inventories will tell us what the present demand and supply are. It is essential to ask more questions about the present situation:

1.   *What is now being done right? How can we ensure that it continues to be done right?*

2.   *What is now being done wrong? How can we correct it for the future?*

Land Use Inventories

Systems models will be expected to provide the following inventories:

1.   *The amount, character, and distribution of recreational land now in use, and the manner in which it is being used.*

2.   *The amount that will be needed to meet expected demand.*

3.   *Of the additional land needed:*

a) the amount and location of unused lands now available for recreational use;

b) the amount and location of potentially valuable recreational lands now being put to other uses, or in danger of being put to other uses—as for urbanization, lumbering or mining.

Standards

Before this information can be put to use, it must be classified, and classification implies the prior existence of a set of standards.

It is appropriate at this point to discuss a commonly used word: optimum. In principle, this word should be avoided by recreational planners. Optimum is an absolute, and there are no absolutes in planning. In recreation, standards may sometimes be arrived at by consensus. To some extent, inventories of land use data tell us what people want by telling us what they do. The role of the planner is to integrate this knowledge with an informed concern for environmental quality, and to ensure that steps taken to satisfy people's expressed desires do not lower environmental quality. Standards must be established accordingly.

What, for example, is the optimum allotment of shoreline per summer cottage? The question demonstrates its own meaninglessness. In certain colonies there are 200 feet of shoreline per cottage, in others 100 or 50 feet, and in still others the equivalent of only 5 or 10 feet of communal shoreline for cottages most of which are well away from the shore. After deliberation, we may decide that a desirable overall average is 75 feet. This will be an arbitrary standard, but it will be empirically defensible; we will be able to show from the inventories and from questionnaires submitted to cottagers that 75 feet is, by consensus, a very nice lot width. It is wide enough to obviate congestion and narrow enough for just the right degree of neighborliness. On that basis we can begin our scenario.

An Illustrative Example of a Summer Cottage Scenario for the Year 2000

First Runthrough

Given the set of assumptions outlined in the preceding paragraphs, we postulate a sixfold increase in the demand for private cottages by the year 2000. Room will have to be found in the Province of Ontario for a million more cottages than are there today, for about as many, that is, as are now distributed over the whole area of the United States. This means a colossal demand for land, for building materials, for mortgage money, and above all for planning skills.

To be able to plan adequately for such a vast increment to secondary housing, we must have an inventory of all shorelines now being used for such housing classified according to density of use, distance from major urban centers, and accessibility. Assuming that 75 feet of shoreline per cottage is desirable, we will find very little unused shoreline left on lakes or rivers within, say, three hours' driving distance of large cities. It then becomes necessary to conduct an inventory of shorelines that are more remote and less accessible, and to suggest infrastructures that will improve accessibility.

Certain assumptions that have been made for the year 2000 will cause us to redefine present concepts of accessibility. Since we are assuming a highly affluent and mobile society, we are also assuming that people will be willing and able to move over greater distances, more rapidly, than they do today. The friction of distance is at present of great importance with respect to summer cottages—as reflected in the high proportion of trips to cottages made on weekends. Weekend trips will be less prominent, partly because vacation time will be longer, but more importantly because a high proportion of the additional million cottages in the province will have to be located beyond weekending distance from their owners. (A remote possibility is that transportation technology will have advanced so greatly that no spot in Ontario will be beyond weekending distance from any other spot. This possibility might well be taken into account in one of the subsequent runthroughs of the scenario.)

Assuming for the moment the relative decline of the weekend trip to the cottage, we will have to be very careful in interpreting whatever parameters about cottage ownership emerge from systems models. We may find that the exponent for distance (d) in the gravity model

$$I = k \frac{M_1 M_2}{d^X}$$

is now something on the order of 2. If it becomes a matter of going far or not going at all, enough people may decide that it is worth travelling the extra distance to lower the exponent of d considerably. It will be necessary to construct flexible models, to equate availability of remote areas, at various levels of accessibility, with varying willingness to travel to such areas.

If it is a matter of going far or not going at all, most people may not go at all, in which case the fashion for cottages will have changed. But as has been pointed out, we are not free to make assumptions about changing fashions except in so far as already established trend lines can be extended into the future. Thus we are forced to make changes elsewhere in the scenario to accommodate the people who still want cottages but refuse to travel any great distance to reach them. Cities could be moved to the resources (through siting among the northern lakes) or resources could be moved to the cities (through provision of new shorelines on artificial lakes).

A more realistic procedure would be to change the standard for length of shoreline per cottage. Instead of 75 feet per cottage, there might be 50 feet, or 25 feet, and so on, and the data would be run through systems models on the new sets of assumptions. We might find that the most likely pattern for the year 2000 will be the cottage subdivision, which is now coming into prominence. Cottages fronting directly on the water will be in the minority; most cottages will be located on streets well back from the water, their owners sharing a communal shoreline having a length of perhaps 10 feet per cottage.

Some people would prefer to live in high-rise apartments near the water's edge than in self-contained cottages on their own lots far removed from the water. Such a development would entail profound changes in the patterns of recreational land use in Ontario. The very look of the landscape would be radically altered; it would no longer be rural, but urban in appearance—in fact it would have the look of metropolis. High-rise, cooperatively owned apartments would be so costly to build that they would be uneconomical if used only for the short summer season, and in any case to leave such buildings unheated through the winter would invite rapid deterioration. Thus changes in seasonal habits would be necessary, and people would use the apartments as year-round vacation homes.

Each change would require further changes in turn. Psychological patterns would have to be radically transformed, for the very idea of owning a summer cottage today is presumably, at least in part, to get away from the city to the country. If the resort looks like metropolis, not much of the country will be left. And if the patterns of seasonality are disturbed, assumptions underlying scenarios for other elements of the recreational pattern—notably the movement of Ontario citizens to resorts in warmer climates in winter—would have to be modified.

Effects on Water Bodies   There is an additional problem to be considered: people who own cottages also own boats—at present, an average of two boats per cottage. Thus, if a high density of cottages is allowed on the shore of a small lake, how are the waters of the lake going to be used? Standards for the number of boats to be accommodated on a given area of water must be made compatible with standards for length of shoreline per cottage. Nor should we lose sight of the problem that pollution from sewage will bring to these waters. Again the need for a well-planned infrastructure, in this case for an adequate system of sewage disposal, is clear.

Following dispersal of cottage development into remote areas, certain lakes will disappear from the inventory of fishing areas as their shores are built up with private cottages. It will therefore be necessary to prohibit cottages upon certain lakes in order to provide for the legitimate needs of fishermen. Systems models will be expected to provide information on the magnitude of these needs.

Second and Subsequent Runthroughs

As assumptions are made about the various sets of options among which people may choose, and the modifications in standards that each type of choice will necessitate, the scenario will have to be modified as well; new data will be fed into computer models, and new sets of parameters will result.

Policy on Standards   If people refuse dispersed cottage development but insist instead on either horizontal (the resort subdivision) or vertical (high-rise apartments along the shore) development within easy drive of the city, it will be necessary to make a decision of another sort: should standards be established that make it possible for only a minority of would-be users to use a facility, or should a higher proportion be allowed to use the facility on the understanding that standards are lowered?

For the purposes of the present scenario we will opt for the latter alternative. In the interests of fairness, we will make whatever recreational resources exist available to as many people as possible, without utterly destroying the desirability of the resources themselves.

Reinterpretation of Parameters   But note the effect this procedure has upon the parameters generated by systems models. The patterns of cottage ownership formulated in the scenario are based on certain assumptions about demand and supply, and those assumptions led to the original set of standards. Affluent, mobile people have indicated that they want *both* seclusiveness and easy accessibility. These variables are mutually interactive, and under the extreme conditions postulated, they cannot be achieved simultaneously. It then becomes necessary to conduct another runthrough of the system, to try to modify the patterns so that incompatibilities are made as slight as possible. A linear programming model which would generate a constraint envelope within which rational decisions could be made would be desirable. Locations for cottage resorts, for example, might be sought at an outer limit of four hours' distance from major cities rather than two hours' distance. The available area would thus be increased fourfold. People would have to travel farther, but not too much farther, and other things would be more to their liking. Additional runthroughs would bring additional refinements, until a final pattern would be selected.

Further Ramifications   Consider the case of people who are not willing to submit to lower standards. Since nearby areas have become so congested, and since uncongested areas are far away, they decide that they do not want to own a cottage. What alternative activity in outdoor recreation will they opt for?

Perhaps they will wish to send their children to summer camps and themselves travel to foreign countries, or spend their vacation time at commercial resorts in Ontario. Our scenario in that case will have to take such patterns into account. The scenarios for the various types of recreational activity will have to be interdependent and since the interdependencies are likely to be numerous, it will probably be necessary to write a computer program to estimate the interconnections.

Complementarity and Compatibility of Planning Among Governmental Agencies

The recreational plan for Ontario will be but one phase of a comprehensive economic plan for the province, and as such it must take into account all other phases of the plan. So, too, must the scenarios.

The Urgency of Policy Decisions Assume, for the purposes of the present illustration, that the spillover of would-be cottage owners from the United States assumes extreme proportions, so that these people would take up all available cottage sites. Should they be allowed to do so?

Two conflicting sets of interests would have to be resolved. First, there are the needs and desires of the citizens of Ontario and of other Canadians. They alone could use almost the total amount of space within two hours' drive of their cities, plus one-half of the remaining space identified in the inventory of unused capacity. Yet the greater the proportion of space taken up by Americans, the greater the inflow of tourist dollars into the Ontario economy. (Presumably, but not certainly; the economic value of a cottage colony to the immediate locality and to the province as a whole has not yet been adequately assessed, and such an assessment would seem to be an urgent task). But if people of Ontario are denied the use of their own lands, not only has a direct injury been inflicted upon them, but also an indirect one; they will surely be induced to travel abroad, and spend tourist dollars outside the country, with unfortunate effects on Canada's international travel account.

Policy on this question will have to be established by the relevant organs of government. One of the chief purposes of a series of scenarios is to alert governmental agencies to the need for developing policy in good time.

Once policy has been set, it will be implemented by a judicious mixture of inducements and restraints. Scenarios will pinpoint areas where each will most appropriately apply. If it appears that it would be desirable to open up a certain wilderness area to cottage settlement, one department might modify its plans for the area to allow such development to take place; another might provide the transportation infrastructure for making it accessible; a third could offer inducements to build cottages there to people who might not otherwise be willing to travel so far by offering attractive mortgage terms; a fourth might restrain industrial development from locating there.

Dispersed Urbanization   Another example of complementarity and compatibility in planning might be locating a dispersed pattern of new cities in the north. One scenario might reinforce considerations generated by other phases of the economic plan for Ontario by confirming the desirability of building such cities at specified locations. Should these cities be built, they will change the scenario in two ways, necessitating further runthroughs. First, people in these cities will wish to use the recreational resources on the lakes near them, so that the distance parameter will be lowered. Lakes that are now very far from potential users will then be very close to them, and again one of the factors of congestion will have been removed. Second, these cities will attract people who may not wish to travel to a distant lake because it is remote from civilization but who will be willing to do so once there is a substantial city near it.

Thus each change in any part of the overall pattern will effect changes in other parts, and it will be incumbent upon planning agencies to ensure that these changes do not work at cross-purposes. There must be new forms of land use control and political organization to ensure that the insights gained from the scenarios result in fruitful, coordinated planning of Ontario's recreational future.

Afterword

You will no doubt have been struck, as I was when I reread the above paper just prior to its publication, by the great difference between the world in which it was written and the world we now live in. The world of 1968 could still look forward to *bigger and better;* at least, the official world could. We could plan for more of this, more of that, and our chief problem was, where would we put it all, and how would we contain the pollution? But even then I knew better, and was remiss in not saying so. Even then, and for years previously, I knew, as undoubtedly every reader of this book also knew, that we were on a delirious joyride, and that the joyride had to end—sometime. But no doubt many readers were surprised, as I have been, at how soon the joyride came to an end—or seemed to. Nowhere in the above paper do I hint at the implications, for recreational planning, of so easily foreseeable an event as the energy crisis we are living through as I write, which may be phony, or the energy crises to come, which surely will not be.

After all, what has been our topic? Vacation homes, second homes, summer cottages. The best name for these dwellings was coined many decades ago by Henry James, in an essay about (I think) Newport, Rhode Island: He called them "inessential houses." Exactly; they *are* inessential; and when the real crunch comes, they will be the first to go.

The last words I should like to give are the final paragraph of a paper I wrote in 1965:

> ... I am not able to be altogether optimistic about the future of recreational travel. The one thing that I am willing to say with any show of certainty about our new migration is that it cannot last. In time the curve of its growth must flatten out; it may even turn down, and the amount (let alone the quality) of travel will grow less instead of greater. In this, as in many other respects, I am forced to believe, we are living in a most unusual and transitory age, one that does not foreshadow the future but instead offers a contrast to it. In recreational travel we may be experiencing that Golden Age to which future generations will look back with longing—unless, of course, standards change so radically as to make our descendants ask: "Why did they bother?"[1]

References

1. Roy J. Wolfe, "Recreational Travel: The New Migration," paper delivered at the Third Delos Symposium, Athens, Greece, 1965.

Chapter   18

Simulating Urban Spatial Growth

Hugh A. Millward
University of Western Ontario

ABSTRACT: *Simulation of a range of possible urban forms can test the coherence and soundness of alternative spatial arrangements of the city's parts. Four scenarios covering the next thirty to forty years are examined for their possible implications for urban form: (1) a surprise-free future based on extrapolations of current trends; (2) a conservationist future that emphasizes environmental protection; (3) an expansionist future that favors the use of increased wealth by private individuals; and (4) a science fiction future that foresees a breakdown of societal norms with less emphasis on individual possessions. Trends and their spatial effects are outlined for each scenario.*

In attempting to forecast the future, we necessarily place great emphasis on the city, since the great majority of mankind will live within large urban areas. But the city of the future will almost certainly be entirely different from its present counterpart in both size and form. By simulating future urban forms, land use planners may gain insights useful in formulating long-term structural plans and helpful in testing the robustness (flexibility) of such plans. This is not to say that we should predict the future, accept our prediction as inevitable, and adapt ourselves and the city to it. Rather, we need to discern a *range* of possible urban forms, each of which is an alternative outcome of present societal choices.

An Extrapolative Approach

How might we approach this task of predicting urban forms? It is far simpler to replicate the past than to predict the future. We are able to compare simulation of the past with the present forms, and so gain a measure of correspondence. We can also *extrapolate* the trends that we discern in the present and recent past into the future, for much of the future is incipient within past and current trends, and the rest is highly unpredictable. This approach constitutes a "no surprise" scenario: it yields a future we tend to plan for that makes all other variants seem surprising.

Urban form changes in two major ways—by adaptations in internal densities and land uses, and by internal infilling of vacant land and additions about the edges. Both types of change are important, but it is sufficient to illustrate forecasting approaches with reference to the latter type only. This is partly because we lack comprehensive knowledge of changing urban form, but also because major structural changes come through new additions to the city, and most new additions locate on virgin land on the periphery. By simulating the sequential allocation of past additions to the city, we build up an understanding of the major variables influencing locational decisions. We also learn how these variables have changed in relative importance through time. By discerning such underlying trends, we become able to project their relative importance and their effects into the future.

The Temporal Trend

The temporal trends that underlie locational process are evident in a case study of West Nottinghamshire, England. West Notts is an urban unit comprising four towns and a number of villages in a close-knit community of about 150,000 people. If we lay a grid over the area, with each cell representing a square 500 meters on a side and then classify all cells by the time period during which they become predominantly built-over, the outcome appears at first glance to be disorderly (figure 18.1). However, we can see that later developments located adjacent to pre-1875 villages, partly because of proximity to workplace and market. Also, there is a "neighbor" effect; sites adjacent to existing developments are usually attractive because of the availability of urban utilities (water, sewers, gas) and amenities (schools, neighborhood stores, and so on). Other developments have located at random points in response to a multitude of factors, most of which are negative in the sense that they force development elsewhere; examples are public and private parks, mineral workings, areas of rough topography, and water bodies.

Only a certain proportion of the available (vacant) cells become developed in any one time period, and this selective allocation of the urban

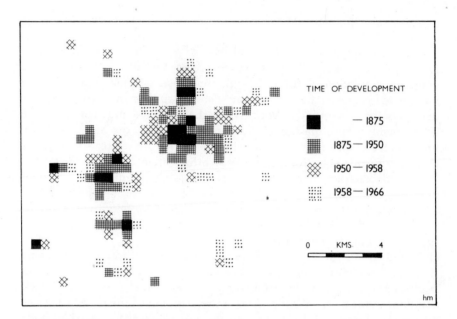

Figure 18.1 West Nottinghamshire: Historical Development, 1875–1966.

increment depends on factors such as those mentioned above. Statistical analysis permits us to approximate the effect that each factor exerts independently. We can infer, for instance, that the presence of development in a neighboring cell raises a cell's probability of having been developed between 1875 and 1950 from 0.05 to 0.30. Trends are evident in most major variables: distance from town centers becomes less important through time as personal mobility increases; the neighbor factor declines in importance as the relative costs of installing utilities are reduced. Very rough and very flat lands remain undesirable for urban development, whereas noxious facilities such as sewage plants and collieries exert an increasingly negative effect and preclude development in their immediate vicinities. Most important of all, zoning becomes very significant in the latest period. In fact, planning policies now completely overshadow the other factors.

Some Simulations of the Past

By combining the statistical effects of major factors influencing the past location of urban development, we are able to map the probabilities of development for the cells in our matrix during any time period.[1] We can then say, for example, that although only some cells were developed during a certain time period, other cells were equally attractive and had an equal probability of being developed, but were not because of randomizing factors in the allocation process. This random element is largely due to the unpredictable nature of human behavior; most decision makers, whether they be developers, industrialists, or house buyers, do not have complete information on all factors involved, and cannot discern slight variations in locational desirability. Also, of course, differing tastes and preferences permit people to be quite "irrational" if they wish to be.

If people *were* completely rational, and had full information, they would develop only the most desirable areas, choosing them one by one from the best downward. A simulation based on such behavior could be termed *deterministic*. In contrast, a simulation which attempts to incorporate human error and free will is a *stochastic* model of reality. By taking the suggested actions of key factors, using them to compute indexes of attraction, and then allocating development according to either a deterministic or stochastic framework, we can simulate the historical development pattern in West Notts.[2] Such simulations are *postdictive* rather than *pre*dictive, but if they replicate lineaments of the actual historical pattern, we can use the same method and extrapolate indexes of attraction to predict future urban patterns. In all simulations the pre-1875 pattern is taken as given, and development in subsequent periods is allocated according to the initial pattern.

The deterministic simulation is obviously far more regular than the real world situation (compare figures 18.1 and 18.2). Nevertheless, the deterministic simulation replicates many important features, particularly the distance and "neighbor" effects. Deterministic simulations produce the most reliable postdictions because all random variations take place around this "average" solution. With the stochastic model, a different result is obtained each time the simulation is run, because of the randomizing element which is its essential feature. Consequently we present only the first run of the model (figure 18.3). The stochastic simulation accords well with our intuitive ideas about how cities develop. A comparison with the historical pattern (figure 18.1) shows the essential similarity of form, and one might imagine that both patterns were produced by the same process. This is the only criterion necessary to establish the worth of the simulation, and similarity of process in both timing and siting does seem evident. To assist our estimation of the relative value of the simulations we might carry out some simple tests of correspondence. Although certain problems arise in correlating spatial forms, the results tend to validate our subjective appraisal. The deterministic simulation is more reliable, with a 65 percent correlation. The stochastic model is somewhat less accurate with slightly below 60 percent correlation for most runs.

Considering that these results occur using a cell size of only 25 hectares (approx. 0.1 square miles), the correlations are quite reasonable; indeed, if we aggregate the simulated and actual patterns into 1 square mile units both types of simulation have a correlation with reality greater than 80 percent.

So far we have managed to simulate the historical growth of an

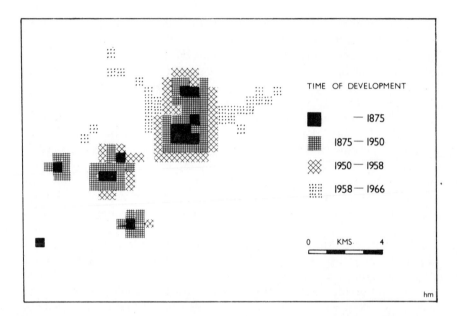

Figure 18.2 Deterministic Simulation of Land Development: West Nottinghamshire, 1875—1966.

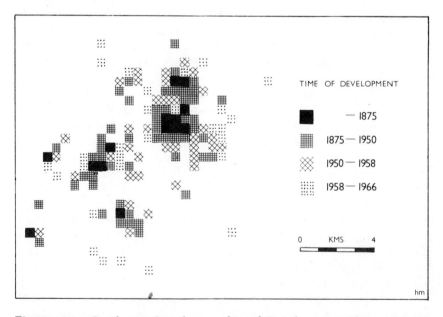

Figure 18.3 Stochastic Simulation of Land Development: West Nottinghamshire, 1875—1966.

urban area with reasonable accuracy, realizing en route the necessity of incorporating a random element to model human error and individual preference. Since we do have reasonable postdictive ability, it is not presumptuous of us to apply simulation methodology in a forecasting exercise with the aim of outlining a "no surprise" urban future.

A Simulation of the Future

In projecting current trends into the future we must beware the danger of "naive extrapolation," in which unthinking projection leads to obviously untenable results.[3] The "straight-line" mentality was amply demonstrated by European demographers of the interwar period, who feared that the populations of Britain and France would drop to only a few millions by the end of the century. Such forecasting attempts warn us that even surprise-free projections (which would of course be most surprising if vindicated) require an intuitive understanding of probable futures.

In this context, we must grasp the notion of "leadtime" with respect to both technological and social innovation. Just as Kahn and others have listed the likelihood of specific innovations during the coming decades, so we need to compile listings and probabilities of adoption for "spatially relevant" innovations. To use Janelle's (chapter 15) terminology, innovations affecting urban form would be those with "space/linkage consuming" and "space/linkage adjusting" characteristics. Particularly important among these are the introduction of new transportation media and the adoption of new value systems by consumers, producers, and planners. Such aspects may be incorporated in surprise-free scenarios as trend-induced innovations and changes similar to the "multifold trends" that form the basis of Kahn's seminal work.

Earlier we identified some variables that determine the spatial allocation of urban development, and mentioned that in the main they exhibited specific trends through time. One important factor in site attractivity was the site's distance from the town centers—the distance people were willing to locate from their workplaces, stores, schools, and other amenities. We attribute the decreasing effect of distance to an increase in personal mobility, which has allowed the desire for suburban living to be gratified. However, we can already discern that planners and local governments as well as energy considerations are beginning to severely restrict individual mobility.

Planning has made bold attempts, in fact, to contain urban areas within green belts, and to preclude development from "green wedges". In general the community applauds these efforts. Land use planning has also altered the historical trend by attempting to maintain large recreational and low-density institutional units as open spaces *within* urban areas. These features are included in this attempt to extrapolate the future. One way in which this is done is to attach a negative effect to rough land, thereby

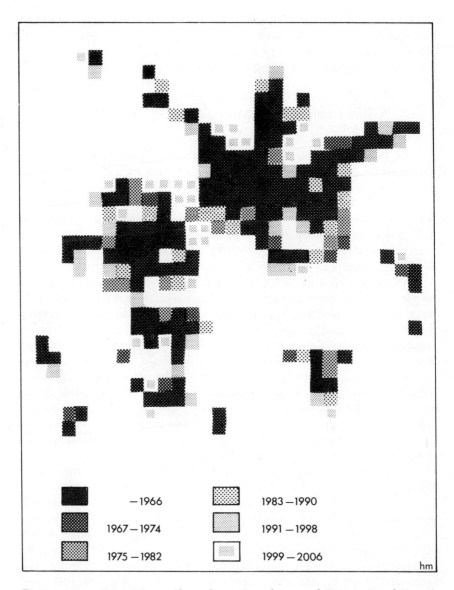

Figure 18.4   West Nottinghamshire: Simulation of Future Land Development, 1966—2006.

preventing development along valley sides and creeks which are likely to be maintained for recreational use. In the West Notts simulation other effects of planning have been modelled by projecting current zoning allocations into the future.

Besides planning and distance effects, we might also look at the economics of subdivision and industrial park development, since economies of scale and continued insistence on integrated design features will almost certainly keep the neighbor effect operative. Also, the dispersal of decision making powers which previously affected the siting of local authority "council housing" in our study area will be eroded as such authorities are integrated into Great Britain's new two-tier local government. When such factors are taken into account, the effects of major parameters are projected for five eight-year periods, from 1966 to 2006. These coefficients in turn determine the attractivity indexes for each time period. To complete the spatial simulation process we also need to know how much land the developers will require. Residential land needs are computed by dividing the anticipated population by desired gross density; calculations along similar lines are possible for industrial, retail, and other land uses.

The "surprise-free" scenario is based on a population of 285,000 by 2006, and allows development for population increase and for the overspill of residents from congested central areas (figure 18.4). A stochastic model was employed here; nevertheless growth is highly regular in comparison to historical trends—this is largely due to planning constraints which are evident in the holes and wedges within the developing form. The planner's desire to "tidy up" the urban configuration is also evident in the increasing regularity of outline, and in the absence of rural development noncontiguous to the existing urban mass. The simulation of the first period, 1966-1974, mirrors very well what has actually occurred since 1966. There are a few specific areas where the simulated pattern is obviously in error, but in general the map is a reasonable picture of future urban form. The historical and projected growth patterns present a graphic portrayal of past exponential growth (figure 18.5). Continued exponential growth is not projected for the future; planning "barriers" are erected to contain growth in certain areas and to direct it to others. Barriers are located where the development isolines run together to form thick bands.

At this point you may be saying to yourself "Yes, I accept that these maps represent reasonable surprise-free pictures of the future, but anyone with sufficient insight could arrive at similar pictures intuitively, without computer simulation." Such an opinion is probably justified at present, but as we build greater complexity into our models of reality and incorporate more factors, the rigor required by computer-aided simulation will become increasingly desirable, and it will allow us objectively to compare different scenarios.

Goal-Oriented Forecasting

Most early attempts at forecasting were concerned with predicting *the* future, the events that would actually occur. By setting themselves this objective, forecasters necessarily produced "surprise-free" projections

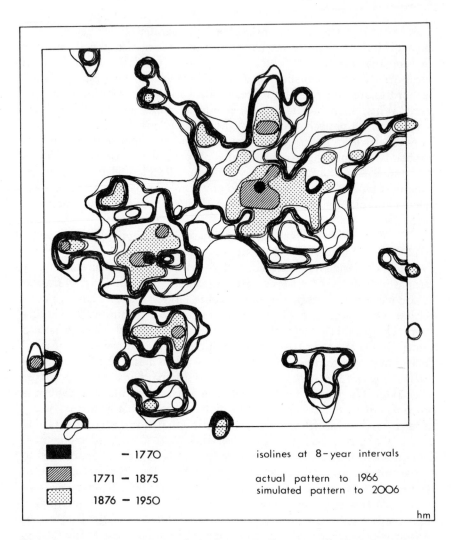

Figure 18.5 West Nottinghamshire: Diffusion of Spatial Growth, 1771–2006.

similar to the one just outlined. As forecasting has developed, however, extrapolative techniques have become considerably more sophisticated.[4] Many innovations that formerly would have induced fundamental (and therefore surprising) changes to the societal milieu can now be included within a surprise-free framework. In transportation, for example, the trend of speed against time for any one technology is an S-curve, with exponential growth and eventual flattening. When one medium of transport such as a railway stops improving, some new technology such as the aircraft is likely to begin its own exponential increase. If such individual curves are plotted together an overall exponential increase will be evident in a curve enveloping the several individual S-curves (that is, in an *envelope* curve).

The envelope curve tends to be highly predictable, but its use in extrapolation must be qualified by two important considerations—the danger of specificity and the presence of absolute constraints. In the transportation example, the macro-variable described by the envelope curve is speed, which is a sufficiently nonspecific measure for prediction. By contrast, measures of capability for individual technologies become quite irrelevant as the technologies become obsolete.

Given a suitable macro-variable the extrapolator must determine whether it is extensive or intensive. He needs to know whether the measure is approaching an intrinsic constraint. Such constraints may be absolute, such as the velocity of light, or time-dependent, in the sense that no further improvement is possible until some related technology advances. One further point worth checking is whether a parallel lagged relationship is evident such as the relationship between the speeds of combat and transport aircraft; in which the speed of transport aircraft lags behind combat aircraft speeds at a constant ratio.[5] Possible parallel lags in urban form are evident between American and European cities, for example in the size of suburban shopping malls.

The multiplicity of techniques labelled extrapolation can produce worthwhile pictures of future technology. Insofar as technology affects urban form, extrapolation techniques should be combined with simulations of urban form, and the results can be termed surprise-free. But extrapolation works under a major limiting assumption—namely, that individual and social desires and goals will remain constant and growth-oriented. Yet social change and innovation is in many ways more important than technological change. Therefore we require some means of evaluating possible and probable trends in social goals, and the impact such trends will have on urban form.

Goal-oriented technological forecasting states a need and then seeks to identify how it might be filled. It has been used by NASA to identify research necessary to achieve given objectives. Goal-oriented forecasting works backward from the objective, introducing progressively greater specificity, and notes those elements lying outside the current knowledge base.

To apply goal-oriented social forecasting, we state an objective or set of objectives, such as environmental protection, and then work backward to discover the implications of this goal. Some implications in the environmental protection case would be minimal pollution, maximum land preservation, and minimum industrialization, and these secondary objectives will in turn have implications for the form and extent of cities.

Research on urban futures must proceed from such questions as, "Given certain overall societal goals, which urban forms are most likely, and how desirable will they be?" Such research is difficult because the spatial effects of goal implementation are unlikely to be intuitively obvious. The complicated interrelationships of phenomena within large systems ensure counterintuitive "perversities."[6] For instance, urban freeways aggravate traffic congestion more than they relieve it, because they induce demand in greater measure than they supply capacity. Before we introduce such technologies, therefore, we need to be aware of their effects. We might, for example, suggest that society must choose between two relatively opposed ethics: "conservation" and "expansion" (figure 18.6). We might define these ethics explicitly by associating conservation with minimum economic and population growth, maximum environmental protection and related factors, whereas expansion would be concerned with maximum economic growth and the free application of technology.

Given such definitions of our ethical choices, what effect will any particular weighting of societal goals have on major social and technological indicators? For example, what changes in birth rates and GNP per capita can we expect given a completely dominant conservationist ethic (figure 18.6, scenario 1), a completely dominant expansionist ethic (scenario 3), or a continuance of the present ethical mix (scenario 2)? A Delphi exercise along these lines could be prepared, and a panel of experts asked to estimate proportional changes between now and the year 2000 in such factors as:

> Birth rate
> Average educational level
> Diversity of life-styles
> Life expectancy
> Length of working week
> Automation of production sectors
> Rate of technological innovation
> Social cohesion

Such measures are reasonably nonspecific, yet they do have implications for urban form, generally in an interrelated way. Thus increased educational levels might depress birth rates, thereby reducing urban expansion. Increased technological innovation might, through increased automation and consequent reduction of the working week, make proximity to workplace less important than it is now. We could also ask about changes in indexes relating specifically to urban form, such as:

> Recreational space
> Average population density in new housing areas
> Proportion of all housing rented
> Average speed of intraurban public transport
> Proportion of new housing financed by public authorities
> Average life of new urban structures

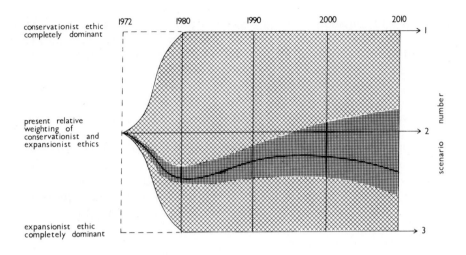

conservationist ethic
completely dominant

1972   1980   1990   2000   2010

present relative
weighting of
conservationist and
expansionist ethics

scenario number

expansionist ethic
completely dominant

Figure 18.6   Graph of Ethical Possibilities Presenting Three Scenarios.

Different proportional index changes would be evident for each of the three "standard" scenarios, and experts' opinions could be averaged. The standard Delphi procedure is to recirculate average figures to respondents and ask them to reconsider their initial opinions. However, none of the three standard scenarios is likely, and to induce consensus on the most likely ethical trend we could ask our Delphi panel to plot the trend on the graph. Such trends may be cyclical. The current trend toward conservation, for example, could be reversed in the immediate future, prominent again after 1980, and reversed again at the century's close (figure 18.6). Confidence limits for such curves can be indicated by shading that identifies the range of ethical mix we feel society is more than likely to have at a given time. Obviously, such confidence bands widen as we look further into the future. Indeed, beyond thirty or forty years from the present, the ethical dichotomy itself may well become obsolete. Averages of such trends constitute yet other scenarios that also imply different changes in listed measures. All scenarios are relevant to urban form, and we must evaluate relevance through *impact analysis*, and discover what forms might be, and which form is most desirable.

Such an impact analysis would be a computer simulation similar to that described earlier, but would also model changes in internal density and land use. We can denote locational processes by specifying the effects of particular factors and by computing indexes of attraction. But how are we to account for land use planning, which will obviously play a major role in the future? The community as a whole has certain land use goals derived from overall societal ethics. The planner's objective is to translate these community aims into viable land use configurations. Individuals within the community, however, will often have conflicting aims, such as segregating themselves from other ethnic groups, or acquiring property which might otherwise be used for parks. Conflicts between the community and the individual will be resolved to the advantage of one or the other, and we must incorporate such relative power situations in our simulations of the future. Having simulated evolving urban form in this manner, though, we will still have the problem of evaluating results. Overall density measures, indexes of social segregation, measures of building age, and frequency of land use conflict can be computed and compared with societal objectives. But the extent to which the adoption of those objectives influences such measures is given only by the "surprise-free" projection (scenario 2). If the conservation ethic results in a more compact city than is otherwise likely, we can evaluate it as desirable in this respect. If counterintuitive effects result in more diffuse forms, some other ethical choice might be more satisfactory.

Urban Futurescapes: Contrasting Scenarios

The following notes outline four urban form scenarios for the next thirty or forty years. Obviously, many facets of the future city will be similar regardless of ethical trends, and we have noted only those aspects peculiar to each. The final scenario presents some features suggested by science fiction writers. *In the long term* science fiction is likely to provide better forecasts than rigorous simulation procedures. Forecasting is still more an exercise in logical deduction than a straight mathematical calculation, and must continue to make substantial inputs of imagination. Science fiction futures are generally based on ethical possibilities quite outside our conservationist/expansionist scheme. For this reason they provide a useful and necessary contrast to other kinds of extrapolation.

Conservationist Future

Assumptions. Material wealth static or somewhat lower than at present. Emphasis on society rather than the individual, and on the development of ethical conformity and harmony of interest. Considerably reduced industrial and technological sectors, with possible rejection even of beneficial scientific offerings. Environmental protection and redevelopment leads to new roles for the city.

Trends	*Spatial Impact*
Greatly reduced industrial sector, with rigorous constraints on siting.	"Cottage" industries integrated into residential sectors, but noxious fa-

Emphasis on quality and craftman-ship.

cilities completely segregated and perhaps located underground. Industrial dereliction.

Stable or reduced population. Homogeneous and harmonious society, but possible "reverse Ludditism" (agitation *for* Machines).

Smaller cities with emphasis on upgrading of structures rather than renewal. Breakaway technological communes?

Decreased migration and intensive family structure. Great commitment to local areas.

Increased variety of urban character, with small-scale structures and locally increased densities. Political fragmentation of urban areas into community councils.

Voluntary reduction of mobility, but selective use of mass transport systems and interurban rapid transit.

Freeway networks reduced or demolished. Remaining transport systems planned for service rather than profit, thereby equalizing accessibility.

Decline of large retail centers and emphasis on neighborhood shopping.

Greater spread of retail land uses, with compact and revitalized central shopping district.

Agriculture more dependent on land quality.

Derelict and underutilized land converted to agriculture.

General environmental improvement, with occasional perverse effects. Specifically recreational areas not so necessary, but emphasis on conservation of ecological units.

Piecemeal residential location disallowed. Industry concentrated in "closed units" such as river valleys, so that adverse effects are localized and amenable to solution.

"Surprise-free" Future

Assumptions. Reasonably high increases in both private wealth and public resources over present levels. Continuing mixture of values, some favoring personal advancement and gain, some favoring public action to offset the more obvious cases of deprivation. Continued, but increasingly selective, application of technological innovation, leading to greater leisure and to heterogeneity of lifestyle. Greater stress and disorientation compounded by tempo of change.

Trends

Spatial Impact

Increasing automation and econo-

Large industrial parks relatively

mies of scale in manufacturing industry. Shorter working week. Standardized transportation components.

self-contained and often isolated from the city-location with respect to interurban transport facilities.

Stabilized population. Relatively greater social fragmentation.

Voluntary segregation by lifestyle including construction of "new-town" communes.

Greatly increased migratory patterns. Center city locations attractive.

Rented accommodation desirable. Urban blight in present-day suburban districts.

Variety of personal transport media (including high-speed sidewalks). Lower tunnelling costs and increased demand make urban rapid transit profitable.

Less need for automobile. Remaining freeways underground, releasing surface areas for other uses.

Suburban retail outlets suffer from neighborhood degeneration. Possible direct-to-customer retail systems develop.

Specialized shopping center, often in peripheral locations, but city centers revitalized due to redevelopment.

Agriculture increasingly automated and independent of land quality.

Greater areas of land available for recreation and sale to sectarian "wilderness" and agrarian groups.

Environmental deterioration owing to recreational overuse rather than industrial pollution. Checked locally by establishment of restricted areas. Aggregation of recreational areas, usually along river valleys.

Emphasis on esthetic considerations in residential location. Completely self-contained "environmental" towns developed (often privately). Obsolete urban structures (freeways) cleared for parkland.

Expansionist Future

Assumptions Advances in technology provide a high level of material well-being with substantial increases in real wealth. Societal values favor the use of this increased wealth by private individuals for improving their accommodation, space standards, and leisure activities, but there is little deliberate effort to equalize resources. Increasing fragmentation of society and rapid change produce stresses relieved through new "social" technologies and pleasure industries. Possibility of superficial and chaotic "late sensate" culture.

Trends	*Spatial Impact*
Small number of very large manufacturing complexes located with respect to natural resources. Scientific, educational, and pleasure industries free to locate according to climate, scenery, and so on.	Greater segregation of industrial areas, with many cities virtually free of manufacturing plants.
Reduced population levels and increased social fragmentation.	Cities continue to grow because of increased space requirements. Voluntary segregation by lifestyle.
Greatly increased migration and relocation patterns. Changing expectations and requirements make many buildings functionally obsolete.	Rented accommodation desirable. Massive redevelopment programs. New structures more adaptable, perhaps with built-in obsolescence.
Variety of competitive transportation and communications media.	Distance to workplace and city center unimportant for residential location—new towns cater to specific tastes. Central business districts no longer necessary.
New forms of "fun" shopping.	Specialist shopping areas.
Factory food production	Agricultural land becomes available for private uses. Distinction between city and country largely irrelevant.
Environmental deterioration checked by increasingly profitable anti-pollution industries. All forms of recreational experience catered to, but conservation of ecological units is only marginally economic.	Public involvement in the provision of recreational facilities declines. Macro-landscaping techniques used extensively in redevelopment projects.

A Science Fiction Future

Assumptions   Complete breakdown of societal norms, and fragmentation into orthodox byworld and underworld groupings. Revitalized entrepreneurial and innovative ethic in hippie byworld, characterized by the use of technology for colonization and environmental renewal. Far higher material wealth in all groups, but little emphasis on individual possession.

Trends	*Spatial Impact*
Very large "ortho" industrial complexes with scattered and small-scale byworlder plants.	Segregated industrial areas.
Population levels vary with respect to the present (higher in some areas, lower in others). Ortho and underworld groups remain in present cities.	Existing cities become highly segregated—all large structures interconnected since underworld rules the streets. Byworlder communes vary in permanency but often very large.
Ortho world housed in massive urban "monads" for protection.	Existing suburban areas degenerate and are occupied by underworld. Monads largely self-contained and lead to the decline of the city center.
Ortho use of non-personal communication and integrated mass transit, but flexible personal transport media favored in byworld.	Complete mobility renders location of land uses with respect to distance factors unimportant.
Urban monads include all shopping facilities. Byworld self-sufficient in shopping goods.	Large retail centers obsolete—city centers taken over by the underworld.
Factory food production, with some traditional farming in byworld.	Rural areas become derelict, but byworld recolonization on better land.
Massive environmental deterioration in conventional cities (excepting monads) but byworld communes generally pollution-free. Protected wilderness areas for orthos.	Complete depopulation of badly-polluted areas of the city. Urban recreational facilities deteriorate.

References

1. Information about the influence of these and other variables on the transition of cells from undeveloped to developed status for each of several time-periods was obtained by a least-squares regression analysis. The resulting estimating equations gave values of the development status which, in the main, ranged between zero and one. The use of regression coefficients as probability values for a binary, two-state transition process was tested in the author's Master's Thesis. See "Simulation of Urban Spatial Growth with Reference to London, Canada and West Nottinghamshire, England," (Master's Thesis, University of Western Ontario, 1972).

2. The spatial simulations were performed by a Fortran program written by the author for use on the University of Western Ontario's PDP-10 computer.

3. Hermann Kahn and Anthony J. Wiener, *The Year 2,000: A Framework for Speculation on the Next Thirty-Three Years* (New York: Macmillan, 1967).

4. For a discussion on extrapolative techniques, see Gordon Wills *et al.*, *Technological Forecasting* (London: Penguin, 1972).

5. R. C. Lenz, Jr., in *Technological Forecasting for Industry and Government*, edited by J. R. Bright (London: Prentice-Hall, 1968), Part 2.

6. Jay Forrester, *Urban Dynamics* (Cambridge, Massachusetts: M.I.T. Press, 1969).

Chapter 19

A Delphi Study of Future Developments in Energy Resources and Their Environmental Impacts

Vaclav Smil
University of Manitoba

ABSTRACT   *As a consensus-forming method for systematically analyzing opinions and value judgments, the Delphi technique appears to be reliable and valid. Responses from forty experts are used to analyze long-range developments in energy systems (thirty production, transmission, and transportation methods) and their complex impacts upon the environment (thirty-one protection, planning, and management techniques). The study examines future energy sources, fossil fuels, limits of growth, nuclear energy, transmission, and future energy production locations.*

The Delphi forecasting technique, like many other management and technological innovations, is a product of the cold war. A classified research memorandum written in 1951 was the first use of the Delphi technique. Restrictive security regulations delayed publication of the original memorandum for over a decade.[1] Shortly after dissemination of the original report in 1963, T. J. Gordon and Olaf Helmer conducted the first civilian Delphi study.[2] The study was primarily experimental in intent, but its four rounds of questioning yielded substantive results on six broad topics of interest: scientific innovations, population growth, automation, space programs, forecasts concerning the probability of war, and the nature of future weapons systems.

Gordon and Helmer's 1964 study stimulated considerable interest in the Delphi technique, and since then Delphi has been applied with increasing frequency to hundreds of problems. Military forecasting and long-range corporate planning remain the topics of most intensive application, but published or announced inquiries cover diverse topics such as civil defense policy, evaluation of research projects, advances in clinical drug treatment, and social planning at the community level. Comprehensive bibliographies have been prepared by Turoff and Pill.[3] Delphi is now the second most popular technique in American futuristics; it is not used quite as intensively as scenario writing, but it is used far more frequently than simulation gaming.[4] Delphi's popularity is largely a consequence of the technique's reliability; in the realm of management planning, Delphi appears to be the most trustworthy of the available forecasting methods.[5]

Delphi's reliability and validity are based on three simple concepts: first, anonymous inquiries eliminate the psychological factors inherent in face-to-face interaction. The biasing influences of outspoken individuals, semantic "noise," pressure toward conformity, and bandwagon effects are negated. Second, Delphi is iterative. Controlled feedback makes it possible to reevaluate and, when necessary, revise earlier answers. At the same time, individuals who hold extreme or unusual opinions have the opportunity to explain their thinking. Finally, Delphi is a statistical technique which does not force unanimity. Forecasts are presented in a simple median-quartile format which gives a clear view of both the majority opinion and the optimistic and pessimistic extremes.

Delphi is thus a method of systematically analyzing opinions and value judgments. It must be emphasized that Delphi is only a consensus forming technique; Delphi outputs are no more than opinions which are internally consistent but for which there exist no external verification procedure at the time forecasts are made. Delphi is an open-ended analysis, and its results can be accepted or rejected. Like all forecasting methods, Delphi contains numerous pitfalls. Wishful and emotional thinking, lack of imagination (or, on the contrary, flights of fancy), failure to anticipate changes, and self-fulfilling as well as self-defeating forecasts are just some of the dangers inherent in the use of the technique.

Yet Delphi has several advantages that traditional quantitative analysis does not possess.[6] Judiciously used, it can open new horizons for more rational decision making. There appears to be no other way to evaluate many probabilities and the significance of many possible or desirable future developments.[7] Thus it is an important weapon in the futurist's or planner's arsenal.

The Delphi Panel

Delphi appeared to be the best technique to employ in a long-range analysis of energy developments and their complex environmental impacts. Such a study was initiated in Spring 1970. First, a panel of participants was carefully chosen. Because Delphi is an exercise in opinion and value judgments, a study cannot produce worthwhile results unless the participants are experts whose opinions and judgements are based on extensive knowledge of the subject at hand. Eventually, forty experts took part in the study. They represented all important energy specializations—general energy systems, coal, oil, and natural gas industries, nuclear engineering, environmental protection, air pollution research, and nuclear radiation studies. Their affiliations ranged from government agencies, through the universities, specialized periodicals, industry, and industrial research.The group was very diverse, including, among other specialists, the inventor of the closed cycle gas turbine, a senior editor of the world's largest energy engineering journal, a top administrator of the U.S. Atomic Energy Commission and the International Atomic Energy Association, and a noted biologist recently prominent in power plant location controversies.

Among those who responded to a request for personal data in the final questionnaire, 48 percent held doctoral degrees, 37 percent had Master's degrees, and the remainder held Bachelor's degrees. The panelists' mean and the median number of years' experience in their current professions were 21. Twenty-eight (70 percent) of the participants were Americans, eleven were Europeans (United Kingdom, France, Switzerland, West Germany, and Belgium), and one was from Japan. Forty experts took part in the study. Twenty-five answered all three rounds, eight answered only two, and seven replied to only a single round of questioning.

The topics investigated in the study fall into four categories: 1) long-range prospects for energy production and environmental protection; 2) the probability of events with deleterious environmental effects during the 1970s; 3) the limits to growth of traditional technologies; and 4) priorities in the realm of energy-environment problems. The three rounds of questioning, which took almost a year to complete, resulted in surprising as well as sobering conclusions. The most important results of the study—the forecasts dealing with long-range probabilities concerning sixty-one technological, managerial, and social innovations—are summarized in tables 19.1 and 19.2. Some of the conclusions with important spatial implications are discussed in greater detail below.

TABLE 19.1   Consensus on Energy Production, Transmission and Transportation (50 Percent Probability Estimates)

Number Item	Quartile-Median-Quartile
1. Fuel cells for small-scale power generation	1980-1980-1987
2. Use of nuclear explosives in the production of	

natural gas and oil, geothermal heat etc.	1980-1980-1993
3. Coal gasification or liquefaction	1979-1982-1984
4. 'Fail-safe' nuclear power generation	1976-1983-1995
5. High temperature gas reactors (A-K cycle)	1979-1984-1990
6. Extra high voltage transmission on very long distances (at least 1,000 kv and 1,000 km)	1979-1985-1990
7. Fast breeder reactors	1981-1985-1990
8. Cyrogenic transmission systems using underground superconducting cables	1983-1985-1995
9. Large scale shale oil recovery	1983-1986-1996
10. Fossil fuel fired magnetohydrodynamics	1981-1988-1990
11. Development of all practically feasible hydroelectric sites in populated regions	1982-1988-2000
12. Techniques for economical recovery of additional 25 percent of crude oil from known resources	1983-1988-1998
13. Fully automated underground coal mining	1983-1988-2000
14. Cryogenic pipeline transportation of natural gas	1986-1988-2000
15. Simple solar furnace for home power generation in tropical and subtropical regions	1986-1990-2000
16. Low cost high voltage underground transmission	1988-1990-2000
17. Microwave power transmission	1990-1993-2000
18. 'Fail-safe' systems for drilling and producing hydrocarbons at any water depth	1987-1995-2002
19. Direct conversion—thermionics	1985-1998-2010
20. Utilization of low thermal difference systems	1990-1999-Never
21. Controlled thermonuclear power	1990-2000-2000
22. Efficient storage of electric energy in large quantities	1990-2000-2010
23. Laser power transmission	1990-2000-2010
24. Large and efficient tidal power plants	1992-2000-Never
25. High temperature gas reactors with thermal cycle other than helium	2010-2010-2020
26. Widespread use of geothermal power	1990-2020-Later
27. Relay of solar energy via satellite collectors	2000-2020-Later
28. Solar energy devices for bulk power generation	2000-Later-Never
29. Cyrogenic superfluid transportation of mechanical energy on long distances	2020-Later-Never
30. Utilization of gravitational energy (antigravity)	Later-Later-Never

TABLE 19.2 Consensus on Environmental Protection, Planning and Management (50 Percent Probability Estimates)

Number Item	Quartile-Median-Quartile
1. Energy sources become the great pawn in international politics	1971-1971-1975

2. Environmentally motivated higher price of energy   1973-1978-1983

3. Acceptance of the idea that all consumers share responsibility for pollution and its cost   1975-1978-1980

4. Safe, large scale disposal of radioactive wastes   1975-1980-1990

5. 'Nonpolluting' internal combustion engine   1976-1980-1990

6. Abolition of 'growth for growth's sake' concept   1977-1980-2000

7. Practical, economical methods of stack gas desulfurization   1978-1980-1985

8. Effective, harmless control of accidental oil spills   1978-1980-1985

9. Dry cooling power plant towers   1976-1981-1986

10. Development of waste heat utilization (desalting, heating,
    sewage treatment etc.)   1977-1983-1989

11. Control of water thermal pollution   1977-1983-1987

12. Nitrogen oxides control   1979-1983-1990

13. New car—batteries, fuel cells, steam etc.   1980-1985-1992

14. Offshore siting of large power plants   1981-1985-1997

15. Removal of noxious matter from fossil fuels before com-
    bustion   1981-1986-2000

16. Establishment of world wide environmental quality
    standards (air and water)   1985-1988-2000

17. Taxes to alleviate pollution problems (effluent taxes, tax
    incentives for dispersal of people from large cities)   1983-1990-2000

18. Establishment of world wide environmental surveillance
    and warning agency   1985-1990-2000

19. Sound suppression on highways and airways   1986-1990-Later

20. New fast and safe mass transit systems   1985-1992-2001

21. Coordinated international planning of energy con-
    sumption   1986-1995-2020

22. Application of Brayton power cycles to eliminate necessi-
    ty of water cooling   1986-1995-Later

23. Planned decrease of per capita energy demand and con-
    sumption   1988-2000-Never

24. Effective population control   1990-2000-2000

25. Conservation of fossil fuels for other future needs   1993-2005-Later

26. Man will largely destroy his ability to survive in great
    numbers and in great cities   2000-2010-Later

27. Utilization of heat sinks other than atmosphere and
    surface waters   1989-2020-Later

28. Polar siting of large power plants   2005-Later-Later

29. Application of new thermodynamic cycles (other than
    Brayton) to eliminate water cooling   2010-Later-Later

30. Elimination of all fossil fuel fired generators   2016-Later-Later

31. No private powered cars allowed   2017-Never-Never

Future Energy Sources

The Delphi panel's evaluation of the feasibility of various methods of power production are disappointing to advocates of unconventional systems. Solar energy, for example, is often cited as a major future energy source. Yet none of the numerous schemes for collecting and converting solar energy seem to be useful for efficient baseload generation. The irregular flow of radiated energy, the marked daily and seasonal fluctuations attributable to cloudiness and to the annual solar regime, the increasing turbidity of the atmosphere, and the necessity for broad collecting surfaces, most probably exclude large-scale, earth-based solar energy production during the next 50 years. Both the 50 percent and the 90 percent Delphi probability estimates of the date of occurrence of large-scale solar energy generation were beyond the year 2020 (Item 28, table 19.1). Satellites combined with microwave transmission may be a more tractable method for capturing large amounts of solar energy. The eventual introduction of such systems depends heavily on developments among competitive earth-based methods, and this explains the very pessimistic forecast of the Delphi panel. The panel in this study settled on "Never" as their estimate of the median 90 percent probability date of occurrence. Tidal power offers scarcely greater possibilities according to the panel. Although the Rance River plant in France proved the feasibility of large-scale tidal power operations, the panelists forecast that high investment costs will preclude most projects (Item 24, table 19.1). Again, the 90 percent median date of occurrence was "Never." Moreover, "Never" was also the modal answer, accounting for almost one-third of the 50 percent probability responses.

Similarly, geothermal power apparently offers little hope (Item 26, table 19.1). Six nations (Italy, New Zealand, the United States, the Soviet Union, Japan, and Mexico) now generate geothermal electric power, and although good prospects for geothermal plants exist in at least another twenty nations, developments are likely to be spotty and small-scale in the aggregate, although they may be of considerable local importance.

Low thermal energy differentials, for example, the use of thermal differences in tropical seas (where surface waters are about 80°, and waters at depths of 2000 feet are about 40°) are another potential source of future electric power. Conceivably, gravitational energy could be harnessed in the form of anti-gravity, and other sources such as neutrino absorption, ocean wave generation, and wind energy could be tapped at some date in the future. The Delphi panel of experts, however, evaluated these alternatives as being even more unlikely solutions to our power needs in the foreseeable future than are solar, tidal, and geothermal power (Item 20, table 19.1).

Generally speaking, there was consensus among the panelists that future competition among energy-producing techniques will strongly resemble the current situation. Fossil fuels and nuclear energy will continue to be the most important modes of power production. Both technologies will, naturally, undergo substantial changes whose pace and timing will determine their relative importance. But overall, the future of energy production will be more evolutionary than revolutionary.

Fossil Fuels

Fossil fueled power generation will be improved by full-scale introduction of direct conversion methods. It is unlikely that we will see all of the proposed direct conversion schemes applied in power generation, but several of them are certain to be put into operation within the next thirty years. The most promising thus far is small-scale generation using fuel cells. The panel forecast 1980 as the year in which a decisive breakthrough in fuel cell technology will occur (Item 1, table 19.1), with subsequent widespread use before the end of the century. Substation fuel cells would be remotely controlled and their primary function would be to deliver power during peak load periods. Their major advantage is that they offer reserve capacity without the necessity to solve transmission difficulties and to develop new generating sites, which are scarcely available now in any case.

Magnetohydrodynamic generation could raise power plant thermal efficiencies to the 50 to 60 percent range. Doing so would mean that fewer new plant sites would be required, fossil fuels would be used more efficiently, and thermal water pollution would be significantly decreased. The panel forecast the 1980s as the period of significant breakthroughs in magnetohydrodynamic technology.

Innovations in the use of fossil fuels, however, cannot in themselves ensure that fossil fuels will retain a strong competitive position. Economies of scale must be realized in order to keep investment and operating costs reasonable. Based on current trends, the sizes and capacities of fossil fuel power plants may be predicted with reasonable certainty for the next two decades. Thus by 1980, we can expect the world to possess over one hundred power plants with capacities above 2,000 megawatts. At least a fourth of these could have capacities greater than 3,000 megawatts, and several of the largest stations will exceed 4,000 megawatts and will approach the 5,000 megawatt mark. In contrast, the largest power plant in the United States today has a capacity only slightly over 2,000 megawatts.

Such innovations and increases in the *use* of fossil fuels must, of course, be matched by comparable progress in the *provision* of the fuels. According to the Delphi panel, the 1980s also will see the development of virtually automated underground coal mining where conditions are suitable. At the same time, surface mining productivity will be increased by improvements in coal mine shovels; maximum bucket capacity will reach between 300 and 500 cubic yards before 1980. Simultaneously, unit trains will make coal transportation easier. The Delphi panel estimates the maximum size of unit trains at 30,000 tons in 1975 and 40,000 tons in 1980. Such trains will be fully automated, unloading quickly through bottom drops or by rotary dumping, and will run about 700 to 900 miles daily. Over shorter distances, slurry pipelines will be used increasingly for coal transportation.

The hydrocarbon production and transportation industries will be equally affected by innovations and economies of scale. During the 1980s, innovations should result in a 60 percent petroleum recovery, which will be a 25 percent increase over current recovery rates. Nuclear explosives may well be routinely used to increase the recovery of oil and gas deposits. The search for new hydrocarbon reserves will continue on all continents but exploration and commercial production will increasingly shift to offshore areas. This worldwide shift will be based on new techniques of offshore drilling which will provide the industry with the capability to drill and produce hydrocarbons at practically any depth.

Petroleum tankers will undoubtedly achieve a maximum size of 500,000 dead weight tons during the 1970s and they may grow even larger. Liquified natural gas tankers, an innovation of the 1960s, will constitute a fleet of at least fifty large ships by 1980, with individual ship sizes ranging up to 150,000 cubic meters. Large diameter pipelines will carry hydrocarbons over transcontinental distances as well as underseas. The increased scale of tanker and pipeline operations will result in larger capacity petroleum refineries. Whereas the largest refineries are now capable of handling 15 to 25 million tons of petroleum a year, the panel forecast refineries with annual capacities of 40 million tons by 1980.

We can look forward, then, to an impressive array of changes which will undoubtedly strengthen the position of fossil fuels in the next several decades. At the same time, the realization that technological capabilities have certain inherent disadvantages makes it obvious that we are entering a period of serious difficulties.

Limits of Growth

One important constraint on further growth is the fact that certain technological and economic limits are now being slowly, but inexorably, approached. The panelists estimated the largest feasible size for turbo-generators in fossil fueled power plants at 2,000 megawatts. They thought 1,500 feet will be the maximum height for power plant stacks. Total installed power plant capacity will most likely not exceed 6,000 to 8,000 megawatts. The largest feasible diameter for crude oil pipelines is about 72 inches (1,800 millimeters). These limits enable us to put current steep growth-curve slopes in broader perspectives. They clearly indicate that development cannot continue indefinitely at exponential rates. Most of these growth limits in the fossil fuel industries will be reached, according to the Delphi panel, within the next ten to fifteen years.

A second, and ultimately more important constraint, is the broad set of environmental considerations which have assumed critical importance for the future development of any energy resource. The methods now used to extract fossil fuels and convert them into usable energy are among the worst despoilers of the physical environment. They cause gaseous and particulate air pollution, thermal and hydrocarbon pollution of waters, devastation of the landscape, and esthetic eyesores, to name just a few of their more evident manifestations. Many of these complex problems can be solved or at least substantially alleviated in the coming decades, and in fact the Delphi panel was rather optimistic about the industry's abilities to overcome such difficulties.

Waste heat utilization, for example, could bring thermal water pollution under control during the next decade (Item 10, table 19.2), especially when coupled with dry cooling towers (Item 9, table 19.2) in more efficient generation schemes such as direct conversion. Stack gas desulphurization (Item 7, table 19.2), fuel oil desulphurization before combustion (Item 15, table 19.2), high efficiency electrostatic precipitation, and nitrogen oxide control could significantly reduce power plant air pollution within the next twenty years. Such efforts may be greatly facilitated by successful large-scale coal gasification, which would produce a high caloric "pipeline" gas. The Delphi panel forecasts such a breakthrough within seven to ten years (Item 3, table 19.1).

Effective and biologically harmless methods of coping with accidental oil spills, increased navigational safety for tankers through closely supervised navigation, and binding international agreements prohibiting deliberate waste dumping in the oceans, could improve heavily polluted near-shore areas.

Yet the technological feasibility of measures to protect the environment is only part of the story. The other part, the economic and social profitability of instituting measures which the forecasts indicate are clearly possible, is far more important. Judged from this viewpoint, the future of fossil fuels is by no means secure. Virtually all pollution control methods cited above will be very expensive, and none of them is 100 percent efficient. Indeed, in many cases efficiencies of 70 to 80 percent are the upper performance limit. Certain pollutants, such as carbon dioxide, are impossible to eliminate as long as fossil combustion continues. Others, such as the finest fractions of fly-ash, could be eliminated from the environment only at enormous cost. And once economies of scale have been pushed to their maximum limits, demands for new generating sites and more raw materials will increase, and pollution will intensify.

Finally, even if total energy consumption grows slowly or moderately, planetary demand for energy will be between 25 and 40 billion metric tons of coal equivalent within the next fifty years. This compares with a 1970 consumption of 6.8 billion metric tons of coal equivalent. If all of this energy were to come from fossil fuels, the extraction, transportation, and handling of such quantities of material defies imagination. It is becoming increasingly clear that the *logistics* of fossil fuel use, rather than the technology of extraction, combustion, or environmental protection, is the crucial factor limiting their use. This is not to argue that fossil fuels will no longer be used. They will certainly continue to provide a large share of our energy in the coming decades. But large as their role looms, even assuming they can cope with more restrictive environmental policies and increasing production costs, we must rely in the long run on more intensive use of nuclear energy.

Nuclear Energy

Nuclear power generation will assume an ever-increasing share of the future energy market. Timing and capacity estimates may be inaccurate, but the overall trend is irreversible. Nuclear generation is by no means devoid of environmental, safety, technological, and economic problems. But the informed consensus of the Delphi panelists is that such problems are not insurmountable and that nuclear power is the energy wave of the future.

Some details of the Delphi questionnaires give evidence on this point. When asked for a priority ranking of urgent energy-environment problems, the item "radioactive wastes and emissions" was ranked tenth, lower than the air pollution effects related to fossil fuel combustion, internal combustion, engine emissions, accidental oil spills, waste accumulation, and problems attributable to domestic heating. Thus in the minds of energy experts, one of the more serious problems usually associated with nuclear energy is not of major consequence.

Similarly, whereas probability estimates concerning environmental episodes in the 1970s foresaw severe urban air pollution, and a catastrophe involving a fully loaded jumbo tanker as almost certain to come (median probabilities of 90 and 70 percent), the panel thought that the occurrence of radioactive contamination outside a reactor building because of failure of a nuclear power plant protective system had a median probability of 5 percent.

This very low probability implies a public risk of 0.05 fatalities per year per million of population, or about 5.7×10^{-12} fatalities per person per hour of exposure. This risk compares quite favorably with known technological dangers involving great numbers of people in long exposures. When the risk of death from disease (on the order of 10^{-6} per person per hour) for a large population is taken as a baseline, the two basic transportation media (certified air carriers and motor vehicles) expose the population to about the same risk. Natural disasters expose population to fatal risks on the order of 10^{-10} per person per hour. Thus even if current estimates of nuclear power plant risks are underestimates by two orders of magnitude, the danger from a nuclear power plant would be only slightly higher than the risk of individual accidental death from hurricanes in the Gulf of Mexico region or from tornadoes in the American Midwest. To the extent that the Delphi panel's risk estimate is accurate, one is more likely to be killed by a hurricane or a tornado, and far more likely to be killed in an airplane crash or automobile accident, than by radiation from a nuclear power plant catastrophe. Such comparisons show clearly that the social utility of nuclear power with respect to accidental catastrophes is high.

Delphi also predicted that technological breakthroughs in the safe, large-scale disposal of radioactive wastes are imminent. Virtually certain control over by-products of nuclear generation was predicted for within thirty years (Item 4, table 19.2). The panel forecast development of fail-safe nuclear generation as early as 1990.

Water reactors have been successfully used for large-scale base-load generation, and future market penetration depends largely on taking advantage of scale economies. The Delphi panel estimated the median limit of the current generation of nuclear power plants at 10,000 megawatts in 1990. If reliable heat control can be achieved, this capacity could easily be surpassed by more efficient generating systems. The first of these promising targets for the American nuclear industry is the fast breeder reactor which the industry hopes to develop in the 1980s. The major advantages of the breeder reactor are its ability to produce more fuel than it consumes and the fact that it uses economical low-grade uranium and thorium ores which are in abundant supply. The U.S. Atomic Energy Commission plans to introduce breeder reactors in the mid-1980s; the Delphi panel forecast a high probability of introduction for the same time (median estimate was 1985).

Finally, there exists a fair possibility that controlled thermonuclear fusion will be achieved within this century. The Delphi panel as well as other informed sources think that this breakthrough will occur in the 1990s. Successful thermonuclear fusion is almost beyond our present comprehension. From what we know, it would supply us with a virtually inexhaustible, highly efficient (60 percent or more), inherently safe, low pollution energy source (see chapter 2).

Transmission

Energy production and consumption and regional differences in demand imply profound changes in transmission systems in the next thirty to fifty years. Ultra high voltage (1,000 kilovolt alternating current) transmission over very long distances (1,000 kilometers) is virtually certain to be routine during the next decade. The panel's 50 percent median estimate for these innovations is 1985; the 90 percent median is 1989 (Item 6, table 19.1). Direct current transmission will take place over even longer distances and at higher voltages (1,500 to 2,200 kilovolts over trans-continental distances).

Further transmission developments will be based on electromagnetic and cryogenic applications. The Delphi panel forecast that the 1990s will see a possible breakthrough in microwave transmission (Item 17, table 19.1), and they estimated that the first decade of the twenty-first century will be the period in which laser power transmission will become feasible (Item 23, table 19.1).Cryogenic systems using underground superconducting cables might be in service even sooner; the Delphi 90 percent probability median estimate is the year 2000 (Item 8, table 19.1).

Future Locations

Unless stack gas desulphurization systems are rapidly developed, coal fired power plants that burn high-sulphur coal will soon retreat to remote locations in sparsely populated areas far from the urban regions of intensive energy demand. The best current examples of such locational decisions are the power plants concentrated in the four corners of Arizona, Utah, Nevada, and New Mexico. But even sites in remote areas create environmental problems and objections. In any event, such mine-mouth locations (similar examples occur in western Pennsylvania, rural Illinois, and the Tennessee Valley Authority region) stimulate high voltage ties.

Seashore and river locations should become valuable again because desulphurized oil use will increase and water transportation is essential for delivery of that commodity at low prices. An interim solution would locate plants offshore from the leeward sides of continents, but such offshore locations will probably be used sooner for floating nuclear power plants, especially off the eastern shore of the United States. The major incentives for such locations, which are now technologically possible, are the problems caused by thermal pollution and, above all, the absence of suitable land sites.

Should sulphur dioxide removal methods become highly efficient, high sulphur coals would no longer be objectionable. Sulphuric acid, sulphur, and fertilizers would be the final saleable products of such removal techniques, and the markets for these commodities could become locational attractions. Effective sulphur dioxide control combined with reliable particulate removal and NO_x reduction would make it feasible for large power plants to return to locations close to load centers, thus economizing transmission and right-of-way costs. Safety regulations and accumulated experience with nuclear power plants make the risks of accidental contamination negligible, and as advanced cooling and heat utilization systems go into operation, nuclear power plants could also move closer to load centers, perhaps locating on the outskirts of cities.

Advanced fast breeder plants and, somewhat later, fusion generators would most conveniently be located in high capacity seashore nuclear parks. Such power plants could serve as centers of large agricultural and industrial complexes. Energy could be used in chemical production and manufacturing without transmission losses, while waste heat could be used to facilitate highly efficient agricultural and maricultural activities.

Breeder and fusion power will make electricity by far the major form of energy. Superconducting cables, microwave, and laser transmission on intercontinental scales via stationary orbit satellite, will make it possible to move energy anywhere on the earth's surface. Currently we have continental power networks and a competent technology, which, despite current problems, seems capable of supplying our power needs for decades to come in an economically and environmentally sound way. In the remainder of this century and in the first decades of the next millennium, we can build a global network based on efficient, virtually nonpolluting plants that will deliver relatively cheap energy in quantities which could do much to eliminate the inequities evident in today's global society.

Even the boldest technological solutions—fusion power, satellites, and laser transmission—are not precluded by the laws of nature. The achievements of technology and the directions it takes have always been determined more by social and political behavior than by inherent natural limits. Future energy policies will be as sound and as successful as our future human policies. Forecasting exercises such as this Delphi study can disclose alternatives and chart the limits of our imaginative horizons. But it is our current and future *choices* which will turn those alternatives into fulfilled dreams or shattered prophecies.

References

1. N. Dalkey and O. Helmer, "An Experimental Application of the Delphi Method to the Use of Experts," *Management Science* 9 (1963): 458—467.

2. T. J. Gordon and O. Helmer, *Report on a Long-Range Forecasting Study* (Santa Monica, California: RAND Corporation, P-2982, 1964).

3. M. Turoff, *Design of a Policy Delphi* (Washington, D.C.: Office of Emergency Preparedness, TM-123, 1970); J. Pill, "The Delphi Method: Substance, Context, a Critique and an Annotated Bibliography," *Socio-Economic Planning Science* 5, (1971):57—71.

4. J. McHale, *Typological Survey of Future Research in the United States* (Binghamton, N.Y.: State University of New York, 1970).

5. G. A. Steiner, *Top Management Planning* (New York: Macmillan, 1969).

6. R. S. Quade, *On the Limitations of Quantitative Analysis* (Santa Monica, California: RAND Corporation, P-4530, 1970).

7. D. G. Rowlands, "Technological Forecasting: A Reply," Long-Range Planning 2, (1969): 78—79.

Chapter   20

Futuristic Fads and Fancies: Some Shortcomings in Futuristic Studies

George Macinko
Central Washington State College

ABSTRACT: *There are serious psychological, social, and philosophical shortcomings in futuristics. Widespread ecological ignorance is apparent, and the much touted "systems approach" is commonly neglected in practice. Scholarship is often careless, language is obtuse, and sources obscure or omitted. Distinctions between necessary and sufficient causes, between what is feasible and what is desirable, and between the "probable future" and the many "possible futures" are frequently ignored. Scenarios should be designed to promote maximum human satisfaction, not maximum allowable population densities. What is at stake is not so much man's survival, but rather the survival of a humane way of life.*

My original intention in preparing this chapter was to document the widespread ecological ignorance evident in much futuristic writing and to suggest some of the adverse consequences of this shortcoming. By so doing I hoped to demonstrate that many of the settlement patterns advertised as possible for the twenty-first century are only pseudo-alternatives because they are subject to limiting ecological factors. To take but one example: it is widely assumed among some futurists that the world's population will continue to grow at its present rate well into the next century, and that by the turn of the century from 75 to 95 percent of this population will reside in urban centers. It is further assumed that in presently "underdeveloped countries" such growth will be made possible by major advances in agricultural productivity which will free man from his age-old attachment to the land. Massive doses of inorganic fertilizers are necessary to attain the high yield agriculture prerequisite to such shifts in settlement. Little attention is paid to evidence of the undesirable side effects of this fertilization, although it promises to overstress the nitrogen cycle in the soil and thereby create serious water problems. Eutrophication caused by the overfeeding of algae from fertilizer runoff poses so serious a threat to the water systems needed for water supply and waste disposal that the use of inorganic fertilizers may have to be cut back in the developed nations and limited in the underdeveloped.[1]

The above example discloses that futuristic writings, though making prominent mention of the "systems approach," commonly neglect to incorporate it in practice. When one attempts to balance increased food production against eutrophication of waters (and the possibly dangerous increased levels of nitrates in drinking supplies) resulting from the increased fertilization proposed, then the "system" imposes some constraints on action. And, of course, the more factors in the ecosystem we consider, the more constraints we find.

My original intention of eliciting some dimensions of the ecological framework within which future settlement must occur was abandoned in favor of this subject—the psychological, social, and philosophical shortcomings of the dominant trends in futurism. I decided on this shift in emphasis after I read an earlier version of Hans Carol's chapter 16.

Carol closed his paper by asking how useful the scenario approach was in charting a desirable path into the future. This question reinforced a similar one posed by Ronald Abler who asked what characteristics distinguish the most desirable geography of the future. These questions, in conjunction with Carol's reminder that scenario writing involves *constructive, scientifically controlled imagination*, suddenly exposed the doubts that accompanied my reading of many futuristic works. That is, not only does much futuristic writing violate the condition of scientifically controlled imagination, but, also, it is only marginally constructive in that it is only minimally concerned with the characteristics of the most desirable future geography. It chooses instead to outline those conditions whereby man can assure himself of a wide range of repellent future prospects. This tendency is noted very nicely by the Berkeley geographer, Daniel B. Luten, Jr., who, in personal communication to me characterized one of the more prominent futurists by saying, "he seems to be trying to devise ways of packing more and more increasingly miserable people into the world."

I wish to challenge the agenda that now dominates futurism; I maintain it not only ignores fundamental ecological considerations, but also chooses to bypass psychological, social, and philosophical warning lights as well. In choosing to concentrate on the latter aspects I recognize my vulnerability; nobody has the exact knowledge necessary to definitively close the argument. But the social risks attendant upon postponing such a discussion are so grave that I am encouraged to press on with this task. To begin, I should sketch some of the scholarly shortcomings of the futuristic movement. I wish to emphasize that not all futurists will exhibit the traits described. Nonetheless, I believe my depiction of futurism is representative of its most widely known practitioners and thus of its most popularly disseminated pronouncements. In what follows I refer to popular writings as well as the more specialized literature because I am convinced that man's future environment will be largely determined by the collective actions of individuals who depend on the mass media for information.

Futurism

Elsewhere[2] I examined the work of Constantinos Doxiadis, the crown prince of futurism, to demonstrate that an inordinate amount of undisciplined thought is promulgated by his "ekistics" school in the guise of reasoned, ultra-sophisticated studies. In these studies language is often used to obscure rather than to illuminate; unexplained inconsistencies abound; and, in general, scholarship is so carelessly handled as to make evaluation nearly impossible.

These and similar shortcomings are widespread in futuristic literature and find especially ready expression in the writings of those who regularly participate in the Doxiadis-sponsored Delos Symposia. R. Buckminster Fuller, for example, when he is not engaged in a colossal put-on (see the story of the "great pirates")[3] uses language in an obtuse fashion that defies comprehension in order to mask a paucity of substance. Edmund Bacon, the Philadelphia city planner, displays the inconsistency with which futurists treat growth when he fails to follow his own arguments to their logical conclusions. Bacon contends that the projected growth of New York City will soon make it such a distasteful place that Philadelphia will be provided a boon in the form of growth diverted from New York. But it is unclear how the forces of growth, after undermining liveability in New York, are to be prevented from accomplishing the same end when unleashed in Philadelphia at some later date.[4] Finally, Fuller, Doxiadis and company make it difficult to check the sources and authenticity of their information. Doxiadis makes frequent reference to nameless authorities and undesignated in-house studies, whereas Fuller simply omits references to sources.

Technetronics

A recent *Time* essay provides a concise survey of a dominant theme in futuristic thought.[5] According to the futuristic technocrats, we are about to enter the "technetronic" age which will be characterized by industrial productivity of such magnitude that most of the world will be liberated from scarcity. The full dimensions of this liberation are nowhere spelled out, however. In their cornucopian visions the futurists ignore the distinction between necessary and sufficient causes. Material progress through increased production has motivated industrial society for at least a hundred years, but material progress by itself provides no guarantee of happiness. And there is a growing awareness that technological change is a determinant of what is feasible, not what is desirable. Our record of providing clean air, clean water, and esthetically pleasing landscapes has suffered while we have experienced our greatest technological advance.

In the *Time* essay the futuristic technocrats cull some ideas from economist John Galbraith's works to buttress their cornucopian projections, but they ignore the many esthetic, ecological, and social qualifications Galbraith provides. Perhaps one should not be too critical of the highly selective tendencies of futurism, for de Jouvenal notes this to be a widespread tendency of modern thought and action.[6] De Jouvenal distinguishes between what he calls "project tidy" and "irrelevant untidy" modes of thought and action. The cut made to extract coal in a mining operation is neat and tidy whereas the disposal of overburden is untidy, because nobody is concerned with what is judged to be irrelevant to the project itself. While agreeing that futurists have no corner on the selectivity market, I maintain that the extent to which futurism dismisses ecological, psychological, and social concerns establishes new levels of selectivity.

What is a Desirable Future?

The question: What constitutes a desirable future? is largely avoided, at least at the explicit level. Yet futurists are not reluctant to construct scenarios containing a plethora of implicit assumptions of desirability. If, as I maintain, a desirable future depends primarily on the quality of the people making up a society, and if, further, the quality of a people is at least partly conditioned by the environmental setting in which they live, then it is imperative to examine the environments postulated by the futurists. The futuristic thought I criticize is primarily that based on "no alternative", single situation scenarios advanced as predictive or propagandizing devices, which violate both the spirit and purpose of the scenario technique. Futurists who draw scenarios in this limited fashion seem unable or unwilling to distinguish between the "probable future," which will transpire given a continuation of present trends, and the many "possible futures" which remain open if man, judging the probable future to be undesirable, chooses to influence that future by deliberate action.[7]

Visions of the Future

The scenarios sketched by futurists such as Doxiadis, Fuller, and Bacon are essentially extensions of past and present patterns (increasing urbanization, continued exponential population growth, power consumption, and industrial production) into the twenty-first century. All are diametrically opposed to Theobald's contention that the one pattern that can be ruled out for the year 2000 is that it will be recognizable in terms of the present. In his words, "The environmental/ecological/population issue makes it clear that we shall either perceive the issue in a totally new way by the year 2000 or the planet will be under sentence of death through man's own stupidity."[8] Theobald notes that in a world dedicated to growth and prosperity all curves are exponential, but only in mathematics do curves grow to infinity. In the real world they break down gently or catastropically and Theobald urges a fundamental change in values to allow for a gentle rather than a catastrophic ending.

In his book *Eden Was No Garden*, Calder exemplifies the opposing viewpoint which characterizes so much futuristic thinking.[9] He assumes that population will continue to grow at present rates and, therefore, we will have 9 billion people sometime in the first half of the next century. To accommodate these numbers, he proposes new towns and cities of 50,000 to 50 million inhabitants largely located in the oceans, both under and especially on top of the sea, most likely in the form of floating iceships. Food will be provided primarily by farming the ocean, climates will be entirely man-controlled, technology will virtually do away with manual labor, and it will even take over much of the learning process—you will learn while you sleep. In all this, future possibilities are advanced as present or near-future fact with little heed paid to the many non-technical contingencies involved.

This tendency to discount, or not to recognize the potentially serious weaknesses in the scenarios is nowhere more evident than in the area of population growth and settlement density. Meier, for example, sets forth a resource-use strategy designed to speed the influx of rural dwellers into cities so that 90 to 95 percent of the world population will reside in cities. "Large urban regions, made up of constellations of cities, must come into existence to accommodate the influx, some containing hundreds of millions of people." To accommodate such numbers he proposes to organize urban space and facilities on a multi-shift, multi-use basis. "The gross densities of settlement are expected to be about 100,000 persons per square mile. This concentration can be very inconvenient if not comprehensively planned so that virtually all the space is available for human use at all times of the day and night."[10]

Although showing scant appreciation for the power of the exponential, the futurists, if pressed, would concede that there are practical limits to urban crowding and to population density. These limits might be labelled maximum allowable density (MAD). Significantly, the mainstream of futuristic thinking assumes that man can go from his present condition right to the brink of MAD without serious societal dislocation. I believe this assumption to be extremely foolhardy; to dismiss cavalierly the dangers of psychic disorientation and/or personality damage under MAD is an abdication of responsibility.

Some Warning Signals

While one goes far out on a limb trying to generalize about the human condition, the accumulated evidence obtained from studies in animal behavior is now so substantial as to compel attention. John Calhoun's studies of rat behavior under differing levels of population density document the progressive and nearly complete breakdown of social fabric once critical densities are exceeded.[11] Other observations of animal behavior under conditions resembling those designed for humans in futuristic scenarios are scarely more reassuring. Calder would have his future society live in pampered, closely controlled climatic, nutritional, and social settings. Similar conditions are already found on modern hog farms, where pigs are stationed before conveyor belts moving at predetermined speeds carrying food rations designed for optimum fattening at minimum cost. The flaw in this otherwise fully automated system is the propensity of some pigs to go crazy. This requires a human attendant who watches for early symptoms of insanity, removes the victim from his place, and replaces him with another animal as soon as possible. Five minutes is apparently the upper limit of deviant behavior before mass insanity breaks loose.[12]

You may object that hog farms are not designed to promote the happiness or welfare of pigs, which is considered irrelevant to the project of maximum pig fattening. My rejoinder is that many scenarios do not appear to be designed to promote maximum human satisfaction (however that may be defined), but instead to promote maximum allowable density or some other structural feature, with human satisfaction looked upon as largely irrelevant.

With due allowance for animal-human differences, it would appear dangerous to dismiss animal behavior studies as irrelevant. Nor is one limited to animal analogies when suggesting that much of futurism disregards alarming omens. The 1962 "Mid-Town Manhattan Study," reporting on an eight-year cooperative research effort of the Cornell Medical College, concluded that approximately 25 percent of those surveyed were disturbed ("mentally morbid" in the study language) and only one in five persons in Manhattan was considered mentally well.[13] Allowing for the vagaries and uncertainties of survey technique, the ambiguity of human response, and the difficulty in separating cause and effect, it still seems probable that these findings reflect density-dependent conditions.

Recently a German physician, Deitrich Oeter, warned city planners that the trend toward high-rise buildings was allowing economic and technical factors to outweigh basic human physiological and psychological needs. Oeter's studies disclose that housewives and children living on fourth floors of apartment houses in Hamburg are twice as likely to be ill as those on the ground floor. Housewives on upper floors were more prone to mental ills and their children more susceptible to respiratory and circulatory ailments than were their ground dwelling counterparts. Oeter concluded that for families with children the healthiest accommodation continues to be the one-family house with garden.[14]

Humanizing the Future

Unless futuristic scenarios are constructed strictly as academic games they have some relevance to the future because they provide the basis for a conscious choice of that future. Since we can only consciously choose from the variety of futures set forth, it is imperative that the widest array of futures be elucidated in all their strengths and weaknesses. Most futuristic writings present a skewed and very short-term view of the future based on the projection of past and present trends.They ignore the difficulties inherent in the continuation of these trends, and they bypass a wide variety of already present ecological, esthetic, social, and psychological warnings. The result is a set of future lifestyles which, if adopted, may prove socially undesirable or even crippling.

I have barely mentioned the ecological difficulties man faces as his growing numbers attempt to adopt increasingly urbanized settlement patterns at ever higher levels of material consumption. I have even more completely bypassed the dangers of pushing into a future with such a heavy demographic load as to require increased dependency on untested but ever more powerful technologies. I chose not to address myself to the problem of human survival, for I believe that what is at stake is not so much man's survival as the survival of a humane and civilized way of life. I agree with Dubos' assessment of man as the most adaptable of animals.[15] I also agree when he says this very adaptability may, if untempered by wisdom, allow him to adjust to progressively worsening conditions of life. Therefore, I see the task of the scenario writer as not simply projecting the future, but rather attempting to humanize it. The failure to do so may well lead to an ugliness of the spirit unpleasant to contemplate, and to a quality of life th at will be strained if not irreparably impaired.

References

1. B.Commoner, "Nature Under Attack," *Columbia University Forum* 11 (Spring 1968): 17—22. See also P. R. Ehrlich and A. H. Ehrlich, *Population, Resources, Environment* (San Francisco: W. H. Freeman & Co., 1970), ch. 7, esp. pp. 187—189.Experiments disclose that replacing manures with inorganic fertilizers adversely affects the efficiency with which nitrates are transferred from soil to plant. The usual response to this decreased efficiency is to continually increase the level of application of inorganic nitrogen, thereby maintaining high yields but in the process making ever greater supplies of unassimilated nitrates available for drainage into lakes and streams leading to spectacular overblooms of aquatic algae.

2. G. Macinko, "Land Use and Urban Development," in *The Subversive Science: Essays Toward an Ecology of Man,* edited by P. Shepard and D. McKinely (Boston: Houghton Mifflin Co., 1969), pp. 369—383.

3. R. Buckminster Fuller, *An Operating Manual for Spaceship Earth* (Carbondale, Ill.: Southern Illinois University Press, 1969). See ch. 2 for the great pirate story and compare Fuller's position on energy and matter in chapter 6 with, for example, P. Cloud's "Realities of Mineral Distribution," in *Effects of Population Growth on Natural Resources and the Environment,* Hearings before a Subcommittee of the Committee on Government Operations, House of Representatives, 91st Cong., 1st sess., September 15—16, 1969. Reprinted from *The Texas Quarterly,* Summer 1968, pp. 219—238.

4. Magazine section of the *Bulletin* (Philadelphia), November 6, 1966, pp. 23—31.

5. *Time,* January 24, 1969, pp. 19—20.

6. B. de Jouvenel, "The Stewardship of the Earth," in *The Fitness of Man's Environment* (Washington: Smithsonian Institution Press, 1968), pp. 103—104.

7. L. Mumford, "Closing Statement," in *Future Environments of North America,* ed. F. F. Darling and J. P. Milton (Garden City, N.Y.: Natural History Press, 1966), pp. 718—719.

8. R. Theobold. Address given at the Conference on Issues and Priorities for Development of American Northwest, June 22, 1969.

9. N. Calder, *Eden Was No Garden* (New York: Holt, Rhinehart, and Winston, 1967), ch. 8. I find Calder to be among the more restrained of the futurists and perhaps, therefore, am even more impressed by the conclusions forced upon him in his attempt to play the numbers game. That is, while I have no quarrel with people voluntarily electing to live on floating iceships, I do believe a different light is cast on the subject if one postulates the necessity of doing so in response to population pressure.

10. R. L. Meier, "Material Resources," in *Mankind 2,000,* ed. R. Jungk and J. Galtung (London: Allen & Unwin, 1969) pp. 105—114.

11. J. B. Calhoun, "Population Density and Social Pathology," *Scientific American* 206 (1962): 139—148.

12. *Yakima Herald Republic* (Yakima, Washington), September 26, 1970. Similar

behavioral aberrations are reported in more detail in R. Harrison, *Animal Machines: The New Factory Farming Industry* (New York: Ballentine Books, Inc., 1966). See especially pp. 71, 184—5, for deviant behavior of battery-raised chickens.

13. L. Srole *et al.*, *Mental Health in the Metropolis: Midtown Manhattan Study* (New York: McGraw-Hill Book Co., 1962), p. 138.

14. *Yakima Herald Republic* (Yakima, Washington), September 7, 1970, Associated Press release. Note the sharp contrast between Oeter's position and that of Meier (ref. 10 above) who proposes large constellations of cities at densities some four times greater than New York City, virtually precluding anything but high-rise living for the majority of the world's population.

15. R. Dubos, *So Human An Animal* (New York: Scribner's, 1968), ch. 5, 6.

Chapter   21

Geographical Futuristics: Philosophical and Practical Problems

The Editors

ABSTRACT: *This final chapter reviews the book's basic theme. Human extensibility, coupled with time- and cost-space convergence, will free societies from traditional locational constraints. But the technologies that set us free also present serious problems of stress and administration. Similarly, widespread exercise of new geographical freedoms and intensive uses of new technologies could lead to resource exhaustion and environmental pollution. If humane futures are to be designed, the complex philosophical issues revolving around human survival, quality of life, and outlook toward the future must be resolved.*

Once these hurdles are negotiated, several strategic dilemmas remain. Some consensus must evolve as to which group or groups will choose among alternative futures on behalf of society. Relationships between futuristics and planning must be clarified, and tactics that channel individual behavior in the direction of general social goals must be invented if we hope to avoid despotic coercion.

Escape from the administration and overload paradoxes does not free us from the ambiguities, conflicts, and dilemmas that afflict any human activity. Time-space convergence and human extensibility are double-edged, and solving the immediate problems they create simply frees us to worry about more general problems. Despite the power they give us to organize and reorganize space, time-space convergence and human extensibility will not necessarily facilitate the fulfillment of human desires. Moreover, the practice of spatial futuristics raises difficult moral and political questions for it requires that some people make decisions on behalf of others. To devise acceptable strategies for making such decisions will tax our wisdom even more than our ingenuity.

Such dilemmas guarantee that some efforts to develop a vigorous and productive geographical futuristics will fail. What is worse, some attempts will erect obstacles to the spatial goals we seek. However, such difficulties are offset by the benefits to be derived from spatial futuristics. It is clear that societies practice spatial futuristics *de facto* when they do not do so overtly and self-consciously. That being the case, we cannot understand spatial and locational behavior—let alone govern it in the decades ahead—if we do not accept the risks inherent in futuristic analysis.

Extensibility and Convergence

The geographical context in which advanced and developing societies will live, work, and play in the decades ahead is one in which individual horizons will be extended greatly while distance loses its power as a major determinant of human affairs. Sophisticated communications technologies will enable individuals or groups easily to contact others throughout the world without respect to location. Individuals and groups are surrounded by information "fields" from which they receive information. One of the unwritten histories of the modern world (touched upon slightly by Philbrick and Abler in chapters 2 and 3) is the expansion of such information fields from the miniscule purviews of medieval peasants to the more global perspectives now possible via telecommunications media.

At present, global perspectives are still incomplete. We are global receivers but only local senders. The overwhelming trend of current communications technology, however, is to complete our expanded information fields by enabling us to send as well as receive information on global scales. This is the true meaning of the concept of human extensibility. A person who receives information from anywhere on earth extends only his *interest*. A person who can send information at will to any place on earth extends *himself*. By transforming global information fields into transmission fields, communications technology makes it possible for everyone to extend himself over the entire earth. Everyone will soon be everywhere.

Some consequences of extensibility were described in detail by Philbrick, Abler, and McDaniel. McDaniel and Abler (chapters 3, 4, and 10) emphasize the man-machine interactions which make human extensibility possible and indeed inevitable. Philbrick (chapter 7) is more concerned with how changes in human extensibility will affect perception, pointing out that the global perspective we are now formulating will be followed by "in-out" perceptions; people will view the world as a single cultural-ecological unit rather than as a differentiated entity. McDaniel seems more sensitive to potential dangers inherent in human extensibility. He argues that the capacity to extend individual consciousness globally raises the danger that individuals will dilute their identities in the process of extending them. Furthermore, he reminds us that media which permit human extensibility can also rob individuals of their identities by eliminating their privacy.

There is general agreement among Philbrick, Abler, McDaniel and others that economic, social, recreational, and residential activities will soon be almost completely footloose. Unlimited capacities for moving energy, materials, and information to any location on the earth's surface will produce unprecedented locational flexibility. Wolfe (chapter 17) and Sommer (chapter 11) also emphasize the importance of time-space convergence. Bunge's forceful rejoinder (chapter 12) demonstrates that convergence benefits are not equitably distributed in American society. Also, the mobility characteristic of North American society has yet to diffuse to the rest of the world. Finally, Macinko's description (chapter 20) of the physical and logistical side effects implied by continued and expanded mobility indicates that complete mobility will itself create enormous problems.

Nevertheless, the general trend in advanced and developing regions is toward greater locational flexibility. Even when developing nations cannot actively participate in the mobility revolutions which produce time- and cost-space convergence, they will necessarily be affected. Telecommunications and air transportation greatly affect India and her relations with other nations, for example, even if her capacities in such technologies are limited.

Communications and transportation are wreaking radical and fundamental changes on the world's spatial organization. Transportation has been reorganizing the world since the Middle Ages, first on the seas and then, during the nineteenth century, on land. More recently man penetrated the third dimension, air and space. Although some fundamental limits are being approached, time- and cost-space convergence will continue to reorganize terrestrial space. Simultaneously, telecommunications innovations will continue to facilitate human extensibility. The spatial context of the future is a shrunken world in which people can be everywhere at once through telecommunications extensibility or rapid, low-cost transportation. Because space convergence will affect goods and energy movements also, we can look forward to locating almost any activity where we want it to be.

Consequences and Implications

Nothing is an unmitigated evil or good, and extensibility and convergence have already begun to cause problems while they confer benefits. We emphasize three implications of these spatial capabilities.

Locations   When human activities are freed from spatial and locational constraints other factors assume more importance in decision making. The abundance of new options can itself be a constraint; too many attractive choices can easily replace the tyrannies of location and transportation. Even if we devise strategies for coping with numerous choices and thus escape the indecision that numerous alternatives often generate, the problem of choosing wisely remains. Being able to put things where we want them to be can help us build a better world, but only if we are cautious and wise. For example, a wholesale move of office activities to high amenity suburban and exurban locations will only spread congestion and pollution over more territory and further impoverish central cities. Without prudent analysis and planning, our new locational freedoms will do little more than enable us to go from the locational frying pan into the fire.

Stress and Administration   Intensive communication can cause severe stress. Such observers as Alvin Toffler contend that some societies have surpassed their capacity to process information, and will face severe social and emotional pathologies.[1] This particular communication tyranny could be alleviated by encouraging people to withdraw occasionally from the communications maelstrom. People must retain full control over the on-off switches connecting them to others.

Implicit in such individual control is the demise of administration and bureaucracy as they are usually conceived. When individuals control their extensibility, they collectively control the world; extensibility is antithetical to hierarchy and bureaucracy. If you can complain to a corporate president, for example, and if you get better results by doing so, there is little point in following regular channels. The president will respond by turning off his switch to complaints and other "trivia" in order to maintain the bureaucracy he commands. But such defensive stratagems will not avail. Concerted human extensibility in the form of public opinion constantly breaches such barriers and makes bureaucrats more responsive to individual messages. Extensibility and hierarchical bureaucracy are incompatible. In the future, administrative structures must be made congruent with actual information flows in order to avoid serious stress.

Bureaucratic or adhocratic administrative structures achieve spatial expression as regions. Chapters 6 through 12 discuss regional problems and explore the administrative implications of alternative sociocultural groupings. The pathologies Warntz (chapter 6) attributes to high density metropolitan living could become more widespread if people do not govern their participation in larger communities. Bunge and Sommer deal more directly with administrative-regional questions: Bunge (chapter 12) describes how urban and exurban regions derived from current bureaucratic structures cause, maintain, and intensify sociocultural problems in North America. Sommer (chapter 11) takes a sanguine view of the metropolitan social fabric, emphasizing the free-form regional structures that will evolve along with fat cities and the mobile parisitopoli. Somewhat further along the administrative continuum, chapters 7 through 10 postulate adhocratic spatial units that coincide completely with information flows. Needs for disconnection, and for the organization of administrative structures so that they match information flows, will produce unprecedented regional voluntarism. Individuals will organize themselves in small regions, large regions, or no regions, as they please.

Cyclical Resource Use Lurking in the background of our discussion are questions concerning the resource base upon which any future locational and administrative edifice is to be built. Janelle (chapter 15) and Millward (chapter 18) addressed some land resource and land use problems that will arise near cities as metropolitan populations increase. Carol's essay (chapter 16) explored interrelationships between administrative-bureaucratic structures and resource utilization. Wolfe (chapter 17) described some recreational regions that will develop adjacent to Canada's metropolitan areas. All of these chapters demonstrate the ultimate interdependence of locational, administrative, and resource constraints. In chapter 20 Macinko questions the ability of the resource base to support the populations and densities envisaged in several popular scenarios. Arguing that limiting ecological factors must be reckoned with, Macinko perceives discrepancies between many forecasts and ecological realities.

To ignore such considerations is to court disaster by making it probable that man will overstep ecological bounds, reduce living conditions to less than humane levels, or both. The ecological questions raised by Macinko and the intellectual problems described by Ryan (chapter 14) cannot be dismissed lightly. Convergence, for example, *may* be a means of escaping undesirable byproducts of the mobility revolution. But it must be demonstrated that extensibility and convergence can solve problems as well as they create them.

Whether these implications of time-space convergence are opportunities or constraints depends on how we perceive and respond to them. If we view locational flexibility as a threat to our large cities and if we attempt to defend existing settlement patterns against competition, such flexibility will certainly cause problems. If we perceive flexibility as an opportunity to solve current problems and create more attractive settlement patterns, it will have beneficial results. Futurists must become more skilled at predicting spatial consequences and more clever at maximizing their beneficial effects.

Philosophical Issues

Discussion of all the philosophical and practical problems we face in the future would require several large volumes. Yet some attention to what many consider to be overriding future problems is essential.

Human Survival   The current interest in futuristic analysis is often motivated by man's fear of his extinction through nuclear warfare or environmental pollution. For reasons that are difficult to identify, this prospect is appalling, almost unthinkable. This is somewhat paradoxical. We all know that we will die and that our children and grandchildren also will eventually die. In directly personal terms, there is little reason to fear the demise of the species. Our fears are probably based on subconscious images of immortality and ideas about the purpose of human existence, but in any case, the bases of our concern with species survival are inadequately formulated.

Our concern with survival of portions of humanity is more tractable, for the threats are often more immediate and the probable consequences clearer. Most of the current concern with forecasting and futuristics derives from the alarming simulation forecasts produced by Forrester and Meadows.[2] Whether such dismay is based upon compassion or on fear by the well-off that their interests are threatened, the social, economic, and population "crashes" predicted by Forrester and Meadows have generated widespread concern.

Cultural-ecological obstacles to human comfort and survival certainly exist. We are currently unable adequately to feed much of the world's population, and in the near future it is probable that we will be unable to satisfy the basic needs of a larger proportion of the world's population.

Yet once again, questions and qualifications can be raised. Many people are convinced that technological innovation will always rescue man from his problems. Arguing that resources are culturally defined, they postulate an infinity of resources. Resources will always be "discovered" when they are needed. Unfashionable as this stance may be, it has yet to be shown that the viewpoint is either valid or invalid. Indeed, the validity of more cataclysmic forecasts about human survival also remains unproved, although we may be unwittingly testing such propositions.

Quality of Life   Survival alone is not enough. If life is inhumane, people are not living but merely existing. At some level of minimal subsistence, the desirability of living can legitimately be questioned. If we intend to provide conditions that promote population growth, it is incumbent upon us to insure that the living conditions of those we "invite" to join us are at least adequate. We must, as Macinko emphasized in chapter 20, look beyond man's physiological needs to his cultural and social needs for living space, recreational space, comforts, and amenities. One does not normally invite guests without taking precautions to see that they are comfortable and well provided for. An alternative, of course, is to cease extending so many "invitations."

Over the short run, the best strategy for improving living

conditions is to reduce rates of population growth. Whether that policy is viable over the long run is unclear. The age structure required for zero population growth, for example, implies social and political conservatism which could themselves constitute serious problems.

       Optimism, Pessimism, and Apathy   Whether one is optimistic or pessimistic concerning the viability and quality of future life depends as much on predisposition as on the evidence, for the evidence we have on the future, like that from the past, is subject to widely varying interpretations.

    Although this collection is generally optimistic, enough caveats and dissenting opinions have been entered to indicate considerable ambivalence concerning the spatial future. Philbrick (chapter 2) and Abler (chapter 3), secure in their convictions that locational constraints will relax significantly, evidently foresee no density or crowding problems emerging from future population growth. On the other hand, Warntz, Janelle and Bunge (chapters 6, 8, and 12) cite current density problems to support arguments that we should avoid future crowding and to justify analytic techniques that clarify density problems. Population distribution is the basic spatial parameter in human affairs, and it should receive first priority from geographical futurists.

    Although it may seem incongruous to say so in a volume devoted to futuristics, benign unconcern with the future is not a wholly untenable attitude. Many people express no great concern about the long-term future. Among those professionally concerned with space and human spatial behavior, futuristics is hardly a burning issue.

    Every generation must tackle the world as it is and solve the problems which confront it. Ultimately, we can no more guarantee succeeding generations a viable and comfortable future than we can guarantee our children successful lives. Even children born with silver spoons in their mouths occasionally spit them out in favor of something less predictable and thus more interesting. Moreover, even if we possessed the capacity to solve the problems which would otherwise afflict the next generation or two, it would probably be unwise to do so. To meet and master *current* problems seems to generate psychological and emotional benefits, and it would be "unfair" to deny our children and their children the challenge of solving their problems for themselves.

    Whereas we cannot guarantee comfort and ease in the future, we can try to maximize the *range of alternatives* that coming generations will have. Such a policy implies judicious resource use. In the same way that killing all the world's whales will surely preclude their use or enjoyment by our descendants, profligate agricultural and urban land uses will constrain the choices open to people fifty years from now. This does not mean we have no claims on currently available resources. Legitimate current demands must be met if there is to be any future at all; blind conservationism is as irresponsible as blind robber-baronism. Arguments that all resources must be preserved for posterity are ludicrous. They reduce mankind to a species of museum keepers. Balancing the claims of the present against the reasonable demands of the future is a delicate business, but one that is essential.

Just as we must use natural resources, we must make locational and spatial decisions despite their long-term effects. Perhaps all that is necessary to practice spatial futuristics is to try to preserve as many future locational options as possible while satisfying our current needs. Geographical futurists might make their greatest contributions by educating themselves, decision makers, and the public to recognize the long "half-lives" of spatial artifacts. The location of a major building or thoroughfare may affect the lives of people for decades, and even centuries.

As with most philosophical issues, definitive answers cannot be proffered. Whether one chooses to be concerned with futuristics and, if one does, whether one takes an optimistic or pessimistic attitude, are matters of inclination and preference. Rational matters should remain unsullied by emotion and personal proclivities, but in practice such methodological purity is impossible.

Strategic Dilemmas

Attempts at spatial futuristics encounter several strategic dilemmas. Some, such as the question of *who* practices futuristics *for whom*, are common to all future-oriented analysis. Others, such as questions about relationships between spatial futuristics and planning, and the selection of optimal tactics for region building, are more specifically the province of those who concentrate on human spatial behavior.

Geographical Futuristics—By Whom and for Whom   If all of us governed our individual actions by considering their collective implications for both the short and the long run, a futuristic literature and profession would be superfluous since futuristic attitudes and practice would be built into day-to-day life. We hazard the forecast that such a state of affairs is highly unlikely. Most of us give scarcely a thought to future consequences of our daily decisions and even less consideration to the effects that will ensue if millions make identical decisions.

Our unwillingness to consider the long-term and collective implications of our individual decisions implies that futuristic analysis will be made by a few people on behalf of society. Choosing one alternative over others requires curtailment of individual freedom. Some individual behaviors will enhance attainment of a chosen future whereas others will retard its attainment. This being the case, policies, propaganda, and laws promoting "desired" behavior patterns and deemphasizing "undesirable" options will be adopted.

The political arena is the forum for choosing among alternative futures and for adopting policies and laws which will promote them. Politics is an inherently futuristic activity. Legislation is almost always designed to remedy current defects or to procure some desired state of affairs. A board of education, for example, recommends that its community's voters approve a bond issue today so that the community will have adequate schools five years hence.

Politics is a useful mechanism for short-term futuristics. From a geographical point of view, however, it has two major drawbacks: first, decisions are usually compromises between two somewhat polar positions; second, politics is too short-sighted. Politicians and their policies must face elections every few years, which guarantees that the political process and the energies of politicians will be devoted primarily to immediate concerns. The inability of politicians to consider ranges of alternative futures and their emphasis on short-run affairs makes politics alone a poor means of choosing among alternative futures.

Yet futuristics is an inherently political activity. The alternative to making futuristic decisions (with their coercive corollaries) in a political manner is to turn such choices over to panels of technical experts. Experts, for all their technical virtuosity, tend to be an overly specialized, rather heartless lot, who are too often contemptuous of feedback from the people most affected by their decisions. In the United States, for example, massive urban renewal and urban freeway construction programs, both heavily subsidized by federal funds, were perpetrated in many metropolitan areas by experts and bureaucrats who subscribed to half-baked and erroneous ideas about how cities work. It remains to be seen whether several affected cities will survive that exercise in spatial futuristics. Had the economic, social, and racial minorities most affected by such decisions had greater recourse to political rather than bureaucratic structures in their attempts to modify and halt such programs, we might have evaded the anguish these programs have caused and will cause for decades to come.

Several of our authors suggest means of avoiding similar problems in the future. In chapter 3, for example, Abler describes technologies that will enable individuals to vote electronically on major issues. Janelle's first essay (chapter 8) discusses the phasing out of bureaucracy as a consequence of greater citizen participation. Bunge (chapter 12) recommends "urban nationalism" to give local groups more control over their futures.

When citizens can more directly influence politics, matters will improve only to the extent that citizens are generally more future-minded. Politicians too must be sensitized to the range of alternative futures and to long-term affairs; technical experts must be made more attentive to the day-to-day realities of life. If this can be done, we might gain the best of both worlds. North American politics is moving in this direction. Executive and legislative commissions of experts are established frequently to investigate difficult problems and report their findings and recommendations to political decision makers. Whereas such panels usually concentrate on current or short-term problems, they provide a fruitful format for considering matters with long-term import.

Should such a hybrid of techniques and politics be the best mechanism for resolving questions about who chooses what future for whom, people interested in promoting futuristics should give high priority to educating politicians and the public to the advantages society would derive from the use of panels of futuristically-minded experts with diverse interests and specialties. Such bodies could propose alternative futures in different realms of cultural, economic, political, and spatial activity, explore the implications of their own proposals, and assess the likely effects of proposed legislation or policies originating in executive or legislative sectors. But choices among alternatives and decisions concerning which effects are most acceptable should remain political decisions. People most affected by choices and decisions will then have opportunities to influence such decisions. Whether these decisions will be made in a representative fashion, or whether we will use communications technology to obtain frequent referenda on important issues, is less critical than is assurance that the groups most affected by futuristic decisions not be at the mercy of futuristic technocrats.

Futuristics and Planning   If one danger of futuristics is equivocation in the face of numerous alternatives, another pitfall is excessive commitment to one or a few alternative(s). It would be folly to deduce a set of alternatives, choose one, and then adhere to it dogmatically for years or decades. If futuristics is to have any value, it must continue to emphasize the range of alternatives. Alternatives must constantly be evaluated and reevaluated.

A productive futuristics will resemble interplanetary exploration. In sending out a planetary probe we aim the shot at a destination to be reached some months hence. We provide the vehicle with corrective steering capacities and reserve power supplies. Thus if our aim is off, corrections can be made en route as such errors become obvious. Furthermore, reserve power and steering capacities make destination changes possible. Futuristics must incorporate similar flexibility. Decisions concerning the location of a facility or the use to which a certain tract of land will be put must constantly be reevaluated in light of ongoing and projected spatial processes. Modifications, revisions, and reversals of earlier decisions—where justified and desirable—must be easy to effect. If anything is worse than neglect of alternative futures, it is slavish devotion to a chosen course of action.

It seems to us that the difference between futuristics and planning lies in the degree to which practitioners of the respective professions consider alternative spatial arrangements. There exists a regrettable tendency among planners to become overly commited to THE PLAN, once it has been committed to maps and zoning ordinances. This drawback is compounded by the fact that many people in planning today have backgrounds in architecture. Architecture has been more an artistic discipline than a science of human spatial behavior at microscales. Thus, esthetic prejudices all too often dominate city and regional planning at the expense of principles of spatial behavior.

Current architecture and planning programs provide their students with firmer grounding in social sciences, and more people now view planning as an iterative design science based on regularities in human spatial behavior. Social scientists' increasing sensitivity to design considerations will also make the respective viewpoints of planners and futurists more compatible. But futurists and planners will continue to have differences of opinion because of the different strategies the two groups use. Futuristics and planning should be complementary, for both are concerned with space and spatial behavior. But a compromise between the positions taken by futurists and planners is prerequisite to more productive interaction.

Tactics for Region Building   Integrating futuristic analysis with goal formulation, planning, and politics is the best way to build efficient and humane spatial futures. The specific tactics futurists will devise to direct behavior toward chosen spatial goals remain to be seen. Given the nature of most social-political systems, the optimal tactic for building successful regions is to harness self-interest. It is more than utopian to think the validity of futuristic strategies will be so self-evident that individuals will eagerly adjust their personal behavior to produce the desired results. All of us are blessed with a good measure of sheer human cussedness, and most of us, when faced with conflicts between private benefits and social benefits, have no real choice but to increase private benefits even at the price of serious social costs.[3]

Attempts to govern private behavior along lines contrary to perceived or real individual interests have not been happy experiences. Prohibition of alcoholic beverages in the United States, for example, was an abysmal failure, as are current attempts to dissuade people from using cigarettes or to prevent them from using marijuana. Because social goals and personal goals are often in direct conflict, devising methods of reaching long-range social goals which are congruent with short-term personal goals will tax our ingenuity to the utmost. But unless futurists, planners, and politicians are clever enough to devise such techniques, they are likely to spend their time tilting with windmills.

A second reason why long-range strategies and goals should be formulated in accordance with personal, short-term interests is the questionable validity of any other approach in complex and interdependent societies. Complicated, tightly integrated social and economic systems seem to defy centralized planning. A slight miscalculation by directors of large, intricate organizations produces great waste; a major mistake is disastrous (for example, the Edsel automobile produced by the Ford Motor Company). Rather than seizing the social bull by the horns and trying to push it toward the region-building behaviors they desire, futurists will have greater impact and incur fewer ulcers if they entice the public to go in a given direction by strewing the path with good things.

Thus we must use a delicate touch in promoting the regions we want for the future. We might decide, for example, to try to reduce population densities and thus avoid the density-related problems mentioned by Warntz and Macinko (chapters 6 and 20). Forbidding migration to large metropolitan areas or trying to deport people to rural regions will not work. Nor, for example, will directives, admonitions, and appeals to conscience reduce differentiation among Bunge's Cities of Death, Need, and Superfluity (chapter 12). The City of Superfluity will merge with the Cities of Need and Death only when it pays to do so, just as people will stop concentrating in metropolitan areas and begin settling in more dispersed locations only when they benefit more from dispersed locations than they would in cities. The task of the futurist who wants to produce locational results is to provide short-run incentives which will cause individuals to behave in ways that should produce optimal regional structures in the long run.

Geographical futurists must sacrifice their political maidenheads if they hope to make futuristics more than an academic exercise. Planning and politics are the arenas in which futuristic decisions are being made. Futurists will affect decision making only if they engage in the often grubby business of formulating programs that will *produce* the castles that futurists are wont to build in the air.

Why Futuristics?

Futuristics might appear to be an innovation in human affairs. But despite the explosion of future-oriented literature that has appeared in the last several years, in some ways futuristics is nothing new.

Futures Unavoidable   Past and current decisions have always affected future options. Future effects are part of any decision, no matter when it is made or whether people realize the implications of their decisions. What *is* new is our *recognition* of the extent to which the past, present, and future are interdependent, and our self-conscious attempts to take future effects of current decisions into account. Futuristics is the objectification of the interrelationships between past, present, and future.

Objectifications (explicit, overt recognitions of previously instinctive, unconscious processes and relationships) are far from trivial. Critical social and cultural breakthroughs are often objectifications of relationships that are blatant *after* someone identifies them. For example, throughout history there have been major conflicts whenever people from different cultural groups came into contact. But until anthropologists invented the idea of culture and popularized its existence, people were trapped within their cultures. Once we realized that culture controls behavior, however, it became an explanatory variable we could discuss. More importantly, the objectification process enabled us to tinker with our own cultural attitudes and to override them. We may, for example, be uncomfortable over the proximity of a visitor from the Middle East who stands much closer to us than he or she "should," given the business at hand. But knowing the way culture controls personal space, and realizing that the visitor's culture demands that he be quite close, a tactful host can dismiss his own discomfort and take no offense at the visitor's "pushiness." He realizes that his guest is not crowding him because of malice or ignorance, but simply because of a cultural habit.

What is occurring now is the objectification of interrelationships between past, present, and future. A plea for futuristics is somewhat misplaced. We are all futurists whether we know it or not, because all our actions have future implications and effects. Our plea thus boils down to an appeal to apply futuristics rationally and self-consciously. To fail rationally and deliberately to consider the future consequences of our decisions is usually to opt for continuation of current trends. Futuristics proceeds whether we realize it or not, and the primary task of committed futurists is to demonstrate that such is the case. Futurists must then demonstrate that rational, self-conscious futuristics is more beneficial to man than blind, hit-or-miss pursuit of life.

There is no guarantee that rational, systematic futuristics is superior to the more relaxed approach that man has traditionally pursued, but it is probable that systematic study will be shown to be preferable. Advanced societies today are much like poorly maintained powerful automobiles that are being driven blindly at open throttle. When the inevitable breakdown or horrible crash occurs, we try to rebuild the car and treat the injured as best we can, but such measures are of little help. Repairs and compensation made after the fact are not substitutes for preventive maintenance and safe driving. To adopt a systematically futuristic approach is to cease driving blindly into the future and to begin driving defensively. The probability of a serious accident will decrease if we simply watch where we are going.

Futures Imperfect   Current trends toward greater human extensibility and time-space convergence make it essential that we quickly develop and apply a robust spatial futuristics. Spatial behavior and spatial conflict were not critical in a sparsely settled world where some isolation existed. Today, the earth's population is large and getting larger, effective distance has disappeared, and isolation has disappeared with it. Increasingly, there are no such things as "local affairs." Everything everywhere affects everything everywhere. Like it or not, we have produced a single, interdependent, tightly-integrated world in which the consequences of locational and spatial behavior at one place reverberate throughout the world. In such a system, it is vital that we know more about human spatial behavior and that we be able to forecast its long-term effects.

Economic constraints on locational behavior are relaxing rapidly, and as they do, the geography of necessity gives way to a geography of choice. Transportation costs, markets, and raw materials no longer determine the location of economic activities. We have developed an information-based economy in which dominant economic activities and the people engaged in them enjoy unparalleled locational flexibility. In this spatial context, amenity and ecological considerations are more important locational factors than in the past. Cities located in amenity regions of North American are growing more rapidly than others, and such trends will intensify as society becomes more footloose.

That amenity and esthetics are becoming more important locational considerations only intensifies the need for spatial futuristics. Thoughtless, shortsighted spatial behavior will ruin attractive amenity environments very quickly. Formerly inaccessible wilderness areas are now ravaged by trail bikers in the summer and snowmobilers in the winter. After only two decades, the bloom is already off the California rose. The very attributes which made Southern California attractive drew so many people so quickly that the amenity qualities of the area were ruined. Given the space-adjusting technologies we now command, there is a close interdependence between spatial behavior and amenity. If we do not become more sensitive to its nuances and govern our behavior accordingly, we shall soon have no amenity regions to protect.

It would be tragically ironic if, having escaped from the tyranny of place, we were to destroy our amenity environments and the possibilities for disengagement they offer. We must seize the administrative opportunity and reorganize ourselves into the regional structures that will best serve our needs and aspirations. Given the importance of space to human beings and the extent to which it determines their humanity, a vigorous spatial futuristics is absolutely necessary.

References

1. Alvin Toffler, *Future Shock* (New York: Random House, 1970).
2. J. W. Forrester, *World Dynamics* (Cambridge: Wright-Allen, 1971); Dennis Meadows, *et al.*, *The Limits to Growth* (Washington: The Potomac Associates, 1972).
3. Garrett Hardin, "The Tragedy of the Commons," *Science*, December 13, 1968, pp. 1243–1248.

Index